INTERNATIONAL PERSPECTIVES ON THE HUMAN FACTOR IN ECONOMIC DEVELOPMENT

INTERNATIONAL PERSPECTIVES ON THE HUMAN FACTOR IN ECONOMIC DEVELOPMENT

Edited by Senyo B–S. K. Adjibolosoo

Westport, Connecticut
London

Library of Congress Cataloging-in-Publication Data

International perspectives on the human factor in economic
   development / edited by Senyo B-S. K. Adjibolosoo.
         p.   cm.
   Includes bibliographical references and index.
   ISBN 0–275–95967–8 (alk. paper)
   1. Economic development—Social aspects.   2. Civil society—
Developing countries.   3. Developing countries—Social conditions.
4. Developing countries—Social policy.   5. Human capital—
Developing countries.   I. Adjibolosoo, Senyo B-S. K.
HD75.I63   1998
338.9—DC21   97–27933

British Library Cataloguing in Publication Data is available.

Library of Congress Catalog Card Number: 97–27933
ISBN: 0–275–95967–8

First published in 1998

Praeger Publishers, 88 Post Road West, Westport, CT 06881
An imprint of Greenwood Publishing Group, Inc.

Printed in the United States of America

The paper used in this book complies with the
Permanent Paper Standard issued by the National
Information Standards Organization (Z39.48–1984).

10   9   8   7   6   5   4   3   2   1

Copyright Acknowledgments

The editor and publisher gratefully acknowledge permission for use of the following material:

Significant portions of Chapter 6 were first published in S. Adjibolosoo, 1995. Rethinking
the Sources of Economic Underdevelopment in Ghana. *Review of Human Factor Studies*
1(2): 1–35.

This book is dedicated to
Mr. F. W. Tete (my father-in-law),
the late Mr. Louis Agbenu
(my middle school standard seven teacher),
and the late Mr. E. R. Quist
(my middle school headteacher).
These three people, in their own ways,
have had significant impact on my life.

they stand like soldiers
swallowing the forest
and their razor-edged words
dangle on their lower lips
as tools for the conquest
their sharp eagle eyes
penetrate the thick foliage
flipping over the leaves
to uncover the slippery beast
their frail shouts parade the woods
to intimidate this animal
while their lean words fly
only to clash and crash
melting like soldering iron
leaving the beast in their mind
                    —Senyo B-S. K. Adjibolosoo

Contents

Tables and Figures

TABLES

FIGURES

Preface

As a detailed evaluation and analysis of the relevance of the human factor (HF) to global economic growth and development, the book maintains that citizenship development through HF engineering is a *sine qua non* to nation building, economic growth, and development. In view of this, the contributors together conclude that the state of a nation's HF affects the rates of economic growth and development. As such, countries that desire to achieve sustained human-centered development must begin their economic development and industrial programs by first concentrating on HF development, and then putting effective development plans, policies, programs, and projects in place to successfully utilize people who have acquired the HF. Using the experiences of the countries whose development processes have been presented, discussed, and analyzed, this book maintains that until the HF is developed countries that aspire to achieve economic growth and development will continue to fail.

In order to continue to develop and promote research materials on the significance of the HF to development, this book presents global perspectives on the HF and its significance to economic growth and development in countries all over the world—developed and developing countries alike. The collected works published in this volume clearly reveal the true significance of the HF in the economic growth and development of nations.

In view of these observations, this book is a must read for people who are interested in development education and community, national, and global development. Above all, national leaders, civil servants, and academicians must read this book to educate themselves about nation building, citizenship development, and the relevance of the HF to international economic growth and development.

Acknowledgments

In many ways, it is nice for one to dream. Yet since no one person can live and do everything all alone, one needs to elicit the help and assistance of many others to make one's dreams come true. Indeed, I have benefited significantly from many people to whom I am very grateful. First, my greatest thanks go to my wife, Sabina Adjibolosoo, and my children, Selassie and Selorm. These three individuals have stood with and by me, through thick and thin, during the writing of this book. Second, I wish to express my sincere gratitude to the following individuals for their tremendous contributions to the preparation of this manuscript: all the authors who have prepared the various chapters, Dr. Benjamin Ofori-Amoah, Mr. Salomon Agbenya, Dr. Harold J. Harder, Ms. Brenda Sawatzky, Ms. Liliana Lara, Mr. David Routly, Reverend Derek Sarpong, and many other colleagues who have contributed in their own special ways to making this book a reality. Finally, I am thankful to Ms. Cynthia Harris, my acquisitions editor, and the Greenwood staff for giving life to this manuscript.

Chapter 1

The Global Scramble for Economic Growth and Development

Senyo B-S. K. Adjibolosoo

Many years ago, certain classical scholars came to believe that nature had placed all humanity under two opposing masters, pleasure and pain. These scholars maintained that while the master of pain unleashes all kinds of affliction and suffering on people, lording it over them, the master of pleasure is determined to help men and women to enjoy all the available goodies of human life on earth. It is in line with this view that Jeremy Bentham and many other classical (liberal) scholars (including their followers) maintained that men and women always strive to maximize pleasure and minimize pain (i.e., all forms of human suffering) simultaneously. This belief led these scholars to argue that the object of public (i.e., social, economic, political, and educational) policy must be the attainment of the greatest happiness for the largest number of people in society. That is, if any social policy is designed and carefully implemented, though its effects may make 20 percent of the population worse off while making the remaining 80 percent better off, that policy would have been deemed to be a huge success. In general, social, economic, political, and educational plans, policies, programs, and projects must assist most people to achieve better living standards for themselves.

Indeed, since the beginning of human life, all humanity has tried relentlessly to improve human welfare and living conditions (Adjibolosoo 1998). In the early beginnings, men and women were faced with a barrage of problems and difficulties that they had to either learn to live with or find solutions to.

Primitive men and women chose to seek solutions to their pertinent problems to enjoy the best of life in their own environments. To make good on their desire, people began to domesticate crops and animals. They became more and more engrossed in the development of tools and other implements with which to either protect themselves or make sure that they had sufficient stock of food available or both. As men and women moved through the various stages of development, they made significant headway in terms of fending for themselves.

The realization that life could be made better and, above all, fully enjoyed, led all humanity to begin a massive scramble for the development of procedures, methods, techniques, institutions, and technologies that would facilitate the process of progress. The desire to gain continuing control over the physical environment, produce and provide for all seasons, conquer hunger and avoid starvation, create a peaceful and livable society, and promote technological advancement led to the determination of men and women to make development happen in all spheres of human endeavor. Clough (1959, 25) observed that the technological evolution of the copper age (between circa 5000 B.C. and 3000 B.C.) led to critical inventions and innovations of which the following were some of the most prominent: smelting technology, the development and expansion of trade and procedures for the exchange of goods and services, division of labor and specialization, and the building and development of huge human settlements. These inventions and innovations provided people with the power and ability to successfully deal with floods, harsh climatic conditions, problems with transportation of goods and services, and buildings for human use and habitation. As such, it is clearly obvious that the human endeavor is aimed at developing an enterprise that will create and sustain ongoing satisfaction and happiness. In this way, the main ideals of development were not only birthed, but also became crystallized and well established.

This chapter is about critical questions regarding economic growth and development. These questions relate to the orthodox view about the factors that cause economic growth and development to happen in countries. In the same way, the chapter asks questions about why some nations develop while others fail to. In what follows, I present discussions regarding the ideals of development we all cherish, human triumphs and failures. In Chapter 13, the significance of the human factor (HF) to the processes of economic growth and development is discussed in detail.

IDEALS OF DEVELOPMENT WE ALL CHERISH

Why do men and women scramble to bring into existence various forms of inventions and innovations? There are a group of factors that together explain why human beings strive to conquer and subdue their environment. To many people, one of the greatest fortunes that can visit any human being is to have and enjoy the "good life." While it is not clear to many scholars what actually constitutes the good life, many people believe and agree that when men and women are able to experience liberty, equity, equality, and justice, and, above all, have the opportunity to enjoy all rights and privileges accorded to them by birth, citizenship, and the constitution, they consider themselves as poised and ready to enjoy the good life.

In reality, the concept of the good life cannot be easily pinned down, since it implies many different things to different groups of people. It is, however, the case that when people are provided with the opportunity and the relevant environment in which they can make the best use of their human abilities, they may be in the position to enjoy the good life. This is one reason why nations, for many centuries, have pursued programs of nation building and development relentlessly—right from the beginning of time to the present day. Though incomplete, the following list reveals some of the critical items that make life worth living and working to sustain:

1. Continuing improvement in human welfare.
2. Sufficient food, clothing, shelter, and belongingness.
3. Liberty, equity, equality, and justice.
4. The existence and maintenance of the rule of law and democracy.
5. A clean and safe environment.
6. Personal peace, safety, and security.
7. The maintenance, protection, and promotion of human rights and responsibilities.
8. Achieving and sustaining human longevity.
9. The ongoing pursuit of human factor development.
10. Personal development (i.e., spiritual, intellectual, moral, physical, etc.).

The pursuit of these ideals has now become the strongest motivating factor in people's endeavors. As people go about their social, economic, political, and educational activities and programs, they do their best to make sure that human effort is directed toward the attainment of these ideals. Since the desire is to live longer and enjoy the good life, public policy is often aimed at the achievement of these ideals.

SUCCESSES AND FAILURES

The search for critical paths to development has been in process since the beginning of human life on earth. For many generations, social scientists of all disciplines have continued to be interested in development theory and human progress. Though this search has been relentlessly pursued for centuries, many theories of economic growth and development have been less successful in serving as the primary foundation for effective development plans, policies, programs, and projects in developing countries. The evidence regarding the effectiveness (in the developed countries) and the weaknesses (in the developing countries) of orthodox development theory in helping to successfully deal with problems of economic development is now overwhelming.

For many decades, development theorists have tried not only to understand how development happens in countries, but also to isolate the various factors that affect the development processes and programs of countries. Having come to believe that they now know precisely the various factors that cause either development or underdevelopment, they proceed to make policy recommendations to developing countries that currently aspire to achieve industrial and technological progress. Yet regardless of the ongoing policy recommendations of development experts, many developing countries still languish and find it too difficult to achieve sustained economic growth and development. This phenomenon has been a great puzzle to orthodox economic development theorists and other social scientists.

The Industrial Revolution brought significant successes and progress to the British in the mid-eighteenth century and beyond. The belief in industrialization and economic growth and development led the British to seek ways to increase their national wealth. During this process, many new ideas, technologies, tools, and other devices were brought into existence to help improve human welfare. Thus, the era of British industrialization experienced significant levels of invention and innovation.

To the British, the thrust of the race for industrialization and the development program was not only to increase national wealth, but also to conquer other lands and use their resources to promote British well-being. Voyages of discovery became prominent and the art of navigation grew and blossomed. The French, Spaniards, Germans, Danes, Dutch, Portuguese, and other European nations jumped on to the bandwagon of colonization. The desire to achieve and maintain national superiority, power, authority, and control over one's rivals led many European countries to comb the globe thoroughly as they struggled to achieve these goals. This event led to the acquisition of colonies in Africa, Asia, North America, Latin America, and elsewhere. Gold, silver, diamonds, and other precious metals and raw materials were derived from the colonies and used to build the metropolitan countries. As such, while most European countries grew richer and stronger, others, including the newly acquired colonies, were made poorer and weaker. Countries in Africa, Asia, and Latin America were drained of their most precious and critical resources. Africans suffered the greatest loss, in that in addition to their resources being plundered, they also lost a significant percentage of their populations to the slave trade.

Regardless of the intensity of this destruction and the extent of pauperization unleashed on Africans by Europeans, scholars of development theory have always believed that the damage done to these countries through colonialism and imperialism could be salvaged by helping them to overcome their problems of economic underdevelopment. Development theorists have written volumes of articles and books regarding how the poor nations can pursue viable development programs to successfully achieve industrialization, economic growth, and development. It is often argued that if these countries could get rid of their (primitive) cultural practices, harness and save more of their marketable surplus, acquire more capital and technical expertise from the developed countries through technology transfer programs, minimize the rate of growth of their population, change their existing economic structures, increase the fertility of local agricultural land, engage in continuing mechanization, provide more education to their people to increase national literacy rates, pursue grassroots participation in the development program and the democratization process, train their people to become less corrupt, and so on, they could also attain sustained economic growth and development.

These recommendations do not go unheeded. Many developing countries have been urged to pursue development programs based on these suggestions. Organizations from the developed nations (i.e., the United Nations, the World Bank, the International Monetary Fund [IMF], nongovernment organizations, etc.), including advanced-country governments, have made significant financial resources and technical expertise available to many developing countries. As help continues to flow in from the developed countries (DCs) to the less-developed countries (LDCs), the case has been made for good planning, policies, programs, and projects. The implementation of these was expected to bring ongoing economic growth and development to stagnating economies in Africa, Asia, and Latin America.

Unfortunately, however, approximately five decades of development planning, policy making, program development, and project implementation have brought little change to the economic conditions in these countries. While most DCs continue to achieve more progress, the LDCs seem to be falling into a deep quagmire of economic underdevelopment. The more they struggle to resurge, the more they get choked in the mire of underdevelopment. This phenomenon is not only frustrating and discouraging to people in the developing world, but it also leaves experts of development theory helpless and confused, unable to comprehend the problem in order to turn the situation around for the better. Their rusty academic tool bags of development theories, ideas, and principles are full, yet unhelpful to the LDCs.

In view of the poor results of orthodox development planning and policy, the critical and nagging questions are as follows: Why is it that though many developing countries possess (or possessed) huge financial capital and other critical raw materials, they are still unable to make sustained human-centered development happen to them? Why does orthodox development theory seem to be finding it too difficult to bring required progress to the LDCs? What is actually missing in orthodox development theorizing and policy recommendations? Countries such as Nigeria, Kenya, Ghana, Zimbabwe, Saudi Arabia,

Kuwait, Iraq, Iran, Haiti, the Philippines, Mexico, the former Soviet Union, Cuba, and many others have all tried to develop but failed, regardless of the availability of their significant material resources.

The failure of these countries to achieve sustained economic growth and development calls for a serious search for answers as to why this has been their plight. Indeed, while some of these countries (i.e., the former Soviet Union, Ghana, Nigeria, Kenya, etc.) were all further ahead of most Southeast Asian countries such as Singapore, Malaysia, Indonesia, and Thailand in the 1950s and 1960s, these Asian countries have significantly improved in the last two to three decades. Their rates of economic growth and development have been extremely significant. This observation brings other critical questions into mind: What is it that these Asian countries are doing right that other developing countries are failing to accomplish? Can other developing countries achieve similar objectives to those being accomplished by Southeast Asian countries? If so, what are the areas to which they must pay significant attention? Correct answers to these questions require that the LDCs discover and fully understand the real reasons for their poor economic performance.

Indeed, if LDCs sincerely desire to achieve sustained economic growth and development, they may have to learn from the experiences of other developed nations. The key problem, however, is that orthodox development theorists are finding it too difficult to decipher the real sources of underdevelopment in the LDCs. Their ongoing speculations have led to development plans, policies, programs, and projects that have rather worsened the problems of the LDCs. Indeed, the LDCs still continue to seek workable solutions to their ongoing economic stagnation and its accompanying problems.

This book was written to provide more detailed and meaningful explanations for why most DCs continue to achieve economic growth and development but most LDCs do not. The contributing authors together argue that the critical factor that makes economic growth and development succeed or fail in countries is the human factor. In this book, the HF is viewed as

The spectrum of personality characteristics and other dimensions of human performance that enable social, economic and political institutions to function and remain functional, over time. Such dimensions sustain the workings and application of the rule of law, political harmony, a disciplined labor force, just legal systems, respect for human dignity and the sanctity of life, social welfare, and so on. As is often the case, no social, economic or political institutions can function effectively without being upheld by a network of committed persons who stand firmly by them. Such persons must strongly believe in and continually affirm the ideals of society. (Adjibolosoo 1995a, 33)

It is this perception about the HF that forms the basis of this book. In Chapter 13, I argue that the LDCs are not growing and developing economically as they should because their labor force lacks the relevant HF traits (Adjibolosoo 1994). In a similar way, most social, economic, political, and educational problems being experienced in the DCs are results of continuing HF decay. As such, they need to first develop their HF before they can dream of achieving sustained economic growth and development.

The chapters in this book together analyze and evaluate the HF foundation of either economic growth and development or economic stagnation and underdevelopment in countries across the five continents. The book takes a detailed look at the state of the HF in each country and how it affects the direction of national economic growth and development. Each contributor to this book presents a detailed analysis and discussion on a selected country and discusses how the level of HF development in that country contributes to its economic growth and development. Each chapter presents materials on national policies and discusses the impact of the HF on each country's past, present, and future development programs; discusses how either HF development or HF decay or underdevelopment has affected the effectiveness of development planning, policy formulation, program development and project implementation in each country under study; discusses the pertinent problems that will never go away in each country until the HF is adequately developed; and discusses what relevant programs must be initiated and implemented to help develop the necessary HF for each country's development program.

As a detailed evaluation and analysis of the relevance of the HF to global economic growth and development, the book maintains that citizenship development through HF engineering is a *sine qua non* to nation building and economic growth and development (see details in Chapter 12). In view of this, the authors together conclude that the state of a nation's HF affects the rates of economic growth and development (Adjibolosoo 1993, 1995b). As such, countries that desire to achieve sustained human-centered development must begin their economic development and industrial programs by first concentrating on HF development, and then putting effective development plans, policies, programs, and projects in place to successfully utilize people who have acquired the HF. Using the experiences of the countries whose development processes have been presented, discussed, and analyzed, this book maintains that, until the HF is developed, countries that aspire to achieve economic growth and development will continue to fail to achieve their intended goals. The conclusion that HF development must be relentlessly pursued by all countries that aspire to achieve economic growth and development is relevant to all countries—developed and developing countries alike.

REFERENCES

Adjibolosoo, S. 1993. The Human Factor in Development. *Scandinavian Journal of Development Alternatives* 12 (4): 139–149.

Adjibolosoo, S. 1994. The Human Factor and the Failure of Development Planning and Economic Policy in Africa. In *Perspectives on Economic Development in Africa*, edited by F. Ezeala-Harrison and S. Adjibolosoo. Westport, Conn.: Praeger.

Adjibolosoo, S. 1995a. *The Human Factor in Developing Africa.* Westport, Conn.: Praeger.

Adjibolosoo, S. 1995b. The Significance of the Human Factor in African Economic Development. In *The Significance of the Human Factor in African Economic Development,* edited by S. Adjibolosoo. Westport, Conn.: Praeger.

Adjibolosoo, S. 1998. *Global Development the Human Factor Way.* Westport, Conn.: Praeger.

Clough, S. B. 1959. *The Economic Development of Western Civilization.* New York: McGraw-Hill.

PART I

THE HUMAN FACTOR: EVIDENCE FROM DEVELOPED COUNTRIES

Chapter 2

Institutions, Development, and the Human Factor: The German "Miracle"

Justus Haucap

Explaining economic growth and development over time is still one of the most difficult tasks in economics. Standard economic theory as advanced by neoclassical economists usually focuses on technological progress and, more recently, human-capital investment (see Becker, Murphy, and Tamura 1990). In practice, however, these conventional neoclassical growth theories have not been very successful. Tremendous amounts of resources have been spent for ambitious development projects, innumerable development programs have been implemented, and again and again policy reforms have been conducted. In spite of these vigorous efforts to accelerate economic development, most of these measures have been rather ineffective and have not led to the economic success hoped for so deeply. As Adjibolosoo (1994) points out, African countries have experienced the failure of development policies based on suggestions derived from orthodox theory.

In the eyes of many traditional development theorists, the missing development in Africa and the failure of actual development policy is caused by insufficient capital funds, rapid population growth, or insufficient infrastructure, to name only a few of the reasons usually given. Other scholars stress some of the key reasons why policy prescriptions are not completely realized.[1] While there are certainly some merits to these points, the dramatic economic success of Southeast Asian countries makes one wonder how good these explanations really are. While the recent history of most of these countries has been a story of rapid economic progress, the economic success of most Southeast Asian countries is not based on conventional development policies. On the contrary, much of the policy advice given by traditional development theorists has been neglected in the same manner as has been the case in most African countries.[2] The actual policies of most Southeast Asian countries have not at all been in accordance with the policy prescriptions of orthodox theory.

It therefore seems that conventional theory is missing some important elements in its attempt to explain economic growth and development. The traditional diagnosis of economic underdevelopment is at best incomplete. As more and more economists acknowledge, the failure of traditional development policy is at least partially caused by the neglect of crucial features of human behavior and development—in theory as well as development policy. Today, criticism of conventional development theory is growing at a faster rate than the developing countries themselves. As North (1994, 359) argues in his Nobel lecture, "Neoclassical theory is simply an inappropriate tool to analyze and prescribe policies that will induce development."

One criticism which has mainly been put forward by scholars of the Human Factor Paradigm (HFP) is the neglect of culture and social structure in economic analysis. As Adjibolosoo (1993) points out, traditional development theory rests on broad generalizations that have no solid foundation: Culture and social structure are either entirely disregarded or viewed as uniform over all countries and nations. However, this is not an innocent assumption. In reality, culture and social structure are different from nation to nation, from country to country, even from region to region. That cultural differences might also be decisive for economic progress was pointed out by Weber (1968) long ago, when he claimed that culture, religion, and social structure have profound effects on economic development. More recently, this point has been taken up by scholars of the HFP, such as Adu-Febiri (1995a), as well as representatives of the New Economic History, such as Jones (1995). According to this view, cultural differences might account, at least in part, for the differences in economic development. Furthermore, in a world of cultural variety, policies that are appropriate and successful in one special case need not be successful under a different cultural setting. Following this line of reasoning, advocates of the HFP emphasize the need for developing an appropriate human factor to help achieve economic growth and development (Adjibolosoo 1995b).

However, what is meant by an "appropriate human factor?" As Adjibolosoo (1993, 142) defines it, the human factor "comprises a spectrum of personality characteristics and other dimensions of human performance that enable social, political and economic institutions to function and to remain functional over time. Such dimensions sustain the workings and applications of the rule of law, political harmony, disciplined labor force, just legal systems, respect for human dignity, sanctity of life and social welfare, and many others. As is often the case, no social, economic or political institutions can function without being upheld by a network of committed persons who stand firmly by it." The human factor, therefore, involves personal characteristics such as integrity, dedication, responsibility, and accountability.[3]

In a similar way, sociologists such as Coleman (1990) and Putnam (1993) emphasize the importance of an economy's "social capital" as a decisive factor for economic performance. Social norms, customs, and ethics might help overcome problems of organizational failure that hinder economic development (see Schlicht 1993). Along the same lines, Clague (1993) argues that rule obedience and organizational loyalty are crucial factors for economic performance. Norms and ethics, however, are not genetically determined by nature, but rather a product of the socialization process. Therefore, advocates of the HFP call for the development of appropriate rules, ethics, and norms by educational means (see Adjibolosoo 1995b).

A second cause for the failure of traditional development theories and policy prescriptions which is strongly related to the arguments of the HFP is the neglect of the incentive structure embodied in economic, political, and social institutions. Advocates of the New Institutional Economics (NIE), such as North (1981) and, more recently, Lin and Nugent (1995, 2301–2370) or Bardhan (1996), claim that institutions matter for economic performance. In neoclassical economics, however, institutions are either completely ignored or regarded as constant over time. While neoclassical models have become more and more abstract and mathematically elegant, the institutional structure of the economy plays virtually no role.

In sharp contrast to neoclassical economics, the main focus of the NIE is on the impact institutions have on economic performance and efficiency. What has been widely neglected, even by most advocates of the NIE until recently, is the important role the human factor plays in economic development. To analyze economic development, however, it is crucial to understand that, though well-designed institutions are necessary for economic development, they are not sufficient. Exactly this point is stressed by proponents of the HFP, such as Adjibolosoo (1995a, Chapter 5). This point has also been made by Popper (1957, 66), who argued, "Institutions are like fortresses. They must be well designed *and* properly manned [womanned]." This means that the institutional structure of an economy and the human factor have to be well suited to each other. On the one hand, a well-educated labor force is of little avail if the institutional structure of the economy does not provide the correct incentives to make use of one's skills. On the other hand, institutions have to be designed in such a way that they are suited to the ethics, norms, and values inherent in society.

Interestingly enough, as proponents of the HFP stress the role of the human factor for economic development, more and more institutional economists have come to recognize that not only formal institutions matter for economic development, but culture, ideology, values, norms, and ethics as well (see North 1994). As Greif (1994) shows in a seminal paper, cultural beliefs may have a significant impact on economic progress. In his comparative study of the Maghribi traders of the eleventh century and the Genoese traders of the twelfth century, Greif argues that the "collectivistic organization" of the Maghribi traders (which resembles that of most African countries) is an impediment to economic development, while the individualistic organization of the Genoese traders (which resembles that of modern Western societies) fosters the development of markets and thereby also economic development.[4] In a similar manner, Kuran (1997) discusses the particular case of Islam and argues that transaction costs are lower for trade between Islamic traders. Since both traders belong to the same religious group and hold the same religious beliefs, their level of trust is higher than the degree of trust between traders of different religious groups. This chapter aims to take further steps toward a more appropriate theory of development that takes account of culture, ethics, and social norms. The importance of both institutional structure and the human factor will then be demonstrated, with particular reference to the German experience after World War II, and the usefulness of the concepts presented will be illustrated by the peculiarities of Germany's institutional structure. For this purpose, we will also review some basic facts of development in Germany, as well as traditional approaches to explain them.

INSTITUTIONS AND THE HUMAN FACTOR

In neoclassical theory, people are usually viewed as strictly rational subjects that do nothing but pursue their self-interest. The picture of the individual as a brainy but heartless calculating machine has been persistent for a long time in economics, though this conceptualization of the *homo economicus* is neither without problems nor particularly realistic. In the recent literature, the concept of rationality and the assumption of narrowly defined self-interested behavior have especially been subject to criticism.

Regarding the rationality assumption, there are at least two different interpretations of the concept. According to the traditional neoclassical view, the concept is to be understood as perfect individual rationality (i.e., decision makers have consistent and stable preferences and make use of every piece of information). This approach is formalized in the context of the theory of revealed preferences and has even been used to explain phenomena like drug addiction (see Stigler and Becker 1977). As Kreps (1990, 745) puts it, "A completely rational individual has the ability to foresee everything that might happen and to evaluate and optimally choose among available courses of action, all in the blink of an eye and at no cost." Admittedly, the rationality concept has been further developed, as for example by Brunner and Meckling (1977, 71), who speak of the "resourceful, evaluating, maximizing man." However, in spite of these elaborations the strong rationality assumption is usually still maintained.

Quite to the contrary, neoinstitutionalists try to approach the conditions of the real world more closely. As Coase (1988, 4) argues, "There is no reason to suppose that most human beings are engaged in maximizing anything unless it be unhappiness—and even this with incomplete success." Therefore, the NIE starts from the assumption of imperfect individual rationality. The concept of bounded rationality does not imply irrational behavior, but Simon (1957, xxiv), who introduced this concept, rather assumes economic actors to be "*intendedly* rational, but only *limitedly* so." However, what is meant by this phrase?

Today, at least two understandings of boundedly rational behavior exist. Some scholars view bounded rationality simply as another constraint on the maximization problem imposed by cognitive limitations such as memory size and computational capabilities (see, e.g., Dow 1991; Meyer 1991; Rubinstein 1993). Others, however, argue that bounded rationality "is not just another kind of utility maximization or something close to it" (Selten 1990, 657). According to Selten (1990, 653) and Gilboa and Schmeidler (1995), human behavior is not guided by a few abstract principles, but is rather case based in the sense that simple decision rules are employed which are chosen on the basis of a few simple criteria.[5] Other economists even consider individual preferences as incomplete and subject to change over time (see North 1978; Myhrman 1989).

Independent of which concept of bounded rationality is applied, it is important to notice that it will be difficult (if not impossible) to specify long-term contracts that specify all future contingencies if it is costly for individuals to gather and process information and make decisions. This, however, leads to another problem, since individuals can be assumed not to be only boundedly rational, but also to behave opportunistically. In the terminology of Williamson (1985, 65), opportunism is defined as "self-interest-seeking with guile." The assumption of opportunism does not necessarily imply that every individual is unscrupulous at any time, but rather that individuals differ in their degree of trustworthiness, which is not transparent ex ante. In the face of bounded rationality, contracts will be incomplete most of the time. Therefore, economic agents will demand safeguard provisions before entering a long-term relationship and undertaking specific investments. Asset specificity and long-term contracts are especially important in the context of economic development where specific investment and long-term relationships play a major role. The more trustworthy individuals are or the higher the probability is to find trustworthy subjects, the lower is the risk premium and the fewer safeguard provisions are necessary. Trust and trustworthiness can, therefore, economize on transaction costs and save on resources important for economic development.[6] As Fukuyama (1995, 27) explains, "Distrust imposes a kind of tax on all forms of economic activity, a tax that high-trust societies do not have to pay." At the extreme pole, a world of perfectly trusting and trustworthy individuals resembles the Arrow-Debreu world of perfect rationality, perfect information, complete contracts, and costless transactions.

Therefore, a more appropriate theory of economic development has to take into account more costs than the pure costs of production. The introduction of transaction costs stands at the core of the NIE. Their role in the process of economic development has been stressed by North, who defines transaction costs as "the costs of specifying and enforcing the contracts that underlie exchange and therefore comprise all the costs of political and economic organi-zation that permit economies to capture the gains from trade" (North 1984, 7). As Furubotn and Richter (1997) point out, transaction costs arise from precontractual activities such as search and inspection, the contracting process itself (bargaining), and postcontractual activities such as execution, control, and enforcement. In addition, the pure costs to reach a decision have to be considered as well, as Myhrman (1989, 48) argues. Decision costs not only refer to the psychological costs of making a decision, but also to the uncer-tainty about future preferences.

In this world of incomplete information and bounded rationality, institu-tions matter for economic performance since they can reduce the complexity of the decision process and eventually economize on transaction costs. Ac-cording to North (1994, 360), "Institutions are the humanly devised con-straints that structure human interaction. They are made up of formal constraints (e.g., rules, laws, constitutions), informal constraints (e.g., norms of behavior, conventions, self-imposed codes of conduct), and their enforcement charac-teristics. Together they define the incentive structure of societies and specifi-cally economies." While a major part of the NIE is rather optimistic about institutional development, arguing that because of the "filter of competition" only the most efficient institutions survive (see Alchian 1950; Myhrman 1989; Eggertsson 1990), others are less optimistic. As North (1994, 360) argues, "Institutions are not necessarily or even usually created to be socially efficient; rather they, or at least the formal rules, are created to serve the interests of those with the bargaining power to create new rules."[7]

After all, even though the NIE realizes the role institutional structure plays in economic performance, the development of informal institutions such as ethics, norms, trust, loyalty, and friendship is only perfunctorily dealt with. Sociologists such as Granovetter (1985, 482) point out that the social context in which transactions are embedded has been largely ignored until recently, even by proponents of the NIE. Stressing the importance of opportunistic behavior, the NIE can be seen as standing in the utilitarian tradition of classical and neoclassical economics, where not only the assumption of purely rational behavior is made, but human behavior is also regarded as taking place in a social vacuum. Agents are depicted as atomized beings that lack any social or cultural relation. Morals, ethics, and norms do not play any role in this world, but agents are rather assumed to unscrupulously pursue their narrowly defined self-interest. The shortcomings of such an approach have been nicely illus-trated by Sen (1977, 332), who noted, "'Where is the railway station?' he asks me. 'There,' I say, pointing at the post office, 'and could you please post this letter for me on the way?' 'Yes,' he says, determined to open the envelope and check whether it contains something valuable."

Obviously, in reality social interactions take place in a different way. Accord-ing to Granovetter (1985), classical and neoclassical economics as well as major parts of the NIE are based on an "atomized, undersocialized concept of human action." Modern sociology, on the contrary, is operating to a large extent with an oversocialized conception of man and woman, according to which people are overwhelmingly sensitive to norms, habits, and the opinions of others. The commonly developed system of norms is again regarded as being internalized through socialization and, therefore, not even perceived as a burden.

As an alternative, Granovetter (1985, 487) develops the so-called concept of embeddedness that avoids "the atomization implicit in the theoretical extremes of under- and oversocialized conceptions. Actors do not behave or decide as atoms outside a social context, nor do they adhere slavishly to a script written for them by the particular intersection of social categories that they happen to occupy. Their attempts at purposive action are instead embedded in concrete, ongoing systems of social relations." This model can be understood as a synthesis between the role-driven behavior assumed in sociology and the selfish, maximizing individual of economic theory.

Experimental work tends to support this view. Several free-rider experiments on private contributions to public goods have come to the finding that test persons were neither contributing nothing, as the free-rider hypothesis of standard economic theory predicts, nor did they spend the socially efficient amount. In most cases, the resulting contribution was rather somewhere in between (see Ledyard 1995, 111–181).[8] Customs, norms, and ethics, therefore, are key factors for economic performance, helping to overcome free-rider problems (see Schlicht 1993). Furthermore, customs and routines simply reduce decision costs (Nelson and Winter 1982).[9]

At this point, the HFP can add some important insights. Norms, customs, and ethics are results of a socialization process. As Adjibolosoo (1993, 146) puts it, "Labor force qualities such as industry, determination, integrity, trustworthiness, reliability, responsibility, accountability, and so on are mostly environmentally (i.e., culturally and institutionally) determined." In this context, Jones (1995) distinguishes three ways in which the relationship between culture and the economy is treated in the social sciences. While economists usually stick to the view of cultural nullity, simply ignoring cultural differences, anthropologists and other social scientists often take the point of cultural fixity, viewing the economy as a subset of culture and culture as changing autonomously. The third stream, called cultural reciprocity, finally acknowledges interactions between culture and the economy. While from this point of view norms have an impact on economic performance, so does the economic performance affect the evolution and decay of norms and habits.

To illustrate the concepts presented so far, we will now shift our attention to the experience of the West German economy after World War II. Especially, the interaction between formal institutions, as, for example, the central bank, and informal institutions, such as norms, ethics, and habits, will be subject to further exploration.[10]

THE GERMAN "MIRACLE"

West Germany's quick and unexpected recovery after World War II and the tremendous growth rates West Germany experienced until the late 1960s are often termed the "German miracle."[11] At the end of the war, major parts of Germany's productive capacity had been destroyed, as well as its infrastructure. The economic situation was disastrous. Millions of people were homeless and jobless, while, in addition, 13 million refugees poured into the country. Under these circumstances, no one dared to hope for a quick recovery at the end of the war. However, only a few years later the West German economy had not only recovered, but was actually growing at a tremendous rate. The gross national product (GNP) more than doubled between 1950 and 1960, and GNP per capita had risen by nearly 80 percent. Income per capita soon exceeded pre-war figures. With 1938 as 100, Germany's GNP per capita rose to 176 in 1962. Unemployment fell from 8.2 percent in 1950 to less than 1 percent in 1962, while the working population rose by 28 percent. Moreover, prices remained almost constant, rising by a total of 9 percent from 1951 to 1962. All in all, an economic miracle had come to pass.[12]

Though miracles are usually defined as events or occurrences that come unforeseeably (or at least unexpectedly) and that cannot be explained by easy means, economists have provided a number of explanations for the German miracle. Certainly, the most striking features of this miracle have been the booming exports of the German economy, the high degree of monetary stability, and the enormous savings rate that made capital readily available and allowed large investments (see Hennessy 1964). While these features certainly explain the enormous growth of the German economy, at least to some degree, the question then is how these features are themselves to be explained.

Indisputably, a key element in the German success has been the inception of Germany's *Ordnungspolitik*, also known as the policy of the "Social Market Economy" (see Watrin 1979; Schmidtchen 1984). This "peculiar German brand of economic liberalism," as Giersch, Paqué, and Schmieding (1992, 16) call it, was implemented by Ludwig Erhard, Minister of Economic Affairs, whose chief adviser was Walter Eucken, the head of the Freiburg School of Economics. His starting point was the question of how the economy and society can be organized both in a humane *and* an efficient way.

To answer this question, Eucken (1952) argued, it is necessary to compare different institutional settings or frameworks. This approach, which Eucken (1952, 180) called "thinking in economic orders," bears a strong resemblance to the comparative institutional approach proposed by Coase (1960).[13]

In Eucken's opinion, it is the task of the state to determine and to guarantee the economic order. In fact, the so-called German Ordoliberals did not demand a minimal state. As Wallich (1955, 115) notes, the Freiburg School of German Ordoliberalism did not plead for a laissez-faire paradise. On the contrary, the optimistic assumption that freedom of enterprise would suffice to ensure competition and stability was specifically rejected. The Freiburg School explicitly advocated a strong state to guarantee the economic order. As Eucken (1951, 72) put it, "The state must influence the forms within which economic activity takes place, but it is not its task to conduct the economic process itself. . . . State planning of the forms—yes; state planning and direction of the economic process—no."

In this context, Eucken (1952, 254) distinguishes two kinds of principles for economic policy. On the one hand, Eucken developed six constituent principles which constitute the competitive order: primacy of monetary policy, open markets, private ownership, freedom of contract, liability, and stability of economic policy. On the other hand, Eucken called for regulative principles to guarantee this order. Based on the experience of the German Reich of 1871 and the Weimar Republic (1918–1933) the Ordoliberals attached equal importance to safeguarding competition and individual freedom against the rise of private power, especially monopolies, cartels, and private interest groups. As Giersch, Paqué, and Schmieding (1992, 28) argue, "In the eyes of the Ordoliberals it was both the lack of adequate safeguards against the rise of private power and the weakness of the state which, in the last analysis, caused the replacement of economic and political freedom by an unrestrained dictatorship."

In accordance with Eucken's constituent principles, especially the primacy of monetary policy, the West German Minister of Economic Affairs, Ludwig Erhard, put through a currency reform in June 1948. Currency holdings and bank deposits in Reichsmark were converted into the new Deutsche Mark at an effective conversion rate of 100 to 6.5. This drastic contraction of the money supply eliminated the enormous excess purchasing power that existed after the war and basically ended inflation. Existing private and public debt was restructured and consolidated. Furthermore, while the monetary reform enabled the *Bundesbank* to gain control over monetary policy, strong institutional safeguards against future inflationary policies were established. Basically, the new central bank, first called *Bank deutscher Länder*, was given independence from the government and all other political bodies. Moreover, the military governments forbade excessive budget deficits. Finally, the currency reform was accompanied by the simultaneous removal of price controls and rationing laws and changes in the tax system geared towards promoting the formation of capital.[14]

However, a tight monetary policy and balanced budgets alone cannot explain the unusual success of the West German economy after World War II. Furthermore, the simple construction of formal institutions and the adoption of a free-market policy does not guarantee quick economic success or recovery. The recent experience of countries in Eastern Europe illustrates this very well. In a similar vein, a comprehensive study by Cukierman (1992) comes to the finding that formal central-bank independence is neither sufficient nor necessary for monetary stability. To reach a desired outcome the formal institutions of an economy have to be well adapted to the informal institutions already adopted by society.

In this sense, we argue that there is more to the German miracle than has been recognized so far. While the institutional policy played an important role for the German success, so did what Adjibolosoo (1993) calls the human factor. Institutions can only work properly if they are well adapted to the underlying culture and ethics of a society. Moreover, as is stressed by advocates of the HFP, for institutions to remain functional they have to be upheld by a network of persons that are not only committed to these institutions, but are also respected and accepted by society. In the case of Germany, Eucken's influence and credibility certainly has not only been due to the fact that he was one of the few outstanding economists that had personally experienced the effects of a centrally controlled economy. Probably even more important was that he had protested against the totalitarian ideology of the Nazi regime.[15] Furthermore, as Acquaah and Adjibolosoo (1995, 111) have stressed in a different context, the legitimacy of a certain policy will be the greater the more it coincides with the way the people affected by this policy see their problem. From this point of view, the general acceptance and legitimacy of the Ordoliberals' economic policy suggestions has certainly also been due to the fact that Eucken's doctrine was "the most home-grown one," as Giersch, Paqué, and Schmieding (1992, 26) emphasize. The concepts of the Freiburg School were based on a deep knowledge and understanding of the (average) German mentality and the informal institutions adopted by most Germans.[16]

To return to Eucken's constituent principles, the primacy of monetary policy and the importance of the 1948 currency reform can only be understood in the context of German history. Having experienced two hyperinflations, the German population was extremely sensitive to any hint of inflation. This policy restraint is certainly a specific German feature and can eventually be explained by the concept of stability culture (Richter 1993). Confidence in the central monetary authority plays an extremely important role in Germany. On this basis, the almost complete independence of the *Bundesbank* is to be understood as a means to regain the people's trust in monetary policy. The monetary policy itself is controlled by the social concept of stability culture.

On a more general level, Wallich (1955) has discussed how the mentality of the German people has contributed to the economic revival.[17] Especially, the willingness to work and save, labor discipline, and the acceptance of sometimes harsh economic policies are worth mentioning. In our terminology, these informal institutions characterizing the German post-war population have been an essential driving force for the German miracle. In the tradition of Weber (1930), Wallich (1955, 20) has argued that "the successive failure of monarchy, democracy, and dictatorship has left the Germans . . . skeptical toward all nonmaterial values." Hence, most Germans were aiming primarily toward material goals. Work ethic and morale can now be understood as a result of the historical experience Germany has faced. Moreover, in the Prussian tradition work was not seen as a job, but rather as a task or even as a vocation (see Caplan 1990). Therefore, Wallich (1955, 331) argues, "Work of all kinds is something almost sacred in Germany. . . . A strong sense of duty prevails, in part perhaps as a Prussian heritage."

This ethical exaltation of work, the high consciousness for high quality, and the tradition of perfectionism among many Germans have certainly contributed to the reputation for high-quality production. As Wallich (1955, 334) puts it, "German thoroughness favors high quality work." As a result, products made in Germany enjoy a high-quality reputation that is almost proverbial and supported by a large body of empirical evidence (see Head 1988; Kühn 1993). The international success of German manufacturers and the lasting export boom is not only due to macroeconomic factors, but also determined by cultural aspects.[18]

Following Wallich (1955, 338), the organization and discipline of the German workforce has also been a crucial element in the overall German success. Social relations are facilitated by strong self-discipline and mutual trust, which economizes on transaction costs (Fukuyama 1995, 231). In the absence of self-discipline and trust, any order must be enforced from outside (e.g., through legal action), so that valuable resources are lost. In contrast, "discipline, reliability, and precision have become habitual with labor" in Germany, as Wallich (1955, 338) points out.

The relations between labor and management were codified as part of Ludwig Erhard's Social Market Economy. Labor relations have been extremely consensual after World War II, which is also reflected by the fact that the number of days lost to strike have been among the lowest in the developed world (see Fukuyama 1995, 216). Reciprocity was institutionalized through rules of codetermination (*Mitbestimmung*) and collective bargaining. Under the rules of codetermination, labor representatives sit on boards of the companies they are working for with access to corporate information and limited participation in governance. The high degree of mutual trust between labor and management is reflected by the fact that the first chairman of Unified German Union, Hans Boeckler, preferred codetermination over nationalization of industry as a positive, constructive force. Hence, the institution of codetermination is to be understood as the attempt to share power between labor and capital rather than to destroy it (see Hennessy 1964, 24). Furthermore, the established workers' councils became influential in promoting good labor–management relations. Finally, the system of collective bargaining between industry associations and labor unions on a sector- or industrywide basis helped overcoming free-rider problems and lowered bargaining costs.

Even in the basic factory-floor relationships, trust between workers and their foreman or *Meister* was institutionalized by various measures, as described by Fukuyama (1995, Chapters 19 and 20). The *Meister* is trusted with great responsibility, and work is organized on a team basis. Workers are often rotated between different workstations as part of the socialization process.

Furthermore, the *Meister* is usually familiar with the work of his subordinates. In this context, the German apprenticeship system of vocational training is important, since it provides the industry with the skill needed for high-quality production. About 70 percent of the German workforce start their career as apprentices, while only 10 percent fail to pass through either an apprenticeship or higher education (Casey 1991, vii). Therefore, vocational training does not bear a certain stigma, as in some other countries. Apprentices are not regarded as "people who failed in the general educational system, but as ones who succeeded in a demanding vocational training track" (Fukuyama 1995, 241). Apprenticeships exist for virtually all professions and consist of a two- to three-year program of practical training and theoretical education. Furthermore, there is quite a number of intermediate certifications beyond the basic apprenticeship. As Fukuyama explains, "These intermediate certifications constitute an entirely separate route to upward social mobility of a sort that does not exist in most other countries."[19] Moreover, it is important to notice that the apprenticeship system plays a crucial role in the socialization process of young professionals and certainly affects the working ethics, norms, and rules governing work relations. Through the apprenticeship system, young professionals get easily accustomed to the existing working ethics.

CONCLUSION

There are certainly more elements to the so-called German miracle and the extraordinary success of the post–World War II German economy than those emphasized in the limited space of this chapter.[20] At this point, at least the writings of Gerschenkron (1962, 1966) and the recent study of Herrigel (1996) are worth mentioning. The main focus of Gerschenkron is on the combination of technological and institutional innovations. As Gerschenkron suggests, economic latecomers, such as Germany, could take advantage of their own backwardness and construct large efficient plants that exploit economies of scale and avoid the problems of competition between several small firms. On the basis of his study of Germany, Gerschenkron then claims that nations could improve their position through political and institutional adaptation in a similar way. In contrast, Herrigel argues that Germany's development was driven to a major extent by small and medium-sized firms that are embedded in a larger system of relations with labor, communal organizations, educational institutions, and local and regional governments and that are much more flexible and less anonymous than large corporations. While there are certainly some merits to these points, both Gerschenkron and Herrigel do not acknowledge the crucial role the human factor and informal institutions have been playing in Germany's development.

It has not been the main purpose of this chapter to produce a comprehensive analysis of Germany's development and to explain every detail of the German economy; rather, this chapter has aimed to demonstrate that there is more to the German miracle than has been recognized so far by most economists. Social relations and culture have impacts on economic performance that are not to be underestimated. Therefore, it is not sufficient to create formal institutions that might work within a certain cultural setting; these institutions must be adapted to the informal institutions adopted by society. On the other hand, formal institutions have an impact on the socialization process. In general, to achieve economic growth and development, formal and informal institutions have to be well suited to each other, or, as Adjibolosoo (1996, 15) puts it, "Both institutions and the HF have to work hand-in-hand to bring positive changes into society."

While in the particular case of Germany the match of formal and informal institutions has produced a "remarkable record of economic growth coupled with a high level of social benefits" (Fukuyama 1995, 243), it will be interesting to see how Germany will cope with the challenges ahead. If Germany is to meet its future challenges it might be necessary to remove the rigidities currently inherent in the system. In contrast to many other countries, in today's Germany most institutions are based on formal law rather than informal consensus. It is, therefore, much more difficult to adjust them during downturns. Economists such as Giersch, Paqué, and Schmieding (1992) or Dornbusch (1993) have already claimed that the end of the German miracle has come. If German formal institutions stay rigid while informal institutions such as norms and habits are changing, this rather gloomy pronouncement may indeed be true.

NOTES

I am most happy to acknowledge the hospitality of the Institute for Management, Innovation, and Organization (IMIO), University of California, Berkeley, where this work was completed. Financial support was provided by the *Deutsche Forschungsgemeinschaft* (DFG) under grant Ri 15–1. Furthermore, I would like to thank Senyo Adjibolosoo and Matthias Klaes for helpful comments, as well as Joachim Keller and Christian Wey for beneficial communications.

1. For a review of reasons given by conventional development theorists to explain the failure of actual development policies in Africa, see Adjibolosoo (1993).

2. Indeed, there is quite a number of economists who argue that the economies of Southeast Asia have succeeded not by following, but by violating the rules of conventional development policies. See, for example, Johnson (1982), Deyo (1987), or Fallows (1994).

3. An excellent introduction to the basic principles of human factor theory can be found in Adjibolosoo (1996).

4. According to Greif (1994), a "collectivist" organization is based on multilateral reputation mechanisms and informal codes of behavior, while an "individualistic" organization is based on bilateral punishment and formal enforcement mechanisms. The effects of the collectivistic ethic are also discussed by Adu-Febiri (1995a).

5. This view is also supported by experimental work which is reviewed in Kahneman (1994).

6. In this context, Giersch (1995, 5) employs the concept of "moral capital," which he regards as a decisive factor for economic performance. According to Giersch (1995, 7), an economy's moral capital is determined by (1) the property moral (respect of property), (2) the contract moral (contract fulfillment), (3) individual moral (responsibility), and (4) public spirit or sense of solidarity. The moral capital can substitute security deposits, mortgages, or hostages and reduce risk premiums paid, thereby making market transactions less costly. For an application of a similar concept of moral capital, see Adu-Febiri (1995b). The importance of both a society's moral capital and its "spiritual capital" is also explored by Adjibolosoo (1995a, 1996).

7. A similar view is held by Olson (1982).

8. As Feld, Pommerehne, and Hart (1994) have shown, even in real-world situations, public goods might be voluntarily provided.

9. The potential interactions between culture and economic performance are more fully explored by DiMaggio (1994).

10. At this point, the work of Perez (1983) is worth mentioning. In her work, Perez explains long-term economic growth and development in terms of matches and mismatches of a society's socioinstitutional structure and technological style. In particular, she postulates that "Kondratiev's long waves are not a strictly economic phenomenon, but rather the manifestation, measurable in economic terms, of the harmonious or disharmonious behavior of the total socioeconomic and institutional system" (Perez 1983, 358). However, while the main focus of Perez is on the interrelationship between technological factors and institutional structure, ours is on the relation between formal institutions and the human factor (or informal institutions).

11. See, for example, Hennessy (1964), Schmidtchen (1984), or Dornbusch (1993).

12. A detailed description of Germany's recovery is given by Hennessy (1964) and, more recently, Giersch, Paqué, and Schmieding (1992).

13. The methodological similarities and differences between Eucken and Coase have been analyzed by Schmidtchen (1984).

14. A detailed analysis of the situation and reforms in West Germany after World War II is given in Richter (1979).

15. As Hennessy (1964, 6, footnote 1) explains, the most arresting fact about Eucken was that he was still alive at the end of the war.

16. The true miracle, therefore, might rather be the fact that Eucken's policy suggestions were accepted and put through against the resistance of international experts. For further discussion see Hennessy (1964) and Hutchison (1979).

17. Of course, a society's or nation's mentality can only be described as average qualities. When speaking of the German mentality, it is not implied that every single German sticks to the characterization given here. Nevertheless, for every culture there are certainly some qualities and properties that are considered typical.

18. However, as Haucap, Wey, and Barmbold (1997) show, in the presence of incomplete information about product quality and the reputation of products, "made in Germany" can also be explained by signaling considerations.

19. The fact that social mobility may be an important engine for economic growth and development has recently been demonstrated on theoretical grounds by Fershtman, Murphy, and Weiss (1996).

20. The extraordinarily high savings rate in Germany, for example, can be traced

back to the Prussian tradition of "starving oneself rich" (*Großhungern*). That means savings behavior is not only affected by economic figures such as income or interest rates, but cultural elements as well.

REFERENCES

Acquaah, M., and S. Adjibolosoo. 1995. The Role of the Human Factor and Co-Management in Managing the Sardinella Fishery of Ghana. *Review of Human Factor Studies* 1 (1): 99–120.

Adjibolosoo, S. 1993. The Human Factor in Development. *Scandinavian Journal of Development Alternatives* 12 (4): 139–149.

Adjibolosoo, S. 1994. The Human Factor and the Failure of Economic Development and Policies in Africa. In *Perspectives on Economic Development in Africa*, edited by F. Ezeala-Harrison and S. Adjibolosoo. Westport, Conn.: Praeger.

Adjibolosoo, S. 1995a. *The Human Factor in Developing Africa.* Westport, Conn.: Praeger.

Adjibolosoo, S. 1995b. The Significance of the Human Factor in African Economic Development. In *The Significance of the Human Factor in African Economic Development*, edited by S. Adjibolosoo. Westport, Conn.: Praeger.

Adjibolosoo, S. 1996. A Guide to Understanding the Fundamental Principles of Human Factor Theory. *Review of Human Factor Studies* 2 (1): 1–26.

Adu-Febiri, F. 1995a. Culture as the Epitome of the Human Factor in Development: The Case of Ghana's Collectivistic Ethic. In *The Significance of the Human Factor in African Economic Development*, edited by S. Adjibolosoo. Westport, Conn.: Praeger.

Adu-Febiri, F. 1995b. Is Africa's Development a Basket Case? *Review of Human Factor Studies* 1 (1): 45–60.

Alchian, A. A. 1950. Uncertainty, Evolution, and Economic Theory. *Journal of Political Economy* 58: 211–221.

Bardhan, P. 1996. The Nature of Institutional Impediments to Economic Development. Working Paper No. C 96–066, University of California, Berkeley.

Becker, G. S., K. M. Murphy, and R. Tamura. 1990. Human Capital, Fertility, and Economic Growth. *Journal of Political Economy* 98: S12–S37.

Brunner, K., and W. H. Meckling. 1977. The Perception of Man and the Conception of Government. *Journal of Money, Credit, and Banking* 3: 70–85.

Caplan, J. 1990. Profession as Vocation: The German Civil Service. In *German Professions 1800–1950*, edited by G. Cooks and K. H. Jarausch. Oxford: Oxford University Press.

Casey, B. 1991. *Recent Developments in West Germany's Apprenticeship Training System.* London: Policy Studies Institute.

Clague, C. 1993. Rule Obedience, Organizational Loyalty, and Economic Development. *Journal of Institutional and Theoretical Economics* 149: 393–414.

Coase, R. H. 1960. The Problem of Social Cost. *Journal of Law and Economics* 3: 1–44.

Coase, R. H. 1988. *The Firm, the Market, and the Law.* Chicago: University of Chicago Press.

Coleman, J. S. 1990. *Foundations of Social Theory.* Cambridge: Harvard University Press.

Cukierman, A. 1992. *Central Bank Strategy, Credibility, and Independence: Theory and Evidence.* Cambridge: MIT Press.

Deyo, F. C. 1987. *The Political Economy of New Asian Industrialism.* Ithaca: Cornell University Press.

DiMaggio, P. 1994. Culture and Economy. In *The Handbook of Economic Sociology,* edited by N. J. Smelser and R. Swedberg. Princeton: Princeton University Press; New York: Russell Sage Foundation.

Dornbusch, R. 1993. The End of the German Miracle. *Journal of Economic Literature* 31: 881–885.

Dow, J. 1991. Search Decisions with Limited Memory. *Review of Economic Studies* 58: 1–14.

Eggertsson, T. 1990. *Economic Behavior and Institutions.* Cambridge: Cambridge University Press.

Eucken, W. 1951. *Unser Zeitalter der Mißerfolge.* Tübingen: J. C. B. Mohr (Paul Siebeck).

Eucken, W. 1952. *Grundsätze der Wirtschaftspolitik.* Tübingen: J. C. B. Mohr (Paul Siebeck).

Fallows, J. 1994. *Looking at the Sun: The Rise of the New East Asian Economic and Political System.* New York: Pantheon.

Feld, L. P., W. W. Pommerehne, and A. Hart. 1994. Voluntary Provision of a Public Good: Results from a Real World Experiment. *Kyklos* 47: 505–518.

Fershtman, C., K. M. Murphy, and Y. Weiss. 1996. Social Status, Education, and Growth. *Journal of Political Economy* 104: 108–132.

Fukuyama, F. 1995. *Trust: The Social Virtues and the Creation of Prosperity.* New York: The Free Press.

Furubotyn, E. G., and R. Richter. 1997. *Institutions and Economic Theory: The Contribution of the New Institutional Economics.* Ann Arbor: University of Michigan Press.

Gerschenkron, A. 1962. *Economic Backwardness in Historical Perspective.* Cambridge: Harvard University Press.

Gerschenkron, A. 1966. *Bread and Democracy in Germany.* New York: Howard Fertig.

Giersch, H. 1995. *Wirtschaftsmoral als Standortfaktor.* Lectiones Jenenses, Heft 2. Jena: Max-Planck-Institut zur Erforschung von Wirtschaftssystemen.

Giersch, H., K.-H. Paqué, and H. Schmieding. 1992. *The Fading Miracle. Four Decades of Market Economy in Germany.* Cambridge: Cambridge University Press.

Gilboa, I., and D. Schmeidler. 1995. Case Based Decision Theory. *Quarterly Journal of Economics* 110: 605–639.

Granovetter, M. 1985. Economic Action and Social Structure: The Problem of Embeddedness. *American Journal of Sociology* 91: 481–501.

Greif, A. 1994. Cultural Beliefs and the Organization of Society: A Historical and Theoretical Reflection on Collectivist and Individualist Societies. *Journal of Political Economy* 102: 912–950.

Haucap, J., C. Wey, and J. Barmbold. 1997. Location Choice as a Signal for Product Quality: The Economics of "Made in Germany." *Journal of Institutional and Theoretical Economics* 153: 510–531.

Head, D. 1988. Advertising Slogans and the "Made-in" Concept. *International Journal of Advertising* 7: 237–252.

Hennessy, J. 1964. The German "Miracle." In *Economic "Miracles,"* edited by J. Hennessy, V. Lutz, and G. Scimone. London: Institute of Economic Affairs.

Herrigel, G. 1996. *Industrial Constructions: The Sources of German Industrial Power.* Cambridge: Cambridge University Press.

Hutchison, T. W. 1979. Notes on Effects of Economic Ideas on Policy: The Example of the German Social Market Economy (in German). *Zeitschrift für die gesamte Staatswissenschaft* 135: 426–441.

Johnson, C. 1982. *MITI and the Japanese Miracle.* Palo Alto, Calif.: Stanford University Press.

Jones, E. L. 1995. Culture and its Relationship to Economic Change. *Journal of Institutional and Theoretical Economics* 151: 269–285.

Kahneman, D. 1994. New Challenges to the Rationality Assumption. *Journal of Institutional and Theoretical Economics* 150: 18–36.

Kreps, D. M. 1990. *A Course in Microeconomic Theory.* Princeton: Princeton University Press.

Kühn, R. 1993. Das "Made-in-Image" Deutschlands im internationalen Vergleich. *Marketing—Zeitschrift für Forschung und Praxis* 2: 119–127.

Kuran, T. 1997. Islam and Underdevelopment: An Old Puzzle Revisited. *Journal of Institutional and Theoretical Economics* 153: 41–71.

Ledyard, J. O. 1995. Public Goods: A Survey of Experimental Research. In *Handbook of Experimental Economics*, edited by J. H. Kagel and A. E. Roth. Princeton: Princeton University Press.

Lin, J. Y., and J. B. Nugent. 1995. Institutions and Economic Development. In *Handbook of Development Economics.* Vol. 3, edited by J. Behrman and T. N. Srinivasan. Amsterdam: North Holland.

Meyer, M. 1991. Learning from Coarse Information: Biased Contests and Career Profiles. *Review of Economic Studies* 58: 15–41.

Myhrman, J. 1989. The New Institutional Economics and the Process of Economic Development. *Journal of Institutional and Theoretical Economics* 145: 38–59.

Nelson, R., and S. Winter. 1982. *An Evolutionary Theory of Economic Change.* Cambridge: Harvard University Press.

North, D. C. 1978. Structure and Performance: The Task of Economic History. *Journal of Economic Literature* 16: 963–978.

North, D. C. 1981. *Structure and Change in Economic History.* New York: W. W. Norton.

North, D. C. 1984. Transaction Costs, Institutions, and Economic History. *Journal of Institutional and Theoretical Economics* 140: 7–17.

North, D. C. 1994. Economic Performance through Time. *American Economic Review* 84: 359–368.

Olson, M. 1982. *The Rise and Decline of Nations: Economic Growth, Stagflation, and Social Rigidities.* New Haven: Yale University Press.

Perez, C. 1983. Structural Change and Assimilation of New Technologies in the Economic and Social Systems. *Futures* 15: 357–375.

Popper, K. R. 1957. *The Poverty of Historicism.* London: Routledge and Kegan Paul.

Putnam, R. D. 1993. *Making Democracy Work: Civic Traditions in Modern Italy.* Princeton: Princeton University Press.

Richter, R., ed. 1979. Symposium. Currency and Economic Reform: West Germany after World War II (in German). *Zeitschrift für die gesamte Staatswissenschaft* 135: 297–532.

Richter, R. 1993. "Stability Culture" as a Problem of Modern Institutional Economics. Discussion Paper, Center for the Study of the New Institutional Economics, University of Saarland, November.

Rubinstein, A. 1993. On Price Recognition and Computational Complexity in a Monopolistic Model. *Journal of Political Economy* 101: 473–484.

Schlicht, E. 1993. On Custom. *Journal of Institutional and Theoretical Economics* 149: 178–203.

Schmidtchen, D. 1984. German "Ordnungspolitik" as Institutional Choice. *Zeitschrift für die gesamte Staatswissenschaft* 140: 54–70.

Selten, R. 1990. Bounded Rationality. *Journal of Institutional and Theoretical Economics* 146: 649–658.

Sen, A. 1977. Rational Fools: A Critique of the Behavioral Foundations of Economic Theory. *Philosophy and Public Affairs* 6: 317–344.

Simon, H. A. 1957. *Models of Man.* New York: John Wiley and Sons.

Stigler, G. J., and G. S. Becker. 1977. De Gustibus Non Est Disputandum. *American Economic Review* 67: 76–90.

Wallich, H. C. 1955. *Mainsprings of the German Revival.* Yale Studies in Economics, Vol. 5. New Haven: Yale University Press.

Watrin, C. 1979. The Principles of the Social Market Economy: Its Origins and Early History (in German). *Zeitschrift für die gesamte Staatswissenschaft* 135: 405–425.

Weber, M. 1930. *The Protestant Ethic and the Spirit of Capitalism.* Translated by T. Parsons. New York: Scribner.

Weber, M. 1968. *Economy and Society. An Outline of Interpretive Sociology.* Translated by E. Fischoff et al. New York: Bedminster Press.

Williamson, O. E. 1985. *The Economic Institutions of Capitalism.* New York: The Free Press.

Chapter 3

The Human Factor in Japan's Economic Development

Mahamudu Bawumia

In the search for the holy grail of economic development, many development economists have examined Japanese economic development for clues. Japan took less than fifty years to emerge as a predominantly industrial society, the first outside the West.[1] Except for the severe interruption caused by World War II and its immediate aftermath, Japanese industrialization grew at a rapid pace. From the mid-1950s, Japan's rate of economic growth was one of the highest and most sustained in the history of nations, averaging, until the 1970s, close to a 10-percent gain per year in real national income. From 1954 to 1964 alone, the decade following the restoration of the Japanese economy to its prewar levels, total production per capita tripled, manufacturing output almost quadrupled, and real consumption per family grew about 50 percent (Lockwood 1965, 10). The transformation of the Japanese economy from less developed to developed status in less than three decades after World War II has been described as the "Japanese miracle." Understanding this miracle has been the preoccupation of development economists and sociologists alike since the 1970s.

Friedman (1988) categorizes the various explanations of Japan's success into two perspectives, the "bureaucratic regulation thesis" and the "market regulation thesis." The bureaucratic regulation thesis holds that the economic bureaucracy in Japan, particularly the Ministry of International Trade and Industry (MITI), directed the development of Japan's high economic growth. A proponent of this view, Wade (1990) has argued that the role of government intervention was key to the success of Japan. The government intervened systematically to foster the development of specific industries in particular. Policy interventions included the targeting and subsidizing of credit to selected industries, keeping deposit rates low and maintaining ceilings on borrowing rates to increase profits and retained earnings, protecting domestic import substitutes, subsidizing declining industries, financially supporting government banks, and establishing firm and industry-specific export targets. For example, with the formulation of the "New Long Term Economic Plan" (1957) and the "National Income Doubling Plan" (1960), in which the aim of government policy was the development of heavy and chemical industries, MITI first designated within the heavy and chemical industries those categories which were to be promoted. These included oil refining, petrochemicals, artificial fibers, motor cars, industrial machinery, airplanes, electronics, and electrical appliances. These industries were then provided with absolute protection and developmental assistance.

The market regulation thesis, on the other hand, propounded by economists of the neoclassical persuasion, holds that Japanese economic successes were the normal result of incentives toward profitable economic activity and were generated by the market. Japanese manufacturing grew so rapidly because industrialists were disciplined by the market and met its challenges effectively. The argument is supported by evidence of considerable competition in Japanese domestic markets, where tremendous rivalry leads to cutthroat competition among manufacturers. The World Bank (1994), for example, argues that Japan's success, as with other East Asian countries, can be attributed to getting the basics right, with private domestic investment and rapidly growing human capital as the principal engines of growth.

Many other explanations have been offered for Japan's success. These include cultural habits of hard work and savings, declining population growth rates, good macroeconomic management, a good banking system necessary to raise the level of financial savings, and investments in human capital.

While each of these explanations for Japan's success has some merit, in this chapter I focus on a previously ignored factor in explaining economic development, the human factor (Adjibolosoo 1995).[2] The human factor encompasses much more than knowledge and ability. Knowledge and ability by themselves are useless if they are not applied, or applied wrongly. It should be noted that the neoclassical definition of human capital does not make a distinction between a population educated to steal and another educated to work. In the rest of this chapter I analyze the role of the Japanese human factor in explaining the Japanese miracle.

CONFUCIANISM AND THE EVOLUTION OF JAPAN'S HUMAN FACTOR

Confucianism came to Japan (from China via Korea) in about the sixth century. At that time, both among the upper classes and the people at large, husband and wife lived separately. The husband visited his wife, but not the other way around. The husband openly had several wives whom he visited in turn; the wife privately received several husbands in turn. The children were brought up by their respective mothers, so the children of different mothers were little more than strangers to each other. They could easily fall in love with each other and marry without any feeling of committing a crime, and at the same time they could easily kill each other (Morishima 1982). In the context of human factor development, one can say that Japan's human factor in this era was at a low level. By the sixth century, however, the Japanese began to try to advance their culture.

Under the influence of Confucian philosophy, Emperor Shotoku Taishi (574–622) proclaimed in his Seventeen Article Constitution that every man in Japan was equal in front of the Emperor. Government officials were also to be appointed not because of their pedigree but according to their character and ability. Offices were no longer inheritable. The first article of the constitution also stated that Japanese society would be organized on the principle of all communal societies: harmony among members. No one should be allowed to form a subgroup within the community to oppose others. Each person should calmly discuss matters to arrive at a decision which is reasonable and desirable from the viewpoint of the society as a whole. To realize harmony within the society, governors at various levels should consult on important matters with the public and make decisions democratically.

Furthermore, civil servants should realize that propriety is the foundation of law and order (Article 4); they should not accept bribes (Article 5); they should appoint the right man to the right position (Article 7); they should come to the office as early as possible and work overtime (Article 8); they should respect and carry out the principle of "work and you will be rewarded" (Article 11); they should not feel jealous over a colleague's good fortune (Article 14); they should administer political justice without which loyalty to the Emperor and benevolence to the people would not prevail (Article 6); they should respect sincerity, which is the mother of righteousness (Article 9); and they should not act from selfish motives but should render service to the public (Article 15).

We see here the beginnings of the evolution of the human factor at a societal level in Japan. Morishima (1982) points out that, on the whole, this Constitution was very Confucian, with the virtues of harmony, propriety, loyalty, benevolence, sincerity, and righteousness highly advocated.

EDUCATION AND LEARNING

After a century and a half of feudal warring, Tokugawa Ieyasu seized power in 1600 and established a shogunate. The Tokugawa regime pursued an isolationist policy. It banned foreign trade altogether, except for one strictly watched Dutch post in Nagasaki harbor. The death penalty was decreed for any foreigner attempting to enter Japan, internal migration was banned, and Christians were rigorously persecuted. Japan went through a more than 200-year period of isolation during which the whole nation was trained in the Confucianist way of thought. During this period, the Japanese were "brainwashed" and molded into a specific type of person by their Confucianist education (Mikiso 1991).

An aspect of Confucianism which aided the development of the Japanese human factor is its rejection of mysticism, incantation, magic, and ghosts. It was an intellectual and rational philosophy. For this reason, Western sciences were able to plant their roots deeply and quickly in contrast to many parts of the developing world today where mysticism and magic are predominant.

Also, Confucian education, against a background of 200 years of bureaucratic control, had trained the warriors to be efficient bureaucrats by the end of the Tokugawa era. Furthermore, they had equipped themselves with the discipline needed by soldiers of a modern army or workers in a modern factory, thus facilitating the commencement of a modern military organization and a modern factory system.

Japanese economic development was stunted during the Tokugawa period. However, the Tokugawa regime established national unity in place of political fragmentation, and created widespread industriousness not unlike the Protestant work ethic. Japan's relative underdevelopment when compared to the West was evident when they saw, firsthand, Western technological and military superiority with the arrival of Commodore Matthew Perry with eight ships off the Japanese coast in 1854. The Tokugawa regime, weak and under pressure, agreed to open trade with the "barbarians."

The regime was subsequently overthrown and the imperial line was restored under the emperor Meiji in 1868. Meiji set about to modernize Japan. The first priority of the Meiji reformers was to acquire foreign learning. Confucianism emphasized learning through the imitation of worthy models. The willingness to borrow and adopt ideas from other societies was, however, tempered by two instinctive questions: "How well does it work?" and "How good is it for us?" Thus, the Japanese developed their own highly distinctive styles of art and architecture to rival those of the Chinese, from whom they initially borrowed the ideas.

Most of the court leaders, led by Iwakura Tomomi, went off for a year and a half to study the political and social institutions of Europe and the United States. Students who returned from the West played a critical role in the modernization of Japan.

They also imported hundreds of foreign experts in various fields, from Western philosophy to lighthouse construction and zoology. The foreign experts proved to be quite expensive by Japanese standards. For example, by 1879, the Ministry of Industry employed 130 foreigners, whose salaries accounted for nearly three-fifths of the ministry's fixed expenditures. They were, therefore, quickly replaced by their Japanese students and assistants or by the Japanese who returned from study abroad. The number of foreign employees in the Bureau of Mines was reduced by one-third between 1873 and 1880. By the turn of the century, few hired foreign experts remained, except as language instructors.

Within months of its creation, the Ministry of Education, established in 1871, pronounced the establishment of elementary education for the benefit of all, "from noble to commoner." The Education Act of 1872, which established universal compulsory education, openly urged, in its preamble, the universal development of character, mind, and talent for the sake of rising and prospering in the world. However, the preamble made no reference to its moral influence.

The Japanese government also established a new organized school system based on Western theory and practice, but in adopting a Western educational system they were not merely imitative. They fashioned a standardized system to meet the needs of the nation as they saw them. In 1872, the government adopted the highly centralized French system, with the country divided into eight university districts and subdivided into middle school and elementary school districts. Sixteen months of schooling were made compulsory for all children. Compulsory education was extended to three years in 1880 and later to six years.

The 1880s marked a period of ideological contention over the substance and methods of national education. The question of moral education was the frequent subject of debate (Gluck 1985). In 1879, Motoda Eifu, the Palace official and Confucian tutor to the emperor, issued the formal call to reestablish "our ancestral precepts and national teachings of benevolence, justice, loyalty, and filial piety as the essence of education" (Takaaki 1972, 140). In the name of the emperor, Motoda drafted a document called "The Great Principles of Education," in which he lamented the results of the new education system:

In recent days people have been going to extremes. In the name of civilization and enlightenment, they pursue only knowledge and skills, thus violating the rules of good conduct and bringing harm to our customary ways. . . . While making a tour of schools and closely observing the pupils studying last autumn, it was noted that farmers' and merchants' sons were advocating high-sounding ideas and empty theories, and many of the Western words they used could not be translated in our own language. Even if such people were to return home after their studies, they would find it difficult to pursue their occupations and their high-sounding ideas, they would be equally useless as officials. (Tenno 1968, 227–228)

Motoda stated unequivocally that "for morality Confucius is the best guide" and prescribed "morality and skills" as the dual objects of education.

By 1882, a shift occurred in education policy. The government decided to put a greater emphasis in elementary education on courses in morals, through which undesirable Occidental influences could be combated and "proper attitudes" inculcated in the masses. The emphasis on the teaching of proper attitudes and morality at the elementary school level, one can argue, was an important step in the development of the Japanese human factor. The change in educational policy resulting in this new emphasis was an implicit recognition by policy makers that human capital alone was insufficient without the requisite human factor in Japan's development.

The role of education in the evolution of the human factor in Japan is captured in the promulgation of the Imperial Rescript on Education of 1890. The Rescript on Education became the focus of a new civil morality based on the premise that national education should serve the state. The Ministry of Education worked to institutionalize moral education in schools, based on the Rescript. From the time the first government textbooks appeared in 1903 through four subsequent redactions until the end of World War II, the schools used uniform and official national texts, not only in ethics but also in history, language, and geography (Gluck 1985, 149). With the Rescript as a moral basis, a corpus of national textbooks, and a body of publicly trained and employed teachers, the Ministry of Education pursued its mission of civic education.

School principals intoned the Rescript on each national holiday, at each school ceremony, and at special monthly convocations held expressly for the purpose. In the lower three grades, the children repeated the words after the teacher in moral instruction class; in the fourth grade and above, they were expected to recite it from memory. In connection with the Rescript's injunction to filiality, first graders were instructed to be sure to tell their parents whenever they left or returned home. In the fourth grade, topics for discussion included "how caring for parents is different from caring for a dog or horse." Third graders learned how to clean the classroom just as they would their home. Lessons on "the spirit of public morality" were instituted and taught to prepare pupils for public life.

Civil morality was thus gradually established among the wider population as the indispensable minimum of civic allegiance. The Confucian social ethic set the bounds of secular moral conformity within which "loyal and patriotic" Japanese were to locate themselves, or at least were expected not to publicly contravene.

INDUSTRIAL TRAINING AND THE DEVELOPMENT OF JAPAN'S HUMAN FACTOR

In establishing a modern school system, the principal aim of the Meiji government was to prepare the young to enter a new industrialized society. In this regard, formal education was not the only approach. Quasi-secondary schools, youth schools, and "miscellaneous" schools, concurrent with the expansion of vocational curricula in the public secondary schools, became important supplements.

The first steps of the Meiji leaders for economic development included a systematic estimate of skill needs. These were based mainly on *Opinions on Industry*, a survey of potential industrial development by national and local leaders and administrators carried out in the 1870s and published in the 1880s (Taira 1971, 393). The early policy makers soon concluded that Japan's needs for skill and vocational training could not be left to the haphazard workings of demand and supply in the labor market, but rather required coordinated, programmed efforts in both the public and private sector of the nation.

Throughout the first two decades following the Meiji Restoration, the new government and its agencies took virtually sole direction of the training of employees within the newly founded factories, arsenals, and offices—just as it did for the whole initial push to industrialize. In hopes of accomplishing this, the Meiji government decreed, early on, both the abolition of all previous barriers to labor mobility and an end to the long-established guild system among the traditional shielded trades. Training relied heavily on instruction by foreigners of recruits in new work sites. Later, as the foreigners left, the more skilled Japanese workers directly instructed young recruits on the job. Most prominent of these vocational programs was the training of employees in the government-owned state enterprises during the 1870s and 1880s.

From 1870 to 1885, modern industrial training in Japan was promoted under the direction of the central government, mainly by the Ministry of Industry, which set up its own schools for telecommunications, steel and iron production, handicraft training, lighthouse keeping, and mechanical engineering. Over time, these programs became increasingly sophisticated and were gradually upgraded. The Department of Engineering of Tokyo Imperial University, established in 1887, evolved from one such program (Levine and Kawada 1980). At the same time, of special significance for training fully skilled workers were the arsenals and shipyards under the control of the army and navy ministries, which established systematic programs, particularly in the fields of metallurgy, mechanics, construction, and textiles. Levine and Kawada's (1980, 231–241) account of human-resource development in the cotton textile industry is illustrative.

Training female operatives in textiles began with instruction by French engineers at the government-owned Tamioka mill, established in 1872. In this early program, girls were "drafted" from families of samurai and wealthy farmers and merchants from various parts of Japan to serve as examples of the "new workers" in modernizing Japan. Once trained to follow factory discipline, these model workers were to return to their local communities and instruct other young females destined to work in local mills. The Tamioka system stressed manual dexterity on the job, continual attention to the tasks of the job, acceptance of the supervisor's absolute authority, competition in work efficiency, use of dormitories for group living, and classroom instruction for general education in subjects such as ethics, arithmetic, and dressmaking.

The Tamioka system served as the model to be emulated for many years. As the textile industry spread in the 1880s and 1890s, and as the government turned over its factories to private enterprises, the employment of females as operatives grew rapidly. Most of the females had low education levels and thus the dormitories served as means for additional schooling. Hirano Cotton Spinning Company, for example, established a formal elementary education school for its female recruits in Osaka in 1887. It hired teachers from local public schools to provide instruction. The curriculum at Hirano covered Japanese composition, reading, dressmaking, penmanship, and ethics. Formal classes lasted two hours every morning and evening, after an exhausting twelve-hour work shift.

Formal training programs initiated in Japan's modern cotton textile industry during the 1920s were part and parcel of the more general industrial rationalization movement of that period. With cotton textiles manufacturing as Japan's most important industry, no longer could companies run the risk of employing poorly educated, low quality, and unstable workers to operate the advanced technologies and intricate organizations. Direct management control, based on systematic policies and research, became increasingly necessary. The big mills began to set up equivalent public elementary schools for the young women in their employ. The companies usually supplied textbooks and materials and offered curricula at both the lower elementary level, which was compulsory under the law, and at the higher elementary level. This education was nontechnical, with subjects such as morals, history, flower arranging, cooking, and housekeeping, to prepare the girls for marriage.

A far more systematic approach to technical training was adopted by the 1920s. At the Tokyo Cotton Textile Company, after receiving a rigorous physical examination the inexperienced recruit took oral tests and listened to orientation lectures covering general factory organization, work regulations, and authority of superiors. She then received one to two weeks training in the basic motions of cotton spinning work and the application of these motions to her particular job. Simultaneously, she attended classes taught by technical supervisors or experienced female workers in techniques for improving skills, preventing accidents, and learning the names and operations of all the machines in the mill. In all of this, there were constant reminders of the need to observe strict discipline in the mill and dormitory.

Except for the continuation of traditional craft apprenticeships in hopes that such skills would be useful in new industries, few other important instances of systematic training for new technologies and organizations appeared in the private sector during these years. Not until the government began to divest itself of ownership of industrial plants and enterprises in the 1880s were training functions for modern industry also transferred for private development. The importance of this early leadership by the government was that public enterprise had set a pattern for enterprise-level training programs; and, in a sense, the government has, through its own enterprises, remained a pattern-setter up to the present.

THE HUMAN FACTOR IN THE JAPANESE FIRM

In the economic theory of the firm, neoclassical economics assumes that all firms are identical, with profit maximization as the primary goal. In this treatment of the firm, important insights into how a society's values influence the organization and structure of firms is lost. The kind of companies that have evolved in Japan are different in structure and organization from their English and American counterparts. In the latter, company–employee relations are characterized by the acquisition of skill by the individual and the subsequent purchase by the company of that skill, which is then combined with other factors of production to make a product which the company sells. A worker leaves the company if he or she considers that he or she could be more profitably employed by another.

In Japan, both for the company and the individual, employment is essentially a lifetime commitment, similar to marriage. Therefore, when assessing an individual's suitability for employment, a person's character, sense of loyalty, and potential ability to contribute to the company over the long term are regarded as more important than immediate productivity and skill. Given this emphasis, workers do not waste their efforts in a short-term sprint (the rat race), but maintain sufficient stamina to do their best to contribute to the company in the long term. Assisting colleagues serves to enhance the appreciation of a worker and therefore boosts his or her long-term rating. These are factors missing from traditional neoclassical analysis.

The view of society which was held in prewar Japan, that society was not the scene for individualistic competition but rather a place for collective struggles where one team competed with another, was something which the Samurai of Japan had grown used to during the course of the Tokugawa period. In a Confucian society, each individual must strive to demonstrate his or her loyalty to the society to which he or she belongs. The extent of his or her loyalty is measured in terms of the degree to which he or she is prepared to sacrifice himself or herself. Employees in Japan experience considerable job satisfaction when they believe that they have made a special demonstration of their loyalty to the company; they achieve a greater job satisfaction by working overtime than by their work during regular hours.

Moreover, the Japanese company strengthens itself by promoting the employees' feelings of loyalty toward the company and by providing them with extensive training. Therefore, when company members have banded together in this way, even if talented personnel were to be recruited from another company there would be almost no way in which they could play an active part, and the company would be unwilling to destroy the unity among existing company employees. It is harmony between company employees and their dedication to the company which are regarded as important, rather than competition between individual employees. The employees of those companies which constitute the "national team" of Japanese industry compete with their foreign rivals as a single, united body, and competition among large enterprises to become a member of this national team and be in receipt of various favors from the government is equally fierce. In this sense, Japanese society is a fiercely competitive society, but it does not produce competition between individuals; the individual has to work on the battlefield of group competition (Morishima 1982).

CONCLUSION

Many factors have been suggested as being responsible for Japan's spectacular economic growth after World War II. The bureaucratic regulation thesis holds that the role of government in picking and nurturing winners was paramount. The market regulation thesis, on the other hand, holds that Japanese economic successes were the result of incentives toward profitable opportunities provided by the market.

This chapter has discussed the evolution of the human factor in Japan and its role in Japan's economic development. While government policies and market forces can explain the Japanese economic miracle, they are only secondary explanatory variables. The primary variable underlying Japan's economic development was a well-nurtured human factor.

The impact of Confucian philosophy, with its emphasis on loyalty, filiality, benevolence, dedication, sincerity, righteousness, and imitation of successful models, cannot be underestimated in the evolution of Japan's human factor. It must be noted that Confucian philosophy alone was not a necessary or sufficient condition. The attempt by various Japanese rulers to build a nation on Confucian principles led to an inculcation of various elements of the human factor in the Japanese population. Emperor Shotoku Taishi's Seventeen Article Constitution emphasized harmonious decision making, communal organization, hard work, honesty, and sincerity.

The Meiji era saw the attempt to build upon Japan's Confucian heritage with an emphasis on the imitation of other successful countries and an education system based on the dual goals of skills and morals. This was practically enforced at all levels of education and industrial training.

Industrial training was promoted under the direction of the central government, mainly by the Ministry of Industry, which set up its own schools for telecommunications, steel and iron production, handicraft training, lighthouse keeping, and mechanical engineering. In the cotton textile industry, for example, formal education was provided by the cotton companies outside of working hours. Employees, like students, were to be well-versed in the Rescript on Education. This Rescript, promulgated in 1890 with an emphasis on morals, was the main thrust of the attempt to inculcate the human factor within the formal and informal education systems and society at large.

It is my contention that the markets or government regulations would not have been successful in Japan or elsewhere without the foundation of a solid human factor base. We should therefore look to Japan's acquisition of the necessary human factor elements as the foundation upon which successful market or government-led policies were built. Emperor Meiji's reign lasted from 1868 to 1912. Within this span, Japan transformed itself from a semifeudal society into a modern nation state. There was a period of economic growth between 1913 and 1938 which ended with the devastation of World War II. The war destroyed the nation's infrastructure, industrial machinery, and naval power. However, Japan was to experience a period of "miraculous growth" between 1953 and 1974. Even though the war had destroyed Japan's physical infrastructure, its human factor was still intact.

NOTES

My thanks to professor Adjibolosoo for his relentless and encouraging pursuit of this chapter. All errors and omissions are mine.

1. Rosovsky identifies Japan's transition to modern economic growth as taking place between 1868 and 1885. See Rosovsky (1966, 91–139).

2. Adjibolosoo (1995) defines the human factor as a "spectrum of personality characteristics and other dimensions of human performance that enable social, economic, and political institutions to function and remain functional over time. The human factor attributes involve dedication, responsibility, and accountability in implementing measures toward development."

REFERENCES

Adjibolosoo, S. 1995. *The Significance of the Human Factor in African Economic Development.* Westport, Conn.: Praeger.

Friedman, D. 1988. *The Misunderstood Miracle: Industrial Development and Political Change in Japan.* Ithaca: Cornell University Press.

Gluck, C. 1985. *Japan's Modern Myths: Ideology in the Late Meiji Period.* Princeton: Princeton University Press.

Harbison, F. H. 1973. *Human Resources as the Wealth of Nations.* New York: Oxford University Press.

Kandasha International. 1994. *Japan: Profile of a Nation.* Tokyo: Taimedo.

Levine, B. S., and H. Kawada. 1980. *Human Resources in Japanese Industrial Development.* Princeton: Princeton University Press.

Lockwood, W. W. 1965. *The Economic Development of Japan: Growth and Structural Change, 1868–1939.* Princeton: Princeton University Press.

Mikiso, H. 1991. *Pre-Modern Japan: A Historical Survey.* Oxford: Westview Press.

Morishima, M. 1982. *Why Has Japan Succeeded? Western Technology and the Japanese Ethos.* New York: Cambridge University Press.

Okhawa, K., and H. Rosovsky. 1965. A Century of Japanese Growth. In *The State and Economic Enterprise in Japan,* edited by W. Lockwood. Princeton: Princeton University Press.

Richardson, B. M., and T. Ueda, eds. 1981. *Business and Society in Japan: Fundamentals for Businessmen.* New York: Praeger.

Rosovsky, H., ed. 1966. *Industrialization in Two Systems.* New York: John Wiley and Sons.

Taira, K. 1970. *Economic Development and the Labor Market in Japan.* New York: Columbia University Press.

Taira, K. 1971. Education and Literacy in Meiji Japan: An interpretation. *Explorations in Economic History* 8 (4): 371–394.

Takaaki, Y. 1972. Zenchosaku Shu. *Keiza Kenkyu* 13 (1): 140.

Tenno, M. 1968. Passion, Society and Education. In *Economic Growth: The Japanese Experience*, edited by L. Klein and K. Okhawa. Nobleton, Ont.: Richard D. Irwin and Irwin Dorsey.

Umetani, N. 1971. *The Role of Foreign Employees in the Meiji Era in Japan.* Tokyo: Yamakawa Shuppansha.

Wade, R. 1990. *Governing the Market: Economic Theory and the Role of the Government in East Asian Industrialization.* Princeton: Princeton University Press.

Weiss, J. 1989. *The Asian Century.* New York: Facts on File.

World Bank. 1994. *The East Asian Miracle: Economic Growth and Public Policy.* Washington, D.C.: Oxford University Press.

Yamamoto, S. 1993. Japanese Traditions and Japanese Capitalism. *Asian Survey* 10: 937–952.

Chapter 4

The Human Factor Dynamics of Singapore's Socioeconomic Development

Francis Adu-Febiri

Contemporary Singapore is a far cry from the Singapore of three decades ago. Before the 1960s, Singapore was a nonindustrialized, underdeveloped colonial island. Its expulsion from the Malaysian Federation in 1965 pushed it into a crisis. Singapore's trade with Malaysia shrank dramatically (Wong 1996, 2) and unemployment soared as Britain pulled out and closed its bases (Chan 1971, 43). Furthermore, ethnoracial tensions and communist activities in the region threatened the very survival of Singapore. The survival and crisis outlook of Singapore has changed significantly since the mid-1970s. The 1980s have seen rapid socioeconomic transformation in Singapore, making the city-state one of the four little dragons of East Asia.

What accounts for this socioeconomic miracle in Singapore? Existing explanations have focused on (1) macroeconomic and political factors and (2) social engineering processes at the expense of appropriate human factor characteristics.[1] With regard to macroeconomic and political factors, the emphasis has been on the ideology of social and economic pragmatism, a strong state, a high volume of foreign direct investment, a high rate of gross domestic savings and investment, a present world materialistic cultural value, higher educational levels and a more even gender distribution of educational opportunities, and high levels of vocational and technical skills (Lee 1996; Chan 1989; Brown 1994; Deyo 1992; Evans 1987; Tsao 1986). The social-engineering-processes account of Singapore's socioeconomic development emphasizes how the state has successfully used the mechanisms of education, housing, family, the mass media, and parapolitical organizations to develop good citizens for nation building (Hill and Kwen Fee 1995). This account, however, neglects the HF characteristics of the first-generation leadership of Singapore, the main catalyst for the country's success in social engineering for nation building.

This chapter contends that Singapore's development literature has neglected the primary factor of socioeconomic transformation. Necessary as they are, an appropriate policy, a strong state, materialistic values, large volume of capital, higher educational attainment, high levels of vocational and technical skills, and effective social engineering processes are insufficient to create and maintain a sustained socioeconomic transformation. It takes people with the appropriate HF characteristics to successfully harness and utilize the aforementioned resources for sustainable socioeconomic development.

In effect, in order to adequately understand and explain Singapore's socioeconomic showcase, we have to go beyond the veneers of macroeconomic policy, the strong state, cultural values, formal education, vocational and technical training, and social engineering processes. The undercurrents of the rapid socioeconomic transformation of Singapore are people who have successfully acquired and applied the appropriate HF and its invaluable principles of economic growth and development. Apart from relevant knowledge and skills, many Singaporeans have acquired the necessary HF in relation to community consciousness, loyalty, patriotism, trust, hard work, self-discipline, commitment, integrity, honesty, accountability, responsibility, innovativeness, vision, and the like. The social engineering processes emphasized by Hill and Kwen Fee (1995) have been the means to produce these qualities in Singaporeans. However, the main source of these qualities was the intricate interactions between the HF characteristics of the first-generation leaders of Singapore and the dramatic change in their development philosophy necessitated by the 1965 crisis.

To substantiate this claim, section 2 of this chapter presents a brief historical background to the many development problems prevailing in Singapore at the time of its expulsion from the Malaysian Federation. The third section discusses how Singapore's development crisis of the mid-1960s necessitated a change in the development philosophy of the country's leaders, and how this change combined with HF characteristics to initiate and implement social engineering processes to deal with and overcome these development problems. This section stresses the significance of the HF, particularly its human quality component, in the problem-solving processes. The fourth section concentrates on Lee Kuan Yew's HF characteristics and shows how these have contributed significantly to Singapore's socioeconomic transformation.[2] In the last section the current problems of Singapore are examined from the HF perspective. Policy recommendations are provided, emphasizing that it is only through the ongoing development and implementation of HF engineering programs that Singapore can sustain its socioeconomic transformation processes.

SINGAPORE: A HISTORICAL BACKGROUND

In 1963, Singapore, then a British colony, voted to join the Malaysian Federation. Singapore joined Malaysia mainly because the political leaders of the city-state at that time "did not believe that Singapore could survive as an independent nation" (Hill and Kwen Fee 1995, 17). Notwithstanding these leaders' fears to form an independent state, Singapore "gained independence reluctantly on expulsion from Malaysia in 1965" (Hill and Kwen Fee 1995, 18). The fear that Singapore could not make it on its own brought Lee Kuan Yew, the People's Action Party (PAP) leader, to tears. He literary wept on national television on the expulsion day, August 9, 1965. The leadership had no choice but to accept a state without a nation and without a viable economy. Britain's declared intention to close its military bases in Singapore in 1967 plunged the already shocked city-state into a crisis.

The good news, however, was that the PAP leadership recovered from their shock and responded positively to the crisis situation. The PAP proceeded not only to formulate "a new economic strategy of self-reliance, but also to articulate for its citizens the difficult circumstances in which it found itself as part of a nation building exercise" (Hill and Kwen Fee 1995, 19). Pragmatism or the "ideology of survival," based on the philosophy of maximum utilization of Singapore's human resources, emerged out of the dismal circumstances. The leaders, using this philosophy, succeeded in mobilizing Singaporeans to build one of the fastest-growing economies in Asia and the world.

In the 1970s and early 1980s, Singapore's economy grew very fast, recording an average growth rate of 9 percent annually. The rate of growth of the economy dropped to 6.8 to 8.3 percent in the 1990s because of decline in external demand. Yet Singapore still remains one of the rapidly expanding economies in Asia. Currently, Singapore operates an "open entrepreneurial economy with strong service and manufacturing sectors and excellent international trading links" (Generalized Statistics on Singapore 1993, 5). Besides economic growth, Singapore has successfully developed a united nation out of a multiracial and multiethnic population.[3] The vision of the first-generation Singaporean leaders to foster HF development in the country held the key to the attainment of the phenomenal socioeconomic transformation in Singapore.

THE HUMAN FACTOR AND SOCIOECONOMIC DEVELOPMENT IN SINGAPORE

In the 1940s and 1950s, Singapore's political leadership worked very hard to prepare Singapore to join Malaysia to create a federation at independence. As mentioned, the leaders of Singapore believed that it could not survive economically as an independent country. The main premise of this belief was that Singapore did not have a large enough population and land base, as well as enough requisite natural resources, for socioeconomic transformation. The underlying assumption was that a country needs a large number of people and a significant volume of natural resources within its boundaries in order to be economically viable. When Singapore was expelled from the Malaysian Federation in 1965, the leadership was compelled by necessity to rethink this assumption. Out of this hard rethinking emerged the pertinent realization that the key to socioeconomic transformation of a country is the HF. Specifically, the leadership of Singapore realized that, with the availability of the appropriate HF, Singapore would successfully harness its natural resources and effectively access vital external resources to supplement the country's local resources. It is this realization which motivated the first-generation leaders of Singapore to concentrate on developing the HF since the late 1960s.

At the time of independence, the level of HF development in Singapore was very low. That is, the Singaporean scientific knowledge base, human quality, and vocational and technical skill levels were very low (Tammey 1988). A large majority of Singapore's population were illiterate farmers, fishers, and traders. With the HF philosophy becoming the core of the development thinking of Singapore's leaders, they utilized their HF characteristics to systematically cultivate and foster the appropriate HF characteristics among the general populace. Specifically, the PAP, led by Lee Kuan Yew, chose to manipulate economic incentives, penalties, ideas, and values, as well as coercion, to influence the conduct of the population and to mobilize it for socioeconomic development (Hill and Kwen Fee 1995, 22). The Singaporean program for HF development was pursued through the social-engineering agencies of education, the mass media, the family, and grassroots parapolitical associations (Hill and Kwen Fee 1995, 23). Through these agencies, the PAP leadership was successful in assisting Singaporeans to acquire and use high levels of scientific knowledge, vocational and technical skills, and human qualities. These pertinent factors not only attracted multinational capital into the country, but also turned it into a vital development resource.

The highly educated and technically skilled Singaporeans did not connive with multinationals to transfer resources out of Singapore because of the levels of the HF characteristics they possessed. From the mid-1960s, Singapore's leadership emphasized that a prosperous nation is built by people who have acquired the necessary human capital and are also good citizens. Good citizens, in the context of Singapore's multiracial reality and ideology of economic pragmatism, are people who are tolerant, self-disciplined, community conscious, loyal, moral, hard working, honest, committed, dedicated, punctual, self-confident, responsible, and accountable. The Singaporean state leadership was primarily concerned with the cultivation and fostering of HF development in its citizens. Singapore's multiracial and bilingual policy, education system, housing policy, and political praxis reflect this as the vision of the state.

The importance of multiracialism and bilingualism in Singapore cannot be overemphasized. Singapore's leadership views multiracialism as a guiding principle in policy development. It believes that for a multiracial society like Singapore to attain a level of unity and harmony necessary for socioeconomic development it has to create inclusive-oriented and loyal citizens. Thus, multiracial and bilingual policy is implemented in Singapore as a powerful force against ethnoracial discrimination. Another important objective of Singapore's race and ethnic relations policy is to prevent "deculturation" of its citizens (Hill and Kwen Fee 1995, 92). According to Lee Kuan Yew, "a person who gets deculturalised . . . loses his [or her] self-confidence" (Hong and Yap 1993, 37). In effect, besides providing a harmonious atmosphere for economic activities, the multiracial and bilingual policy of Singapore aims at developing citizens who are self-confident and also loyal to the state. These citizens are always expected to acquire and use HF characteristics to foster nation building and economic development.

Education in Singapore is not only designed to give graduates knowledge and skills, but also to foster good citizenship in a multiracial society. Thus, the cultural pluralism and bilingualism enshrined in Singapore's educational system reinforce the state's political ideology of multiracialism, purporting to cultivate loyalty and self-confidence among the populace. The fact that Singapore's educational system puts a great emphasis on HF engineering is evident in Lee Kuan Yew's comments on the 1979 education report presented by Goh:

The first subject concerns good citizenship and nationhood. What kind of man or woman does a child grow up to be after 10–12 years of schooling? Is he a worthy citizen, guided by decent moral precepts? Have his teachers and principals set him good examples? Imparting knowledge to pass examinations, and later do a job, these are important. However, the litmus test of a good education is whether it nurtures good citizens who can live, work, contend and cooperate in a civilized way. Is he loyal and patriotic? Is he, when the need arises, a good soldier, ready to defend his country, and so protect his wife and children, and his fellow citizens? Is he filial, respectful to elders, law-abiding, humane, and responsible? Does he take care of his wife and children, and his parents? Is he a good neighbor and trustworthy friend? Is he tolerant of Singaporeans of different races and religions? Is he clean, neat, punctual, and well-mannered? (Goh 1979, iv–v)

In short, what Lee Kuan Yew is advocating for his country is "education for living, and civics" (Hill and Kwen Fee 1995, 90). This entails the cultivation and fostering of not only human capital, which is emphasized by neoclassical development theorists and practitioners, but also moral capital, spiritual capital, aesthetic capital, and human potential (Adjibolosoo 1995, Chapter 1).

In order to produce the required quality of citizens, Singapore's educational system incorporated "shared values," that is, amalgamated religious ideas and social philosophies into the educational curricula in the 1980s (Hill and Kwen Fee 1995, 200–201). The specific rationales for making shared values an integral part of the educational curricula were (1) the existence of signs of HF decay such as dishonesty, theft, snobbery, self-gratification, and decline in the work ethic (Tammey 1988, 116); and (2) the notion that the economic success of Hong Kong, South Korea, and Taiwan are attributable to their implementation of the Confucian practice of ethics (Hill and Kwen Fee 1995, 201). The shared values are, therefore, introduced to help Singapore to produce in its citizens appropriate HF characteristics of hard work, honesty, trust, community consciousness, social discipline, self-reliance, tolerance, loving kindness, and compassion (Hill and Kwen Fee 1995, 201–204; Kuah 1991, 34). To a large extent, Singapore has succeeded in using its educational system to help develop the HF in its citizens. For example, according to Tammey (1988, 117), "One of the ministers speaking of his admiration for the moral probity of his former classmates at a religiously affiliated school, noted that they had successful business careers, and that, being trustworthy, bankers trusted them" (also quoted in Hill and Kwen Fee 1995, 201). Citizens who acquire and apply these HF characteristics play a significant role in Singapore's rapid socioeconomic transformation process.

Singapore's housing policy is also used as a social engineering process for the cultivation and fostering of the appropriate HF characteristics in its citizens. The state builds family-unit houses for both the lower- and middle-income classes, regardless of their racial and ethnic backgrounds. The occupants purchase these houses by making affordable monthly payments. With people from various ethnoracial and social class backgrounds mixed together in these state-created housing estates, coupled with Singapore's equity policy, healthy ethnoracial and class interactions are encouraged. These interactions have helped Singaporeans to develop ethnoracial as well as social class awareness and sensitivity, and, for that matter, the essential HF characteristic of tolerance. In effect, this social engineering strategy has significantly contributed to the decline in ethnoracial and social class tensions and conflicts in Singapore.

Apart from its social integration function through the fostering of tolerance, Singapore's public-housing policy significantly contributes to the development of loyalty in the citizens. Public-housing schemes in Singapore have given the opportunity to about 87 percent of the population to own houses inexpensively. Housing ownership is known to expand people's "commitment to the prevailing social order by the development of personal stakes in its survival" (Agnew 1981, 457). In the Singaporean context, the government uses the public-housing program to cultivate the essential HF characteristics among its citizens.

Since the 1970s, Singapore's housing policy has become an increasingly refined adjunct of social engineering "to encourage desirable social values, internalize social control, support general economic policies, and maintain the PAP's political dominance" (Hill and Kwen Fee 1995, 122; Castells, Goh, and Kwok 1990, 245). Specific qualities developed by the housing policy include loyalty, responsibility, community consciousness, and hard work. As Wong and Yeh (1985, 231) correctly observed, "The underlying philosophy [of Singapore's public-housing program] is that if one owns an asset in the country, one would stand to defend it." And according to Hill and Kwen Fee (1995, 121), in the Singaporean context, the collective use of housing facilities helps create the desire and interest in people to engage in grassroots organizations (i.e., Citizens' Consultative Committees, Residential Committees, and Town Councils, etc.) that work to promote both community and national interests. Together they work to engender the vital HF characteristics of community consciousness, loving kindness, care, and mutual respect among many Singaporeans. Salaff (1988, 243) adds, "This painless road to property ownership ties a family into debt and credit relations that require them to work steadily for years to come." This is commitment. The care for old relatives entailed in the public-housing program of Singapore also makes the younger generation develop a sense of responsibility (Hill and Kwen Fee 1995, 122).

The success of such massive social engineering programs in Singapore has depended very much on a leadership possessing appropriate HF characteristics. The case study of the leadership qualities of Lee Kuan Yew that follows clearly reveals that the HF characteristics of Singapore's first-generation leaders have contributed in no small way to the socioeconomic development of Singapore.

THE ROLE OF LEE KUAN YEW IN SINGAPORE'S RAPID SOCIOECONOMIC DEVELOPMENT

When Lee Kuan Yew assumed the leadership mantle of Singapore in the 1960s, the situation looked bleak and the future full of uncertainties (Wong 1996, 2). Before age thirty-five, when he became Prime Minister, Lee Kuan Yew had acquired a high level of human capital. He had graduated from the London School of Economics and Cambridge University as a top economist and lawyer (Josey 1974, 30–33). With his considerable intellectual skills and knowledge of international economics and geopolitics, Lee Kuan Yew had the necessary background to be a successful leader of Singapore in a global village where international capital virtually rules. While these intellectual skills and knowledge base were necessary for his success, Lee needed something more than human capital to become an effective statesman. The level of his human qualities was absolutely an essential factor for a transformational leadership. Lee Kuan Yew, fortunately, had sufficient qualities of determination, hard work, loyalty, patriotism, integrity, honesty, self-discipline, responsibility, accountability, and vision. These are the basic factors that developed Lee's strong character, providing him with the confidence to step into Singapore's socioeconomic doldrums and transform it into a flourishing society.

Lee Kuan Yew's strong personality traits are mainly products of interaction between his upbringing in Asian values and the Japanese occupation of Singapore in the 1940s when he was growing up. The Japanese maltreatment of Singaporeans, including Lee himself, made him resolve to do everything possible to prevent Singaporeans from becoming "the pawns and playthings of foreign powers" in the future (Josey 1974, 2). Hence, when Singapore was expelled from Malaysia in 1965, Lee Kuan Yew "quickly picked himself and his party up [and] set out with determination to take Singapore on the road all alone" (Wong 1996, 3). This determination was firmly steeped in Lee's loyalty, patriotism, and integrity. According to Minchin (1990, 239), when Singapore's attempts to be part of the Malaysia Federation failed, "Singaporeans realized that whatever Lee Kuan Yew was doing, even if it turned out wrong, he was doing it for the benefit of Singapore and all Singaporeans." Lee further demonstrated his patriotism and integrity when, in 1990, he voluntarily stepped down from being the prime minister to a senior minister when he realized that he would do better as an advisor to the government than as the head of government (Wong 1996, 6). Many leaders in the world, especially in Africa and Latin America, would cling to power even when it is clearly detrimental to the socioeconomic advancement of their countries.

Accountability is another strong dimension of Lee Kuan Yew's character. He is one of the initiators of the "return to sender" ideology of Singapore (Hill and Kwen Fee 1995, 246–248). This ideology is reflected in the "family values" and "civic society" project of the 1990s (Hill and Kwen Fee 1995, Chapter 9). This project was initiated as a government response to the negative reactions of significant segments of the electorate to the government's selective reproduction policy and close association with the Housing Development Board. This government response is indicative of a sensitive interventionist state and, therefore, a concrete illustration of the belief of Singapore's leadership in accountability of government leaders to the grassroots. Lee Kuan Yew's belief in accountability and the democratic process is reflected in the following quotation: "If I [Lee Kuan Yew] were in authority in Singapore indefinitely, without having to ask those who are being governed whether they like what is being done, then I have not the slightest doubt that I could govern much more effectively in their own interest" (Minchin 1990, 2).

The fact that Lee Kuan Yew possesses the necessary personal character that fosters hard work is indisputable. He has worked relentlessly hard for his country since the 1950s. Currently he is a senior minister who works diligently to provide relevant advice to the government of Singapore and other governments in Asia (see Lee 1995, 11; Chiang 1995, 3). Knowing that hard work is essential for socioeconomic transformation, Lee Kuan Yew has endeavored to build into the Singaporean culture a strong work ethic (Wong 1996, 6). Such hard work is connected with self-discipline, which is the bulwark against political corruption and misappropriation of state and community resources. Lee Kuan Yew has a good amount of self-discipline. So far he has not faced any accusations of political corruption and embezzlement of public funds. Wong (1996, 8) notes that Lee Kuan Yew's "influence is ingrained in the whole of the political culture and institutions and over almost all aspects of Singaporean society today." Lee Kuan Yew's efforts have brought Singapore this far mainly because of his acquired HF characteristics (i.e., his knowledge base, intellectual skills, and human qualities). With these characteristics, Lee Kuan Yew has been able to serve as a positive role model for Singaporeans and encourage the cultivation of the appropriate HF ingredients in the people through education, training, and parapolitical programs. With this quality of people, Singapore is able to mobilize its other resources to create an efficient infrastructure that attracts substantial foreign direct investment as well as preventing such capital from causing unreasonable foreign-exchange leakages.

It is important to note, however, that Lee Kuan Yew is not a "perfect" individual. One of his main weaknesses is the intolerance underlying his overwhelming personality. Lee Kuan Yew's intolerance of the viewpoints of his opponents is evident in the dominance of PAP in Singapore's politics since independence. He has been a prominent leader of this domineering political party since its emergence. The weak opposition Lee Kuan Yew's strong personality has created in Singapore works against Singapore's realization of its full socioeconomic potential. Political intolerance limits the choices and freedom of citizens, thus creating tensions in communities and workplaces. The energy expended on resolving such conflicts could be used to increase productivity and improve the quality of social life. Moreover, intolerance restricts the opportunity of opposition members to contribute their quota to the nation-building process. To release energy from all segments of society to facilitate sustainable development, the essential HF characteristics must be cultivated in the political leadership of Singapore.

Another challenge Lee Kuan Yew's Singapore faces is how to successfully manage the new set of problems that the success of the city-state has created. These problems include increasing expectations of the people and what to do with huge annual budget surpluses (Wong 1996, 7). The next section addresses this problem of how to manage success in Singapore.

THE PROSPECTS FOR EFFECTIVE MANAGEMENT OF SUCCESS IN SINGAPORE

According to Wong (1996, 7), the problems of managing success are feeble compared to the problems Singapore faced when Lee came along over forty years ago. Management of success is problematic, nonetheless. Without the availability of the appropriate HF characteristics, huge economic surpluses and higher expectations of the population could plunge a nation into social unrest, corruption, and eventual economic decline. Huge budget surpluses could create laxity on the part of the leadership and the people. Work ethic could degenerate. Politicians, bureaucrats, and managers may start appropriating parts of the surpluses for their personal benefit and that of their families. In such a context, perception of government not meeting the high expectations of the people would produce general disenchantment, particularly among the relatively underprivileged groups such as the lower classes, women, youth, and ethnoracial minorities. Opportunists could easily capitalize on this condition to instigate insurrections or stage *coups d'etat* and thus cause political instability. As the cases of Africa and Latin America show, political instability brings disruption into the economy.

It is in this light that the current direction of Singapore toward a shift in the management of the country to a new technocratic leadership could be a dangerous move. According to Hill and Kwen Fee (1995, 24), the hallmark of the second-generation leadership of Singapore, led by Goh Chok Tong, is "the power of competent authority in which the claim to influence is based on the expertise and technical competence of the political elite." From the analysis of the significant role Lee Kuan Yew has played in Singapore's development, it is clear that for transformational leadership to materialize, leaders must possess not only "expertise and technical competence," but also the critical HF characteristics.

In order for Singapore to successfully manage its socioeconomic miracle, therefore, it needs to continue relentlessly with its social-engineering programs to groom its new leadership and the population to acquire and apply the appropriate HF characteristics. Specifically, the following strategies are recommended:

1. Election and appointment of political leaders should be based not only on technocratic competence, but also on the possession of the necessary HF characteristics.

2. People appointed to serve on Singapore's Housing Development Board, Economic Development Board, and Central Provident Fund should possess appropriate HF characteristics.

3. Singapore's Public Housing Policy should continue to promote HF engineering.

4. The educational system of Singapore should persist in the implementation of moral and cultural education.

5. Parapolitical organizations should continue to cultivate and foster appropriate qualities in people at the grassroots.

6. The state must give families the necessary encouragement to play their traditional role of HF socialization.

7. Singapore's political leaders must acquire and apply the essential HF characteristic of tolerance.

Can Singapore effectively maintain the cultivation of the appropriate HF characteristics among its citizens through the existing HF engineering programs? So far, Singapore's political leadership has used the educational institution, the economic institution, housing programs, parapolitical organizations, and the mass media to manipulate material incentives, penalties, ideas, values, and coercion to achieve its HF engineering goals. However, given the increased educational attainment of Singaporeans and the growing democratic ideology of the new world order, these conventional methods of HF engineering are insufficient to generate the required level of acquired HF characteristics to sustain the country's socioeconomic success. Singapore needs social rituals techniques to complement its existing HF engineering mechanisms. According to Collins (1992, 46) social rituals, by bringing people together and encouraging intensive interactions among them, generate special emotional energy that could be channeled to accomplish social goals. As a social technology, social rituals have been effectively used to cultivate and foster the appropriate HF characteristics in many societies (see Adu-Febiri 1995, 80–97).

In order for Singapore to prevent or effectively deal with the social problems its economic success may create, the judicious and pragmatic implementation of these HF engineering programs to supplement existing ones is a must. When this recommendation is adhered to, Singapore will effectively meet its growing challenge of success management.

CONCLUSION

In the 1950s and 1960s, Singapore and many African and Latin American countries were at a similar socioeconomic development stage. What did Singapore do, and what is it doing, differently from these other countries that has transformed it from an economically precarious situation into a socioeconomic showcase? Singapore has a leadership, particularly Lee Kuan Yew, who possess appropriate HF principles of development and have systematically cultivated and fostered such principles in the Singaporean populace.

The development crisis of Singapore in the mid-1960s compelled the first-generation leadership to change the country's development philosophy and strategy. Since independence in 1965, the appropriate HF characteristics of Singapore's leaders have helped them organize a massive social-engineering program using the educational system, public housing, parapolitical organizations, the mass media, and the family to create good citizens from its multiracial population. These good citizens are the critical resource that Singapore's leadership has mobilized to create the necessary infrastructure and stable institutions that attract and retain foreign direct investment and generate domestic investment capital and efficient intersectoral linkages in the economy. These, in turn, have birthed the economic miracle.

Singapore's economic success has been achieved at the expense of political tolerance and civic society. In addition, the success has brought in its trail the challenge of how to prevent the increasing expectations of the people and enormous budget surpluses from creating social problems that could destabilize the society. Technocracy alone is unlikely to be an effective means of managing Singapore's economic success. The need for continued HF engineering to complement technocracy is necessary if Singapore is to transform its economic miracle into sustainable development. Social rituals combined with education and training programs can play a significant role in HF engineering processes aimed at producing sustainable development. It takes well-prepared people to create and maintain sustainable development.

NOTES

1. The human factor is given a new meaning by Adjibolosoo (1994, 25–37). According to him, it is an unchanging fact that "to be effective and efficient in the production process, the people of a nation must also acquire unique human qualities and/or characteristics that encourage and promote economic progress (such as discipline, dedication, responsibility, accountability, integrity, and the like). It is these attributes and many others akin to them that contribute to a successful or unsuccessful utilization of acquired knowledge and skills. Human capital is, therefore, a small segment of the HF."

2. Lee Kuan Yew has been the most prominent political leader and statesman of Singapore since the 1950s.

3. Singapore's population is comprised of 76.4 percent Chinese, 14.9 percent Malay, 6.4 percent Indian, and 2.3 percent other (Generalized Statistics on Singapore 1993, 2).

REFERENCES

Adjibolosoo, S. 1994. The Human Factor and the Failure of Development Planning and Economic Policy in Africa. In *Perspectives on Economic Development in Africa*, edited by F. Ezeala-Harrison and S. Adjibolosoo. Westport, Conn.: Praeger.

Adjibolosoo, S. 1995. *The Human Factor in Developing Africa*. Westport, Conn.: Praeger.

Adu-Febiri, F. 1995. Human Factor Engineering for Development in Africa: The Role of Social Rituals. *Review of Human Factor Studies* 1 (2): 80–97.

Agnew, J. A. 1981. Home Ownership and the Capitalist Social Order. In *Urbanization and Urban Planning in Capitalist Society*, edited by M. Dear and A. J. Scott. London: Methuen.

Brown, D. 1994. *The State and Ethnic Politics in Southeast Asia*. London: Routledge.

Castells, M., L. Goh, and R. Y-W. Kwok. 1990. *The Shek Kip Mei Syndrome: Economic Development and Public Housing in Hong Kong and Singapore*. London: Pion.

Chan, H. C. 1971. *Singapore: The Politics of Survival 1965–1967*. Singapore: Oxford University Press.

Chan, H. C. 1989. The PAP and the Structuring of the Political System. In *Management of Success: The Moulding of Modern Singapore*, edited by K. S. Sandhu and P. Wheatley. Singapore: Institute of Southeast Asian Studies.

Chiang, Y. P. 1995. Asian Influence Will Rise Says SM Lee. *The Straits Times Weekly Edition*, 11 February, 1.

Collins, R. 1992. *Sociological Insight: An Introduction to Sociology*. New York: Oxford University Press.

Deyo, F. C. 1992. The Political Economy of Social Policy Formation: East Asia's Newly Industrialized Countries. In *States and Development in the Asian Pacific Rim*, edited by R. P. Applebaum and J. Henderson. Newbury Park, Calif.: Sage.

Evans, P. B. 1987. Class, State, and Dependence in East Asia: Lessons for Latin America. In *The Political Economy of the New Asian Industrialism*, edited by F. C. Deyo. Ithaca: Cornell University Press.

Generalized Statistics on Singapore. 1993. *The Software Toolworks Atlas*. Version 4.0. Navota, Calif.: The Software Toolworks.

Goh, K. S. 1979. *Report on the Ministry of Education 1978.* Singapore: Government of Singapore.

Hill, M., and L. Kwen Fee. 1995. *The Politics of Nation Building and Citizenship in Singapore.* New York: Routledge.

Hong, L., and J. Yap. 1993. The Past in Singapore's Present. *Commentary* 11 (1): 31–38.

Josey, A. 1974. *Lee Kuan Yew: The Struggle for Singapore.* Sydney: Angus and Robertson Pty.

Kuah, K. E. 1991. State and Religion: Buddhism and Nation-Building in Singapore. *Pacific Viewpoint* 32 (1): 24–42.

Lee, K. C. 1995. SM Lee Invited to Visit Vietnam. *The Straits Times Weekly Edition*, 4 March, 11.

Lee, K. Y. 1996. Singapore Recommends to Brunei Only Proven Investments. *The Straits Times Weekly Edition*, 28 January, 3. Also available at http://www.gov.sg/mti/speech~9.html.

Minchin, J. 1990. *No Man Is an Island: A Portrait of Singapore's Lee Kuan Yew.* Hong Kong: Allen and Unwin, Australia Pty.

Salaff, J. W. 1988. *State and Family in Singapore: Restructuring an Industrial Society.* Ithaca: Cornell University Press.

Tammey, J. B. 1988. Religion and the State in Singapore. *Journal of Church and State* 30: 109–128.

Tsao, Y. 1986. Sources of Growth Accounting for the Singapore Economy. In *Singapore: Resources and Growth*, edited by L. Chong-Yah and P. J. Lloyd. Singapore: Oxford University Press.

Wong, A. K., and S. H. K. Yeh. 1985. *Housing a Nation: 25 Years of Public Housing in Singapore.* Singapore: Maruzen Asia.

Wong, T. 1996. Lee Kuan Yew: An Australian's Perspective. Available at http://www.ss.rmit.edu.a...wong/TeresaWong_Austpers.

Chapter 5

The Relevance of the Human Factor and a Grassroots Approach to Economic Development: A Case Study of the Antigonish Movement in Canada

Santo Dodaro, Leonard Pluta,
and Joe Amoako-Tuffour

Over the last four decades or so, there have been considerable resource flows from the West to the developing nations by way of technical assistance, capital, person-power training, and food aid. These flows have been aimed at supplementing the resources of the developing countries to promote growth and structural change. Africa, in particular, has been at the receiving end of considerable foreign input into development planning, policy formulation, and the implementation of programs and projects. The flow of expertise, technical assistance, and other resources notwithstanding, the benefits that have accrued to the local populations have arguably been meager at best. Indeed, if the success and failure of development efforts are to be judged by the degree to which they have fostered the realization of the human potential and the improvement of individual welfare, rather than by improvements in macroeconomic aggregates, then the conventional approach must be deemed to have led to the disappointment of many, even in instances where overall economic growth has been recorded. Such a state of events is perhaps best captured by the notion of "growth without development."[1]

In recent years, greater attention has turned to what is generally termed "economic reform." Reforms generally encompass both macroeconomic stabilization and structural changes. By restructuring the framework of economic activities and removing the strictures of government controls as well as impediments to the functioning of the market economy, reforms are expected to raise productivity and, in time, maximize per capita income growth. Missing in these new directions of development efforts, as was the case in conventional development approaches, is how to harness local human resources, individually and collectively, to alleviate local poverty.

The conventional development effort is a "top-down" approach. It aims at the economy as a whole and, with the appropriate macroeconomic policies, relies on sectoral linkages and trickle-down effects to stimulate economic activities. In a market-driven development strategy, reliance is placed on prices as coordinating mechanisms and signaling devices. Simply put, higher prices create higher returns to factors of production and attract additional resources. Economic agents are assumed to respond to appropriate incentives, behaving in such a way as to maximize the returns to commodities and inputs that are bought or sold. Competition forces agents to use factors of production as productively as they can, or else fail.

Underneath it all is the important prerequisite that economic agents have access to economic information and knowledge about economic opportunities. But knowledge about economic opportunities as well as the decision-making ability, or more importantly, the opportunity to exercise it, remain a major problem even for those who may have access to information. The problem is even worse in many developing countries. The dispersed nature of rural communities, characterized by small farmers, small-scale income-generating activities, high levels of illiteracy, inadequate lending and borrowing avenues, poor transportation, and poor overall infrastructure, has meant that individuals are unable to exploit economic opportunities beyond the minimum required to assure survival. Knowledge about productive relations, exchange, and consumption possibilities remain a scarce good. And prices hardly represent an avenue for communication of such knowledge. The result in many places is the prevailing large informal sector, serving large segments of the population who are excluded from, or remain weakly connected to, the formal sector, which is the main arena of macroeconomic policies. Weak economic links hamper sectoral linkages and, unsuspectingly, thwart the effectiveness of many well-intended economic policies. It also means that large segments of the rural poor continue to lack appropriate access to physical resources for development, and to information and knowledge about opportunities for entrepreneurship.

The grassroots approach is a "bottom-up" strategy. It aims at bettering the human condition at the group or community level by pooling material and human resources, particularly decision-making ones. It focuses on the human resources as a whole, ensuring that members participate fully in society by becoming part of the decision-making entrepreneurship.[2] This chapter contributes to an understanding of this view of economic development, which emphasizes the central role of human resources, by using the Antigonish Movement in the province of Nova Scotia, Canada, as a case study. The Movement, born out of the socioeconomic conditions existing in Eastern Nova Scotia during the 1920s, which are quite similar to the prevailing circumstances in many present-day developing countries, is often cited as a successful experiment in grassroots development. Its legacy is the Coady International Institute at St. Francis Xavier University. Every year, the Institute, sponsored by the Canadian International Development Agency and St. Francis Xavier University, has been home to at least fifty international students actively involved in development work at the community or grassroots level in their respective countries and engaged in study in a diploma program in community development and self-help.

Though many factors account for the Movement's success, the appropriateness of its economic strategy, the social cohesion of the stakeholders, and the emphasis on harnessing human resources at the community and local level are major contributory factors. The key components of the last involve the mobilization of entrepreneurship and decision-making capacity at the community or group level, the curtailing of free riders, and the presence of some sort of compulsion to foster collective action.[3] The interplay of socioeconomic and cultural factors in the pursuit of the common social good and the individual human good, without subordinating the latter to the former, provided the essential impetus. The Movement's indisputable premise is that those who are poor lack appropriate access to information and knowledge, as well as decision-making ability or, more importantly, the opportunity to exercise it. All these contribute to poverty, powerlessness, and inertia, leading ultimately to defeatism and further underdevelopment.

The rest of the chapter is organized as follows. In the second section we offer a definition of grassroots development and identify the fundamental barriers to economic development and growth which the grassroots approach is intended to overcome. The socioeconomic environment that gave birth to the movement, as well as the objectives of the movement, form the content of the third section. We examine the strategy of the movement, with emphasis on its fundamental components of leadership, entrepreneurship, knowledge and education, and the harnessing of human resources, in the fourth section. The economic gains and social transformation under the movement are examined in the fifth section. In the last section, the lessons for development are presented.

WHY GRASSROOTS DEVELOPMENT?

Grassroots Development Defined

Providing a precise definition of what constitutes grassroots development is more difficult than would seem to be the case at first, since it represents an approach that attracts an array of ideological and philosophical proclivities. For our purpose, and within the context of the Antigonish Movement, the grassroots or bottom-up approach can be couched in terms of the affirmation or reaffirmation of individual sovereignty over both production and consumption; that is, shifting control over decision making and resources in the economic sphere to the individuals and members of the community as a whole so that basic needs, and other objectives as well, can be met. Thus, the people themselves are involved in the process as decision makers, as contributors of resources, and, ultimately, as beneficiaries, in contrast to the more passive stance inherent in the more conventional approaches to development. Its basic strength lies in its consistency with economic rationality and its usual caveats of broadly defined economic efficiency and welfare or utility maximization.

Grassroots economic activity, like any other, is directed at bettering the human condition and, as such, must be perceived as a means rather than an end in itself. As well, it is not meant to deal simply with marginal economic activities but to focus on the economic mainstream; that is, ensure that all members of a society participate fully in that society by becoming part of the mainstream.[4] Rather than a component of the informal economy, the approach should be seen as a vital part of the formal economy.[5] Rather than constituting an alternative to the more macro-level approach to development, the grassroots approach complements it by focusing on local and regional subunits as opposed to the economy as a whole.

The issues that we have identified are fundamental to the understanding of what constitutes the grassroots approach to development and the economic factors which ensure its viability. It brings the consideration of the whole human factor into the mainstream of economics as well as sociology and politics. To be functional, its organization, structure, and objectives must conform to the existing institutional and technological realities as well as to sound economic theory. The whole approach is meant to be pioneering rather than a return to traditional methods, while fully appreciating the importance of tradition, culture, and the like. In effect, it represents a forward-looking and holistic approach to economic development and progress.

Barriers to Economic Activity

The fundamental barriers to economic development and growth which the grassroots approach is intended to overcome may be specific to individual countries and regions. There are, nevertheless, certain fundamental features which are generally common to all, including the existence of poverty and lack of both human and nonhuman resources. While important, poverty itself is more of a symptom than a cause. Poverty exists as a result of other factors, the most fundamental of these being the lack of access to physical resources and the existence of exploitation. Both can be perceived as the result of the existence of market failure. But this is only part of the story. We must consider the human dimension.

The poor generally lack access to appropriate information and knowledge as well as decision-making ability and entrepreneurship. They also tend to lack self-esteem and confidence in their ability to effect economic and social improvements and are often distrustful of other people and of collective self-help efforts. Fundamentally, all these components contribute not only to the existence of poverty but also to its perpetuation by creating a sense of powerlessness and inertia. The grassroots approach, in its attempt to overcome these barriers, relies on the regeneration of confidence, self-worth, and motivation on the part of each individual, as well as on the pooling of material and human resources. Thus, it naturally focuses on the group or the community. The fundamental inducement which it employs is the desire on the part of economic agents to improve their welfare, especially in terms of meeting their basic material needs and the sense of self-esteem and individual worth generated by making their own decisions and being active participants in economic life.

THE ANTIGONISH MOVEMENT

The Initial Socioeconomic Environment

During the 1920s, the eastern provinces of Canada—Nova Scotia, New Brunswick, and Prince Edward Island—were experiencing a state of economic depression which had its origins in the decline of the "wood–wind–water" economy dating back to the late nineteenth century. In addition, there was a collapse in the industrial sectors brought about by declining demand and ability to compete.[6] The Antigonish Movement was one region's answer to the prevailing state of economic despair. Eastern Nova Scotia's major occupational groups—industrial workers dependent on coal and steel, farmers engaged primarily in subsistence agriculture, and fishermen located in the numerous fishing villages dotting the Eastern Nova Scotia coastline—suffered from the decline.

The urban industrial areas of Eastern Nova Scotia were highly dependent on coal and steel, industries which were increasingly in trouble due to declining demand and increased competition from producers in Central Canada and elsewhere. Moreover, these industrial enterprises were characterized by absentee ownership and monopolistic and monopsonistic conditions as typified by the "company towns." The exploitation and unemployment arising from the declining markets resulted in rapidly deteriorating conditions as manifested in labor unrest, strikes, and increased poverty.

Conditions in the rural areas were equally precarious. Much of rural activity during the 1920s was still of a subsistence sort, even though the degree of commercialization among farmers was increasing, particularly as a result of improvements in transportation and communication. Scarcity of capital—including poor soil conditions—and monopsonistic buyers of produce limited both the degree of commercialization and the potential benefits from it. At the same time, the increase in demand for consumer goods and producer goods put the rural population at the mercy of monopolistic sellers of such goods. Many abandoned the agricultural sector and the lack of employment opportunities in the urban areas compelled outmigration.[7] Fishermen, too, were at the mercy of monopsonistic fish buyers, who established very low prices for the fish, and monopolistic sellers of consumer and producer goods. Often these buyers and sellers were the same people. The greater reliance on the market made the plight of the fishermen even more serious than that of the subsistence farmers, though many fishermen also engaged in farming in the off season.

In the economic sphere, this situation points to a fundamental problem of market failure predicated on (1) the imbalance in market power between the merchant class on one hand and the workers and primary producers on the other and (2) the fact that the Eastern Nova Scotia region, like rural regions in many developing countries, was caught in a period of fundamental transition between traditional and modern economic organization, with the latter being able to exploit the former. Moreover, both of these factors were heightened by the prevailing poor and deteriorating market conditions.

The imbalance in power between workers and primary producers on one hand and the capitalist and merchant class on the other created a situation whereby the latter group was able to appropriate rents and quasirents at the expense of the former, particularly in the primary sectors.[8] Both in the fisheries and in the rural sectors, these economic rents were appropriated by the monopsonistic buyers and monopolistic sellers at the expense of the fishermen and farmers.[9] This, coupled with the overall decline of the region even prior to the Great Depression, created a situation where basic needs were not being met.

The overall decline of the region, the economic power structure, the decline in the standards of living, and the consequent outmigration are characteristics shared by the rural communities in many developing economies. Deteriorating socioeconomic conditions manifest in widespread rural unemployment, widespread poverty, urban drift, inefficient allocation of resources, and, in many cases, a feeling of helplessness and hopelessness. In Eastern Nova Scotia, these conditions created both a dissatisfaction with the existing economic system and an environment receptive to alternatives, particularly alternatives that stressed cooperation, self-reliance, and human dignity.

The Birth of the Antigonish Movement

The Antigonish Movement offered a way out of the prevailing socioeconomic crisis; a way out which was both nonpolitical and people based, so that they could trust it. Moreover, rather than imposing decisions from above, it asked people, who until then were essentially marginalized, to make their own decisions in order to gain control over the socioeconomic environment. It showed people, in a clear and simple way and using the language they understood, how their economic well-being could be improved through their own collective efforts. The main selling point of the Movement among the people was its practical and problem-solving bent. The relative geographical isolation of the region; the social and cultural cohesiveness existing within various communities,[10] and the dynamic leadership of Moses Coady and other early leaders,[11] also contributed immensely to the attraction of the Movement.

The Antigonish Movement, with its ideology of economic democracy and objective of getting everyone actively involved in economic life, appeared ideally suited to resolving the economic problems facing the people of Eastern Nova Scotia. First, its call for group action served to overcome the lack of power which the people experienced when acting individually by allowing them to pool their resources and decision-making abilities to initiate economic activities and, in the process, mobilize and develop additional resources. At the same time, the importance of the individual was not ignored. Second, by stressing the benefits which could be obtained by implementing economic projects and activities, it provided the motivation required to elicit commitment on the part of members of the community at large, not for altruistic reasons, but for reasons of their own welfare maximization. The Movement did not ask people to make sacrifices but, rather, to improve their well-being by making more effective and efficient use of their human and nonhuman resources.[12] Finally, it proposed a strategy which blended well with other human aspirations as well as with the social fabric of the community at large.

Goals and Objectives of the Antigonish Movement

The principles of the Antigonish Movement, formally stated in the 1940s but in fact reflecting its functions from the very outset, are as follows:[13]

1. The primacy of the individual.
2. Social reform through education.
3. Education beginning with the economic; that is, education must begin with the benefits that people can expect to derive from it.
4. Education through group action.
5. Effective social reform through fundamental changes in social and economic institutions.
6. Full and abundant life for everyone.

The importance of these six principles is that they reflect the basic features of the movement and, in particular, the combination of short-term, medium-term, and long-term goals which made it so effective. In effect, the sequence inherent in these principles can be envisaged as follows:

1. The short-term goals, which comprise the basic economic ones, were to be achieved through the implementation of economic projects such as cooperatives, credit unions, and community enterprises. This addressed the most pressing and obvious problems faced by people in depressed areas.[14] Indeed, the basic strategy of the movement comprising adult education and group formation and cooperation was aimed at this particular target.

2. The medium-term goals, which essentially envisaged the integration of individuals into the socioeconomic, political, and cultural environment and, thus, the achievement of full participation in the wider society, were neither as pressing nor as important to the people and hence left for a time further down the line.

3. The long-term goal of a broadly defined full and abundant life comprised the most lofty of human aspirations.

The importance of this sequence is in recognizing that while lofty goals and aspirations are important to the human condition they can best be realized when the most basic of needs and wants are satisfied first. To this end, the Movement was interested in promoting structural change and development, and concentrated on creating the required institutions.[15] Within the context of the existing conditions in the region, the changes sought aimed at improvements in the market mechanism by increasing the power of small producers, consumers, and wage earners; improvements in the allocation of resources and distribution of benefits; increases in the degree of commercialization and diversification, especially in the rural sectors; and promotion and development of resources; that is, bringing new resources into production.

Clearly, the Antigonish Movement was not in fundamental opposition to the market system, but rather acted to remedy the manifest shortcomings of the market in the economically depressed areas and, eventually, to foster greater participation in that system. It stressed that when the market failed to function for the benefit of the people, the people had both the option and responsibility to actively intervene in it. Moreover, the Movement, though stressing the group and cooperation, was predicated on the "primacy of the individual" and recognized the inherent worth of each individual, which is not to be sacrificed. More than any other reason, this differentiates the Movement from communism and socialism, which postulate the primacy of the collective over human individuality and freedom. For the Movement, it was not a choice between private enterprise and socialism. Instead, it was a middle way in which the predictable shortcomings of private enterprise as well as the abuses of the prevailing socioeconomic system could be corrected (Macpherson 1978, 90).

In light of these objectives, the focus on education—particularly education of a nonformal nature and directed at problem solving—and cooperative action was entirely appropriate.[16] On the one hand, the education provided information and knowledge required for effective decision making and institution building. On the other hand, cooperation allowed for greater access to resources and diversification of risk. The central importance attached to education also implicitly recognizes that human resources are fundamental to the mobilization of other resources. Without human resources, particularly decision-making ability and technical knowledge about methods of production, but also factors such as human dignity and the belief that it is possible to effect changes and overcome existing social and economic barriers, there cannot be any employment of other resources.[17]

THE STRATEGY OF THE MOVEMENT

The strategy of the Antigonish Movement was predicated on the following sequence: adult education contributing to the development of human capital and human resources; human capital and human resources mobilizing entrepreneurship at the group level; and group entrepreneurship promoting the mobilization of other resources—both human and nonhuman—for the purpose of production.

The Role of Adult Education

As noted, adult education was essentially the basic tool of the Antigonish Movement. Education is intrinsically linked to the concept of knowledge and, in effect, constitutes the process whereby the stock of knowledge is enlarged. In turn, knowledge—particularly of the sort that is nonformal in its organization and immediate in its impact, as that promoted by the Antigonish Movement—leads to greater self-awareness, critical evaluation of existing conditions, a strengthening of the desire to bring about change, and, eventually, decision making and economic activity.[18]

The importance of education and knowledge in improving living conditions and in improving the working of the economy cannot be underestimated, provided that the education and knowledge are indeed appropriate. Education, and the knowledge emanating from it, constitutes human-capital formation or the building up of "intellectual infrastructure." This human-capital formation or intellectual infrastructure is of fundamental importance to the functioning of the economy as well as to the promotion of economic development and change.[19] Some minimum amount of knowledge is imperative for the efficient allocation of resources as well as for the functioning of the market mechanism in a manner in which all participants can, in fact, gain. In the perfectly competitive markets, full information is assumed to obtain. On the consumption side, this entails knowledge about product characteristics, prices, and so on so that the best possible choices are made for the purpose of welfare maximization. Not only does knowledge facilitate rational maximizing behavior, it also helps to counter or weaken monopolistic and oligopolistic tendencies. The greater the amount and diffusion of knowledge, *ceteris paribus*, the greater the efficiency of resource allocation and the level of social welfare that can be achieved.

Appropriate knowledge and information is also vital to the production process in terms of both the adoption of production techniques and the choice of products and product characteristics. Knowledge is also central to innovation and technical change. In a real sense, technology is synonymous with knowledge, though the latter is considered to be much broader. Knowledge and technology share the characteristic that they are self-perpetuating; that is, knowledge and technology generally generate more knowledge and technology. This is particularly relevant, since it points out their dynamic nature and the fact that their influence is both continuous and ever expanding.

As mentioned, the mobilization of entrepreneurship at the group level was central to the adult education strategy. In its traditional sense, entrepreneurship involves the following functions:[20] discovering economic opportunities by analyzing market conditions and production possibilities based on the perception of wants and needs and required resources; undertaking the task of mobilizing and organizing resources for production; and undertaking the risk involved in any venture. Indeed, the main attribute of entrepreneurship involves the willingness and ability to solve problems. The problem-solving and practical focus of the Movement's adult education program was ideally suited for this. Essentially, it provided the group with the information required to identify profitable opportunities and actions and the motivation and knowledge to exploit them. The process of establishing such group or collective entrepreneurship is more involved than it would seem at first glance. The members of the various groups have to have a realistic idea of what they are capable of and individuals must trust each other. Given the low standards of living of the people, the risks involved in undertaking a project were so great that they could not be undertaken blindly. On the other hand, even small projects, involving very little risk, would not be undertaken without the necessary desire, will, and commitment to take action and to promote improvement. Normally, in circumstances characterized by poverty, exploitation, and a sense of helplessness and human degradation, this desire, will, and commitment is lacking. In these circumstances, passivity and apathy are often the norm, with little action undertaken beyond the minimum required to assure survival. Thus, a critical function of adult education in the context of the Antigonish Movement also involved awakening or reawakening the desire, will, and commitment to action and, in doing so, permitting entrepreneurship to emerge. However, it should be pointed out that in areas where such group entrepreneurship was most successful during the 1930s, the fisheries in particular and the rural areas in general, there was already a good deal of individual entrepreneurship. In part this explains the relatively greater success of the movement during its early years among primary producers vis-à-vis urban industrial workers.[21]

The importance attached to education, knowledge, and information is also clearly consistent with Coady's notion of the importance of "scientific thinking." The Movement was not to be one based on a return to old ways, but one which looked to the future with a pioneering spirit. Indeed, it was designed to be at the forefront of new ideas within the constraint of its fundamental purpose and objectives.

Knowledge for Structural Transformation and Change

In the foregoing discussion we have dealt with the issue of education within the context of the Antigonish Movement at a more abstract and theoretical level. It is legitimate to ask at this stage exactly what type of knowledge was required and promoted by the Antigonish Movement. The type of information required, of course, depends on the type of action which is being contemplated. Thus, for example, rural transformation and commercialization would require knowledge about markets and marketing, the role of money and financing, and the like. In order to facilitate the implementation of cooperative projects, knowledge about institutions such as cooperatives and credit unions would be required. For example, people would need to know how they function and their implications. Essentially, the knowledge that is required is of a practical nature primarily concerning how things work and how things are done. This is the problem-solving type of information dealing with concrete factors of obvious relevance and importance.[22]

Another form of knowledge to be fostered by the education program concerns what we refer to as human and social knowledge, comprising such things as attitudes, habits, and norms, such as motivation, self-confidence and self-knowledge, willingness to cooperate, and so on. These are essentially components pertaining to culture and tradition and are particularly relevant in the context of the Movement's community orientation and the notion of group entrepreneurship. Moreover, the different forms of knowledge (i.e., technical, human, and social) tend to be interrelated and cumulative. Thus, for example, as individuals learn new techniques and master new skills, their perceptions of themselves, their neighbors, and the world around them also tend to be altered. Knowledge that transforms the individual also transforms the group that the individual is part of and has the potential to transform the community and its institutions as well.

For education to have a maximum impact, the knowledge that it generates must be useful or appropriate but, at the same time, it must be widely disseminated. In the Antigonish Movement, this function was facilitated by the Extension Department of St. Francis Xavier University. Indeed, the Extension Department, established in 1928, was the very center of the movement; it can be described as being both its heart and its brain.

The importance and need for such an apparatus as the Extension Department, to assist not only in the generation of new and appropriate knowledge but also in ensuring its widest possible spread or dissemination, stems from the fundamental nature of knowledge. Knowledge, once generated, has the property of a public good (i.e., it is nonrival), meaning that its spread to more and more people does not limit the amount available to any one individual, and, at the same time, it is very difficult to exclude people from obtaining it once it becomes part of the public domain.[23] Moreover, as is the case for all public goods, once it is generated the marginal cost of knowledge is zero or at least very low to those who generate or possess it. However, the cost of actually generating this knowledge is very high. The significance of this is that if the knowledge is to be made readily available then it should follow the marginal cost-pricing criteria, meaning a very low or zero price in the face of relatively high costs incurred in generating it. This makes it unprofitable for any private corporation, dependent on its revenues to survive, to provide it—unless it can be internalized or protected, as in the case of patents, licenses, and professional accreditation, so that they may sell it as a private good and reap benefits from it.[24] However, allowing such essentially short-term monopoly power would defeat the whole purpose of disseminating knowledge as widely as possible. In the absence of an appropriate institutional framework, there would be little incentive for the generation and diffusion of appropriate knowledge and information. Individuals who want it would have to either generate it for themselves or obtain it from others at relatively high cost. Generally, the private benefits would fall short of the private costs incurred, so that such knowledge would not be sought.[25] The Extension Department, not being motivated by the need to generate profits, assisted in both the generation and diffusion of appropriate knowledge and information and, in the process, reduced private costs vis-à-vis private benefits, making it profitable for people to seek it. In the process, of course, the external economies or positive externalities associated with knowledge were also captured.[26]

With extremely meager financial resources, the Extension Department was successful in its task by, in fact, utilizing other resources which were relatively abundant (i.e., the people and their collective experience). The fact that the appropriate knowledge required during the 1930s and, to a lesser extent, the 1940s to implement economic projects and improve people's welfare could be generated from the people themselves was a key component of the Movement's success during its early years.[27] Moreover, a large proportion of these people were the doers who already possessed some degree of entrepreneurial skill; all they needed was a framework.

The Adult Education Strategy

The method employed to generate knowledge and distribute it as widely as possible was centered on the study clubs, constituting not only the simplest but also the most effective institutions for carrying out the process of adult education and cooperation envisaged by the Movement.[28] Moreover, these study clubs, which were by and large unique to the Antigonish Movement, also served other functions, ranging from social to motivational ones. Most important, they were a vehicle for full democratic participation in decision making on the part of the people, decision making which could or would yield readily recognizable benefits.

Though a detailed description of study clubs cannot be undertaken here, and, in any event, would be redundant since they have been fairly extensively documented in the existing literature, a brief discussion would be useful. The study clubs consisted of small groups, generally between five and ten people, who would meet at least once a week. Actual composition (i.e., men only, women only, or both men and women), the election of leaders, and decisions concerning where to meet—generally where it was most convenient—were left up to the individual club. Though the Extension Department provided some broad guidelines, there were no rigid procedures to be followed. They were intended to provide an atmosphere where frank discussion and study could take place with all members as active participants, and this tended to favor meeting in people's homes or other familiar places. In general, these meetings would have both an economic and a social dimension, so that while their purpose was serious indeed, the atmosphere was both familiar and friendly. In a real sense, study and discussion were conceived as being part of the everyday activities of life, as opposed to simply an extraordinary activity for an extraordinary time period.

Though there is no doubt that it played an important role in the success of the study clubs, the Movement tended to deemphasize the importance of leadership. Study club leaders were envisaged as being akin to secretaries and organizers charged with the responsibility of making sure that meetings took place regularly, that study materials were made available, that proper study methods were employed, and that everyone participated in the process of study and discussion (Moses M. Coady and Associates 1943). In practical terms, however, their ability and dedication was extremely important in shaping and guiding the study clubs and in promoting the spirit of cooperation and self-reliance. As well, these leaders were generally instrumental in establishing the study clubs in the first place, and also acted as contacts for the Extension Department.

The role of the Extension Department within this institutional set up was essentially twofold. On the one hand, it provided the initial spark which led to the formation of the study clubs, a function most often achieved as a result of mass meetings held by officers or volunteers of the Extension Department, which provided the necessary fervor and motivation. On the other hand, it also provided both direct and indirect support. Not only did it help to organize the study clubs and provide them with some general direction and guidance but, at the same time, it provided study materials of various sorts, including books, bulletins, and so on. As well, it trained leaders, not only in order to make the study clubs more effective but also to ensure that there would be people around who could, in fact, successfully manage economic projects once these were instituted. Nevertheless, the actual study and project implementation was, by and large, left up to the study clubs and the associated study clubs (i.e., clubs engaged in the same line of study).[29]

In addition, the Extension Department maintained interest in the movement by organizing various sorts of conferences, such as periodic regional conferences and larger rural and industrial conferences.[30] Aside from the interchanges which are normally promoted by conferences, the main purpose of these activities was mainly "inspirational" or promotional, by celebrating the successes and achievements of the Movement and exploring strategies for the future. They served to cement the bond between the people and the movement by integrating the movement more fully with the community at large while, at the same time, providing a sense of being part of something significant (i.e., of being part of a larger whole) and inspiring participants with the powerful vision of enormous future possibilities.

It cannot be doubted that this method was successful, at least during the course of the 1930s. The number of study clubs, which numbered 179 in 1931, when the Extension Department actually began operation, increased steadily to 860 by 1936 and 1,300 by 1939. Moreover, the purpose of these study clubs was to generate economic activities. Thus, rather than an end in themselves, they were envisaged as simply the means to an end (i.e., the creation of permanent cooperative economic institutions). Their function was to mobilize group entrepreneurship, which in turn could undertake cooperative action through the mobilization of resources, both human and nonhuman.

It must be pointed out that not all study clubs reached the stage where economic action was undertaken. Some folded as soon as the initial enthusiasm had waned, some survived primarily as social clubs, some were unable to muster the collective will to mobilize adequate amounts of resources, while still others succeeded in mobilizing adequate resources but for various reasons could not commit them to economic projects.[31] Thus, the success of the study clubs depended less on their number at any one time and more on the number of viable economic projects undertaken. In this respect, the Antigonish Movement must also be considered a success, as the 1930s saw a remarkable proliferation of cooperative lobster factories, cooperative fish plants, credit unions, and so on.[32] However, the focus on economic projects undertaken reveals only part of the success story. These projects not only promoted economic development, but also contributed to human and social development. As the people of Eastern Nova Scotia were creating their cooperatives, they were also developing their own humanity and revitalizing their communities.

The Role of Cooperation

Cooperation went along with education in the mobilization of resources. Its primary intent was to enable members of the community faced with common problems and sharing common goals and aspirations to pool their resources together for the purpose of putting into action viable economic projects. The expected economic consequences of such pooling of resources included an increase in market power both as consumers and as producers, an increase in economic efficiency as a consequence of potential economies of scale which could be taken advantage of, and the creation of new activities as a result of group entrepreneurship.

The achievement of these economic effects, however, also depended on the social and human consequences of cooperation. Of paramount importance was the ability of groups to overcome the so-called "prisoner dilemma" by eliminating uncertainty with respect to the behavior of others and ensuring that both the costs and the benefits would be shared.[33] It was accepted that some would possibly contribute more to the process of study, mobilization of resources, and the like, but, rather than exploitation or a free-rider problem, within a truly cooperative effort based on trust and general goodwill such an eventuality was consistent with Coady's notion of the more talented members of society putting these talents at the disposal of the community (Coady 1939, 10). Thus, rather than looking for a free ride, members would be encouraged to contribute to the extent of their abilities with the rewards of doing so coming in the form of social recognition. Indeed, the combined forces of church and culture gave rise to moral and spiritual foundations that were not only strong enough to survive in the face of human and social turmoil but were also very receptive to group action.

The smallness of the different communities also contributed to the elimination of the free-rider problem. Even in the urban areas of Eastern Nova Scotia it was relatively easy to spot those who were willing to benefit by "cheating." Thus, people were quite willing to work together since they were reasonably sure that all would participate in both the work and the benefits. In economic terms, they could foresee long-run benefits in excess of mainly short-term costs and no free riders.[34]

The Antigonish Movement addressed both the economic and noneconomic dimensions of the free-rider problem through the social and moral regeneration promoted in the study clubs and the implementation of cooperative activities. The geographical isolation, smallness, and social cohesion of the communities also contributed to success. The fact that the people could clearly see the relationship between their actions and the benefits arising from them, both at the individual level and at the community level, also helped to strengthen and accelerate the process.

ECONOMIC GAINS AND SOCIAL TRANSFORMATION

The economic gains arising from the economic activities promoted by the Antigonish Movement can be identified as being of two fundamental types: the reallocation of rents and quasirents and the increase in value added generated by resource mobilization and improved economic efficiency. The establishment of credit unions, processing and marketing of fish and other products, cooperative purchases of inputs, and the like meant a reallocation of rents to the small farmers and fishermen and away from the monopolistic sellers of intermediate inputs, the high interest cost of individual borrowing, and the monopsonistic buyers of output. The increase in value added and in the goods and services available was the result of a variety of things, including greater processing in the primary sectors; expansion into new areas of production, such as fruit canning; the establishment of community industries such as sawmills, woodworking factories, milk pasteurization facilities, and the like, as well as of cooperative stores and buying clubs; and the mobilization of savings through credit unions, and the like. Moreover, there was an expansion in family production, such as canning of fruits and vegetables, clothes making, and handicrafts. These activities were important not only for their direct impact but also for their demonstration and spillover effects.

While hardly a panacea, since it did not solve all the problems of the region, the Antigonish Movement did make a significant contribution to meeting the basic needs of the people and improving overall economic conditions in Eastern Nova Scotia, especially during the depression years. Cooperation allowed primary producers to get better prices for their products through greater control over the marketing process as well as through the increase in value added resulting from the processing activities carried out in local cooperative plants. Moreover, they were, in some instances, able to branch out into other activities and thus to exploit new sources of potential income while at the same time promoting a greater degree of diversification. Consumer cooperatives and buying clubs lowered the cost of goods and services, while credit unions were able to mobilize savings which could in turn be used to loosen the credit squeeze in various communities. The various community industries that were established generated employment opportunities while expanding the menu of goods and services available, including capital goods. Perhaps of even greater significance were the human, social, intellectual, and ultimately moral effects of the Movement. It called for people to be active participants in improving their lot and thus to exercise power over the economic environment and circumstances which shaped their lives and the life of their community. It showed people that they in fact mattered and that, in Coady's words, they could become "masters of their own destiny." Thus, the Movement also countered the general feeling of hopelessness, powerlessness, and, in some cases, even individual worthlessness, as well as the sense of community stagnation and decline which gave rise to the Antigonish Movement to begin with.[35]

Material, social (community spirit, cooperation, and participation), psychological (attitudes and motivation), and ultimately moral (feeling of self-worth, human dignity, and justice) elements are fundamental aspects of the basic-needs approach which, in its broadest manifestation, views development and progress as involving "both a physical reality and a state of mind" and, we might add, soul (Todaro 1985, 87).

CONCLUSION

In this chapter we have primarily focused on the economics of the Antigonish Movement as an example of a successful grassroots development experiment. Our analysis suggests that grassroots movements are essentially unique and must be treated as such. Indeed, we have been careful to point out that many things succeeded because of the existing environment and circumstances. These are factors which are likely to differ between countries and regions and also over different time periods.

While it was not our objective here to provide a blueprint for the economics of the grassroots approach to development, an analysis of the Antigonish Movement reveals that for a grassroots movement to succeed its strategy must be consistent with basic human needs and desires, including the need to develop and exercise free will. The experiences of the movement also point out that the actual institutions and strategies which satisfy the notion of economic rationality for a particular movement must necessarily be conditioned by the underlying circumstances: the nature of the problems that it is addressing, the resources that it can draw on, the technical requirements of various activities, and the cultural, social, and political environment. The activities of the movement also placed great emphasis on the role of group entrepreneurship and the importance of developing the individual and collective will that is necessary for such entrepreneurship to be mobilized.

In our discussion concerning the Antigonish Movement, we have characterized the fundamental problem facing it as being one of market failure. In strictly economic terms, the problem of market failure was envisaged as one related to monopolistic and monopsonistic market structures and unemployment of resources and inefficiency. These, however, were only part of the story. Besides the long-standing economic decline, the economic effects were made worse, particularly within the context of the ideology of the Antigonish Movement, by the failure on the part of the people to understand that competitive markets create economic institutions with the power to alter resource use and the distribution of well-being in society. In Coady's (1939) words, this failure constituted "the great default of the people." The solution to the perceived problems was envisaged in terms of changing the power relationship in the marketplace and mobilizing resources. The strategy chosen was consistent with both these objectives as well as with the available resources.

Finally, the Antigonish Movement shows that the top-down approach to development planning can be complemented by the bottom-up grassroots approach. Development does not have to proceed in one way to achieve sectoral/rural–urban linkages. The Antigonish Movement demonstrates that working toward grassroots improvements, in fact, creates an environment which reinforces the top-down approach. The key task is to facilitate the acquisition of knowledge about opportunities, to improve the transmission of information among the grassroots participants, to mobilize entrepreneurial skills and the decision-making capacity of the community or groups, and to curtail free riders by providing each of the participants with a clear incentive to actively cooperate in achieving goals.

NOTES

1. This is a notion that emanates, for example, from the seminal work by Seers (1972).

2. On the face of it, our approach would seem to be consistent with what Uphoff (1988) refers to as "Assisted Self-Reliance" which entails a fusion of both top-down and bottom-up approaches with the former strengthening rather than weakening the latter. However, as is made clearer later on with respect to the experience of the Antigonish Movement, our notion of assistance is much different from that of Uphoff and others.

3. See Olson (1965) for an excellent treatment of the issue of compulsion.

4. In this vein, Thordarson (1990, 13), in reference to the workings of some grassroots cooperatives in Third World countries, notes that they "are helping to assimilate the so-called 'informal sector' to the mainstream economy."

5. Our notion of grassroots development implies cooperation but is not synonymous with the cooperative sector. Indeed, only cooperatives that are in fact established and controlled by their members can be viewed as strictly grassroots organizations. Cooperatives and other like organizations established and controlled by government bodies have more in common with government enterprise than with the types of organizations that we have in mind.

6. See, for example, MacInnes (1978), Mifflen (1974), and Sowder (1967), among others. For additional interesting insights into the Antigonish Movement and the initial socioeconomic conditions, see also MacPherson (1979, 1978, 1975) and Sacouman (1977).

7. On the issue of outmigration, Sowder (1967) notes that the population of Eastern Nova Scotia declined by 26,607 over the 1891 to 1931 period. In the same vein, Moses M. Coady and Associates (1943, 1) complained that "in one fifty-year period Eastern Canada lost four hundred and fifty thousand of its people to other parts of America."

8. Simply put, an economic rent is the payment made to a productive resource in excess of that which is required to maintain that resource in a particular employment. Quasirents are the same, except that they are temporary in nature. For more discussion on the issue of rents see Blaug (1985) and Krueger (1974), among others.

9. Economic rents, which as a rule can be found in all industries, are normally envisaged as being distributed, albeit not necessarily equally, by market forces among buyers and sellers (among demanders and suppliers). However, as can be shown by consumer and producer surplus analysis, the appropriation of rent depends on economic power. The side that has most or all of the economic power generally also appropriates most or all of the economic rent. In the case of Eastern Nova Scotia in the 1920s and 1930s, the same group appropriated the economic rent from several markets: as buyer of fish and produce, seller of consumer goods, and supplier of credit and producer goods.

10. For example, the Scottish Catholics, the Acadians, and so on. The importance of such a cohesion is recognized in the literature on grassroots development and cooperatives. See Lele (1981) and Korten (1980), among others.

11. On the dynamic personality of Coady, see Laidlaw (1971), Delaney (1985), MacDonald (1986), and MacLellan (1985).

12. Technically, since they were asked to save, study, and work, there was a sacrifice involved, but this was more than offset by the expected benefits to be gained from it.

13. Indeed, it can be argued that the articulation of these principles took place precisely when the movement itself was, perhaps, starting to decline.

14. See Johnson (1944) and Coady in St. Francis Xavier University Extension Department (1945) for the earliest articulation of these principles.

15. The importance of this essential focus on improving the income of the people is critical and generally recognized in the literature as a key element in successful grassroots activity. See, for example, Korten (1980).

16. Institutions, in fact, act as the agents of economic change and development. It is through them that processes such as adult education, cooperation, and so on are carried out.

17. Indeed, appropriate education has come to be recognized in the literature on economic development in general and grassroots development in particular as a key determinant of successful implementation of economic activity.

18. It is interesting to note that this view, in fact, runs counter to the more traditional economic development theories which emphasize capital accumulation. However, it is consistent with some of the more recent literature, particularly within the context of the basic-needs approach, which places the development of human resources ahead of sheer capital accumulation. For a good early exposition of the basic-needs approach, see Streeten et al. (1981).

19. The issue of decision-making ability is raised in the seminal work by Hirschman (1958). Hirschman considered the lack of adequate decision-making ability to be the key constraint faced by developing countries and this served as the basis for his espousal of the unbalanced approach to economic development.

20. Generally, anything which augments the quality or productivity of labor can be considered in the same vein as physical capital. The distinguishing feature of human capital is that it is embodied in the individual and, among other things, entails a decision-making dimension.

21. See Hagen (1986) and Leff (1979).

22. The fact that projects were undertaken earlier does not necessarily imply that the Movement was more successful in rural than in urban areas. However, some of the evidence available for later periods could be taken as suggesting that such was indeed the case. Nevertheless, credit unions, cooperative stores, and the like prospered in urban areas.

23. Related to this sort of nonformal education is what Simmons (1983) refers to as education for self-reliance. According to Simmons, this type of education "teaches groups of people how to study together and become aware of the political and economic determinants of their poverty. They learn how to organize themselves to improve their own circumstances, and in that process they learn to build roads, manage water distribution . . . and grow more food. . . . Through co-operative saving, they reduce their dependence on moneylenders" (p. 264).

24. By their very nature, public goods cannot be adequately provided through the standard market mechanism. For a more complete discussion on the issue see any good text in public finance, such as Herber (1983). Also relevant in this context is the work by Cornes and Sandler (1986).

25. Arguably, a lot of knowledge tends to be embodied in people who can then market it to achieve some particular end or objective. Knowledge obtained through formal education can often be viewed as being of this sort, since those who possess it generally use it to achieve some end, such as getting a job and the like.

26. We can envision a situation in which, even if the education constituted a good investment, the resources required to obtain it are simply not available. The matter may be complicated by the fact that, while benefits accrue over time, the costs are incurred in the present or up front.

27. These externalities or economies arise from the public benefits of education and knowledge exceeding the private ones.

28. This meant not only a saving in terms of resources but also ensured that the knowledge and information generated and diffused was indeed of the appropriate sort.

29. Indeed, these study clubs were the core of the adult education program of the Extension Department of St. Francis Xavier University and hence of the whole

Antigonish Movement during the 1930s. In a real sense, they were the embodiment of the grassroots approach and fundamental spontaneity of the Movement.

30. It was, in fact, at the associated-clubs level that the actual economic projects were implemented.

31. These are well documented in many of the various Annual Reports and other documents of the Extension Department of St. Francis Xavier University (1928–1939).

32. For example, Sowder (1967, 30) notes that "often these study clubs became bogged in useless talk and dissention. When Dr. Coady discussed these early ventures he states that some clubs had to reorganize 'again and again' before any positive results were forthcoming."

33. For example, by 1939 there were 17 cooperative lobster factories, 11 cooperative fish plants, and 170 credit unions. For more details, see Dodaro and Pluta (1986, 1988).

34. The prisoner–dilemma effect arises when there is uncertainty as to how others will behave, leading to a suboptimal outcome as each individual tries to insure himself or herself against the worst possible outcome. For a detailed analysis of the prisoner dilemma, see any of the more advanced texts in microeconomic theory.

35. A free rider is one who shares in the benefits but not in the costs. In the context of the Antigonish Movement it could refer, for example, to fishermen who gain from the higher prices resulting from cooperative marketing of fish by selling to the fish buyers rather than joining the cooperative and participating in the work involved. A complete analysis of the free-rider problem can be found in any public finance text. For additional insights into the free-rider problem within the context of grassroots organizations, see Tendler et al. (1988).

REFERENCES

Blaug, M. 1985. *Economic Theory in Retrospect*. 4th ed. Cambridge: Cambridge University Press.

Coady, M. M. 1939. *Masters of Their Own Destiny*. New York: Harper and Brothers.

Cornes, R., and T. Sandler. 1986. *The Theory of Externalities, Public Goods and Club Goods*. Cambridge: Cambridge University Press.

Delaney, I. 1985. *By Their Own Hands: A Fieldworker's Account of the Antigonish Movement*. Truro, Nova Scotia: Lancelot Press.

Dodaro, S., and L. Pluta. 1986. The Evolution of the St. Francis Xavier University Extension Department and Its Adaptation to Changing Conditions, Part 1. Mimeographed.

Dodaro, S., and L. Pluta. 1988. The Antigonish Movement as a Model of Regional Economic Development. In *Political Economy of Development in Atlantic Canada*, edited by M. A. Choudhury. Sydney, N.S.: University College of Cape Breton Press.

Hagen, E. E. 1986. *The Economics of Development*. 4th ed. Homewood, Ill.: Irwin.

Herber, B. B. 1983. *Modern Public Finance*. 5th ed. Homewood, Ill.: Irwin.

Hirschman, A. O. 1958. *The Strategy of Economic Development*. New Haven: Yale University Press.

Hirschman, A. O. 1984. Grassroots Development in Latin America. *Challenge*, September/October, 4–9.

Johnson, H. G. 1944. *The Antigonish Movement: A Lecture to the Students of Acadia University*. Antigonish, Nova Scotia: St. Francis Xavier University Extension Department.

Korten, D. C. 1980. Community Organization and Rural Development: A Learning Process Approach. *Public Administration Review*. Reprinted by the Ford Foundation.

Krueger, A. O. 1974. The Political Economy of the Rent-Seeking Society. *American Economic Review* 64 (3): 271–303.

Laidlaw, A. F., ed. 1971. *The Man from Margaree*. Toronto: McClelland and Stewart.

Leff, N. 1979. Entrepreneurship and Development: The Problem Revisited. *Journal of Economic Literature* 17 (1): 46–74.

Lele, U. 1981. Co-operatives and the Poor: A Comparative Perspective. *World Development* 9 (1): 55–72.

MacDonald, J. D. N. 1986. *Memoirs of an Unorthodox Clergyman*. Truro, Nova Scotia: Lancelot Press.

MacInnes, D. W. 1978. *Clerics, Fishermen, Farmers and Workers: The Antigonish Movement and Identity in Eastern Nova Scotia, 1928–1939*. Unpublished Ph.D. Diss., McMaster University.

MacLellan, M. 1985. *Coady Remembered*. Antigonish, Nova Scotia: St. Francis Xavier University Press.

MacPherson, I. 1975. Patterns in the Maritime Co-operative Movement, 1900–1945. *Acadiensis* 5 (1): 67–83.

MacPherson, I. 1978. Appropriate Forms of Enterprise: The Prairie and Maritime Co-operative Movements, 1900–1955. *Acadiensis* 8 (1): 77–96.

MacPherson, I. 1979. *Each for All: A History of the Co-operative Movement in English Canada, 1900–1945*. Toronto: Macmillan of Canada.

Mifflen, F. J. 1974. *The Antigonish Movement: A Revitalization Movement in Eastern Nova Scotia*. Unpublished Ph.D. Diss., Boston College.

Moses M. Coady and Associates. 1943. *The Antigonish Way*. Antigonish, Nova Scotia: St. Francis Xavier University Extension Department.

Nurkse, R. 1964. *Problems of Capital Formation in Underdeveloped Countries*. New York: Oxford University Press.

Olson, M. 1965. *The Logic of Collective Action: Public Goods and the Theory of Groups*. Cambridge: Harvard University Press.

Sacouman, R. J. 1977. Underdevelopment and the Structural Origins of the Antigonish Movement Co-operatives in Eastern Nova Scotia. *Acadiensis* 7 (1): 66–85.

Seers, D. 1972. What Are We Trying to Measure? *Journal of Development Studies* 8 (3): 21–36.

Simmons, J. 1983. Education and Development Reconsidered. *World Development* 7 (11/12). Reprinted in *The Struggle for Economic Development*, edited by M. P. Todaro. New York: Longman.

Sowder, E. M. 1967. *The Present Status of the Antigonish Movement in Nova Scotia*. Unpublished Ph.D. Diss., George Peabody College for Teachers.

St. Francis Xavier University Extension Department. 1928–1939. Annual Reports and Other Documents. St. Francis Xavier University Archives.

St. Francis Xavier University Extension Department. 1945. *The Social Significance of the Cooperative Movement*. Antigonish, Nova Scotia: The Department.

Streeten, P., S. J. Burki, M. U. Haq, N. Hicks, and F. Stewart. 1981. *First Things First.* New York: Oxford University Press.

Tendler, J., K. Healy, and C. M. O'Laughlin. 1988. What to Think about Co-operatives: A Guide from Bolivia. In *Direct to the Poor: Grassroots Development in Latin America,* edited by S. Annis and P. Hakim. Boulder, Colo.: Lynne Rienner.

Thordarson, B. 1990. *Banking on the Grass Roots: Co-operative in Global Development.* Ottawa: North–South Institute.

Todaro, M. P. 1985. *Economic Development in the Third World.* 3d ed. New York: Longman.

Uphoff, N. 1988. Assisted Self-Reliance: Working With, Rather Than For, The Poor. In *Strengthening the Poor: What Have We Learned?* edited by J. P. Lewis. St. John, New Brunswick: Overseas Development Council.

THE HUMAN FACTOR: EVIDENCE FROM DEVELOPING COUNTRIES

Chapter 6 ——————————————————————

Facing the Challenges of Economic Underdevelopment in Ghana: The Role of the Human Factor

Senyo B-S. K. Adjibolosoo

The development train boarded by Ghana at independence has covered many miles as of today. Presently, however, this train seems to be moving on very rough and undulating terrain on which the tracks have been built with severely deformed rails. It is not only too circuitous to travel on, but also slippery—filled with hidden mines of economic underdevelopment. Thus, though the wheels of the train are good and revolving continuously, the train seems to be making little progress. Since structural adjustment programs (SAPs) and stabilization policies are founded on neoclassical economic theory, they seem to be focusing on symptoms rather than on the real problems. The financial gas tank of the train's engine is being continually refilled with liquid funds and other resources from the developed nations. What is being ignored, however, is that the gear of the development train has unsuspectingly slipped into the neutral position.

In view of these observations, the main objectives of this chapter are to review past policies, present issues relating to the current state of the Ghanaian economy, and make deductions regarding the primary source of economic underdevelopment in Ghana. By arguing that top-level development experts seem to be confused and oblivious to the true problems of Ghana's underdevelopment, the chapter points out that, until the true problems are identified and dealt with successfully, the Ghanaian economy will not develop regardless of the magnitude of the available financial resources. The chapter concludes that relentless revving and oiling of the engine of Ghana's development train without successfully tackling the existing problems will be fruitless in the long term.

POST-INDEPENDENCE POLICIES:
A HISTORICAL SYNOPSIS

Since independence in 1957, Ghana has relentlessly pursued development planning. As is obvious from the information presented in Table 6.1, the goals and objectives of each plan were clearly stated in relation to social, economic, industrial, and infrastructure development. As such, it can be concluded that the post-independence leaders of Ghana knew exactly what they wanted to do and pursued development planning and policy as the means whereby the intended goals could be achieved. A critical review of these plans reveals that each plan and its accompanying policies and programs were concerned with economic growth and development, job creation, the promotion of conditions for the attainment of higher living standards for Ghanaians, and industrial development (see Table 6.1). As observed by Ewusi (1986, 30), the 1951–1956 plan allocated available funds to four major areas: economic and productive services, communications, social services, and common services. Most of these plans focused on capital budgets for the public sector to the total neglect of the private sector.

The plans also focused on how to attract foreign investment capital. Excellent investment incentives were offered in terms of taxation, profit repatriation, expropriation, and so on. Ewusi (1986, 36–37) observed that foreign investors were granted attractive tax concessions. They were granted the permission to repatriate a significant percentage of their earned profits. Expenditures made on research-and-development activities could also be deducted before taxation. Manufactured products that used significant domestic components were also exempted from export taxes. Imported materials and machinery used to manufacture import substitutes in the country were also exempted from import and customs duties. An agreement signed in 1958 between the governments of Ghana and the United States protected American investors against the risks of expropriation, currency inconvertibility, and severe commercial losses.

Thus, as is obvious from the information in Table 6.1, the development of infrastructure, industrialization, import-substitution programs, self-reliance and self-sufficiency, and the enhancement of sectoral performance clearly stand out. Policy goals have been spelled out explicitly, with no doubts regarding Ghana's development intentions.

Stylized facts have revealed that ongoing development planning, policy-making program development, and project implementation did not have the key to unlock the doors of progress to usher Ghana into sustained economic growth and development. Yet, in the midst of continuing failure and frustrations, Ghana did not give up. From 1966 to the present, Ghana has experienced many different phases of economic policy formulation, implementation,

Table 6.1
The Genesis of Ghana's Development Plans

YEAR	PLAN	OBJECTIVES
1919–1929	The Guggisburg Ten-Year Development Plan	Infrastructure development and the production of agricultural raw materials
1951–1956	The First Five-Year Development Plan	Develop infrastructure Create good social services Lay industrial foundation Increase agricultural output Pursue import substitution
1957–1959	The Consolidated Plan	Consolidate the goals of the 1951–1956 plan
1959–1964	The Second Five-Year Development Plan	Develop all sectors Complete Volta Dam Produce local substitutes Promote construction industry
1963–1970	The Seven-Year Development Plan	Develop infrastructure Promote import-substitution industrialization Advance manufacturing and agriculture
1968–1970	The Two-Year Development Plan	Stimulate economic and cultural development Improve living standards Improve capacity use Acquire managerial experience Develop industrial estates Promote the private sector
1970–1971	The One-Year Development Plan	Develop the public sector Develop industries Identify and promote new growth areas Increase capacity utilization
1975–1980	The Five-Year Development Plan	Diversify industries Pursue self-reliance Promote cottage industries Accelerate industrial growth

and abandonment. A summary of the genesis of policy development in Ghana is presented in Table 6.2, which clearly points out that economic policy making and implementation were more reactive than proactive. Various governments (civilian and military alike) developed and implemented policies that were aimed at dealing with the crises of the time. Exchange-rate controls,

Table 6.2
Policy Chronology

YEAR	POLICY
1961	Exchange rate controls and import licensing to deal with worsening balance of payments.
1967	Devaluation of the cedi and trade liberalization.
1969 - 1971	Though the Busia government continued with import liberalization, some controls and import surcharges remained.
1971	Another devaluation of the cedi.
1973 - 1979	The policy of import controls continued.
1979	Tighter controls were imposed.
1983	The first phase of the Economic Recovery Program (ERP) was introduced in April for the period 1984 - 1986. Another devaluation in August (thirty cedis to one U.S. dollar).
1984	Interest rates rose by 1.5 per cent. In December, another devaluation occurred (fifty cedis to one U.S. dollar).
1985	Wages were increased in January. The budget for this year increased prices on most commodities; registration and license fees increased. There were increased taxes on services and personal income tax brackets were also adjusted in April. The prices of cocoa, cotton, and tobacco were increased by 90 per cent in June. The new investment code was published in July. Hospital user fees also increased. Interest rates rose further.
1986	Since there was another devaluation of the cedi (ninety cedis to one U. S. dollar) in January, minimum wages were adjusted accordingly. In August, lending and deposit rates increased. In September, the foreign exchange auction came into being.
1987	In February, the two-tier exchange rate system was merged. Import duties were reduced on commercial vehicles and capital goods. A World Bank structural adjustment program pursued trade liberalization policies in March. Phase two of the ERP was amended to cover 1987 - 1989.

Source: Roe, Schneider, and Pyatt, 1992, 81-82.

currency devaluation, import controls, wage and income controls, and the introduction of user fees on education, health, and much else were the most frequently implemented policies (see Table 6.2).

Economic policy in Ghana failed to be proactive. As such, these plans, policies, and programs lacked a long-term leadership vision, mission statement, and commitment. The frequent changes in government and leadership exacerbated the lack of direction and objectivity. From 1961 to about the second half of the 1980s, governments acted like community fire departments. That is, all they did was to try to either contain or accommodate pertinent social, economic, political, and educational problems of the day (see Table 6.2). For example, the government of the day acted in response to balance-of-payments problems, exchange rate difficulties, shortages of essential consumer items, worker unrest and agitation for higher wages, inflation, unemployment, and many other causes. Thus, like bush fires that do not necessarily follow any systematic patterns and are therefore able to fool and defeat the plans of many firefighters, these economic problems get out of hand when governments continue to pursue reactive policies in attempts to deal with them. At best, they are only successful at worsening the problems.

Through the years, economic policy was no more than frail attempts to palliate crises in the development program. As such, the primary focus of long-term plans and policies was most often ignored in the short run and finally abandoned in the long run. These attitudes, by degenerating into a policy-hopping syndrome, have denied post-independence Ghana the ability to confront and deal successfully with the main hindrances to economic development and industrial progress.

Since the 1960s, various governments of Ghana have tried to achieve economic growth and development. Policies of both Western and Eastern persuasions have all been tried in the past. The foreign debt situation of the country has also worsened, as has been the case with other developing countries (Lipson 1986, 1988). The debt situation looks as if there is no hope for many LDCs. Yet little has happened to change this picture. In view of this, the IMF and the World Bank try to develop and implement programs to help the LDCs to meet their debt obligations. Both organizations have been extremely active in policy formulation, development, and implementation in Ghana in the last decade and a half.

Stabilization policies have aimed at the minimization of current account imbalances (i.e., debt management), reduction in domestic absorption, exchange rate devaluation, dismantling restrictions and barriers imposed on international trade, and, above all, opening up the country to foreign investors (George 1988; Nelson 1990). Policy reforms usually focus on conditional loans. These loans are conditional on the recipient's willingness to minimize the size of government and its intervention, promote the free-market system, free wages and prices, discontinue credit expansion, devalue the local currency, and so on (Cornia, Jolly, and Stewart 1987; Pickett and Singer 1990; Tarp 1993). Structural adjustment programs demand state effectiveness in such areas as policies regarding trade, banking, and finance; planning; policy formulation, initiation, and implementation; and economic monitoring and data analysis (Picard 1994, 3). The primary objective of these efforts is to reform the public sector to make it more efficient and effective.

In the banking sector, the IMF–World Bank SAPs and stabilization policies (SPs) in Ghana have been primarily concerned with (1) how to strengthen financial institutions and enhance their continuing effectiveness; (2) the implementation of new banking and finance-related laws and regulations; (3) the improvement of management performance; and (4) the introduction of new accounting standards and audit guidelines. The irony, however, is that though many of these policies have not helped the country to achieve its intended long-run economic objectives, little has been done to reevaluate the primary reasons for policy ineffectiveness or failure outside orthodox economic thinking. In the past, policies deemed to be fruitless were abandoned and replaced with new ones on the advice of government policy advisors and foreign experts (i.e., the IMF and the World Bank). We will now evaluate the effectiveness of the SAPs in Ghana over the last decade.

OBSERVED IMPACT OF PAST POLICIES ON GHANAIAN ECONOMY

The SAPs in Ghana have not really achieved any significant success. The continuing pursuit of policies and programs in these directions will not, unfortunately, achieve any significant, positive long-term results because they continue to ignore the critical role of the HF in the development process (Adjibolosoo 1995a, 1995c).

Educational standards, the quality of health-care delivery, and the performance of many other public services are declining in both efficiency and effectiveness. In many cases, the relevant inputs are not readily available because of price escalation brought about by the SAPs. Most people are always under severe suffering due to the implementation of the SAPs and SPs in Ghana. Visits to hospitals by both rural and urban dwellers are declining because the people cannot afford the user fees being charged as a result of the SAPs and SPs. In many cases, those who go to the hospital go when their illnesses have advanced to the final and terminal stage. As such, many go only to die in the hospital. Those who cannot afford to pay the required user fees usually stay and die at home (Kam 1995, A10). Common infectious diseases that can be easily treated kill many because these people cannot afford to go to the hospital in time to be treated. Education is also suffering, in that parents who cannot afford the minimal school fees keep their children at home. While the impact of this phenomenon may not be observable at the present time, its effects will definitely show up in the long term. Indeed, the SAPs, in their enthusiasm to boost short-term output of exports for debt repayment, are actually slaying the goose that lays the golden eggs.

If Ghana hopes to make any long-term progress, the vicious cycle of policy formulation, implementation, failure, abandonment, and replacement (i.e., the policy-hopping syndrome) has to be discontinued. Structural adjustment programs and stabilization policies deal with the symptoms of problems about whose actual root causes leaders have few clues. As such, the challenges the advocates of these policies and programs face far exceed their knowledge, understanding, and capabilities. Picard (1994, 5) noted, "Structural adjustment programs operating within this context have often had a negative impact on human resources and institutional capacity."

The continuing failure to achieve intended objectives has led some scholars to believe that the ineffectiveness of the SAPs and SPs is due to the lack of efficient and effective institutions and other relevant institutional structures (see Lungu and Bwalya 1994, 64). The general consensus is that as soon as capacity building is achieved and institutions are developed, the LDCs will find the path of development easy to follow. This belief has led many scholars of economic development to suggest that policies that can create effective institutional structures must be pursued (Picard and Garrity 1994). It is, therefore, clear why the IMF and the World Bank pursue the SAPs and SPs. Yet the continuing pursuit of policies and programs in these directions will not, unfortunately, achieve any significant results because they continue to ignore the critical role of the HF in the development process (Adjibolosoo 1995a).

THE ORTHODOX VIEW OF POLICY AND PROGRAM FAILURE

Many scholars of development theory have come to believe that when the true ingredients of development are nonexistent a country will find it too difficult to develop. It is often argued, therefore, that developing countries that lack capital, savings, investment, human capital, and the like will continue to experience underdevelopment. In the case of Africa, the World Bank Policy Research Report (1994, 20) observed the following:

There is no single explanation for Africa's poor performance before the adjustment period. The main factors behind the stagnation and decline were poor policies—both macroeconomic and sectoral—emanating from a development paradigm that gave the state a prominent role in production and in regulating economic activity. Overvalued exchange rates and large and prolonged budget deficits undermined the macroeconomic stability needed for long-term growth. Protectionist trade policies and government monopolies reduced the competition so vital for increasing productivity. In addition, the state increased its presence in the 1970s, nationalising enterprises and financial institutions and introducing a web of regulations and licenses for most economic activities. More important, the development strategy had a clear bias against exports, heavily taxing agricultural exports, one of the largest supplies of foreign exchange.

At the moment, these experts are currently dazed and confused because they cannot fully comprehend why their desired SAP and SP medicine does not seem to be producing the expected results. Indeed, at the commencement of both the SAPs and SPs, these organizations and their intellectual experts had little clue regarding how relevant and applicable they were to the Ghanaian situation. To date, policies have been made to deal with exchange rate problems, enhance trade liberalization and improve capacity utilization, promote export production and lower tax rates on export products, reduce government expenditure, and recover costs in the areas of government expenditure on health and education services (see Tables 6.1 and 6.2).

INTERVIEWS: EVALUATION OF
SOCIAL AND ECONOMIC CONDITIONS

In June 1994, I made a research trip to Ghana and conducted a series of interviews in order to obtain people's general and specific impressions about the perceived impact of the SAPs and SPs on the performance of the Ghanaian economy under the economic recovery program. The randomly selected subjects involved in the interviews included both rural and urban dwellers, the employed and the unemployed, and people from both the private and public sectors. The interviews with two individuals are reproduced in the following section. A selection of the comments regarding social conditions, employee behavior, social conditions, attitude change, and education are reported here to illustrate how some Ghanaians perceive the effectiveness of the SAPs and SPs.

Case 1: Current Conditions and Employee Behavior

Author: What do you think about social, economic, and political conditions in Ghana as far as people's well-being is concerned?

Interviewee 1: To tell you the truth, conditions in Ghana now are a bit unbearable. Everybody is sort of unhappy about the trend of affairs—politically, socially, and economically. Cost of living is so high that most people cannot afford easily the basic necessities of life. Yet workers' wages are very low. Right from the word go, there is instability because if income is not commensurate with the cost of living then definitely there is a problem somewhere. In an underdeveloped country such as Ghana, we realize that those who are rich are always getting richer from their investments because they have the money to invest and also live on. However, the vast majority of the people are uncomfortable. People are unable to pay the school fees of their children. Although it is not really a luxury to own a car in Ghana today, it is, however, excessively difficult to have one because maintenance costs are very high and usually unaffordable to the low-income earners. When traveling, we prefer to take the state transport in order to reserve our scarce financial resources to be channeled into buying the basic necessities of life. People are living on borrowed monies these days. It is not healthy for us at all. Doctors are complaining that many people are malnourished. This is because the people do not make enough money to live on a balanced diet. Thus, health problems abound in the country. Even at government hospitals, the fees are very high and as such many people cannot afford to go to such hospitals when they fall sick. Generally speaking, we are all feeling a great discomfort over our development program. It is our hope that something will be done urgently. Otherwise, the problems will compound and swallow many of us. People are not even able to save. Things are getting out of hand.

Author: Given all you have said so far, it seems to me that from your perspective life is becoming very unbearable to the Ghanaian. My concern then is how people are surviving in the country these days.

Interviewee 1: The average Ghanaian is intelligent, very intelligent. Ghanaians have a way of surviving that baffles the minds of those who are outside the country, because when they come from elsewhere with their foreign currency, within a short period of time their money is exhausted and they ask us how we who have lived here all these years are able to survive. We are in the system and because of that we have to cut our coat according to our size. Every family is always trying to devise ways and means whereby its members can at least survive on the barest minimum. This means that we have to eliminate a lot of things, such as personal pleasures, desserts, and the like. We just have to impose checks and balances on ourselves continuously in order to survive the hard economic times. Women do petty trading to supplement the family income. We are only managing with the scanty resources we get from many different income-generating activities.

Author: It is interesting you mentioned Ghanaian intelligence. The part of it that both baffles and bothers me is that since I came into the country a few weeks ago, I have been holding interview sessions with many civil servants. What I am realizing is that certain civil servants are not working in their offices as they are expected to do. In one office, while the female secretary was knitting an apron, her male counterparts were reading the daily newspapers. In some other offices, government employees spend a considerable amount of time trying to figure out the next set of probable national lottery numbers. In situations like these, would you say that people are doing these things because they want to make ends meet by using official working hours to do so? If this is the general practice, how then can civil servants increase their productivity?

Interviewee 1: Your observations concerning the output of workers in the civil service is very correct. The fact is that, in most cases, the inputs needed by civil servants to produce are not available. I heard, for example, that for a period of about three months now there has been no money budgeted for the purchase of typewriters, ribbons, and stationery for certain government offices. In situations like this one, what is the civil servant expected to do there? Nothing! So the intelligent Ghanaian civil servant will have to make use of the time available. If the employees feel they have been around at the office for a number of hours doing nothing, they figure out that they might as well do something else instead. The boss has no justification for giving them any queries because the required inputs are not available for the subordinates to work with. There is also no concentration and peace of mind on the job because the worker is thinking about how to feed his or her children. People have resorted to enjoying themselves in other business-related activities through which they could make additional income to supplement their work incomes. Although the probability of winning the lottery is slim, people still hope that they could be the lucky winners of big income. Marginal productivity in the civil service is quite low. The phenomenon you have described will be very difficult to deal with because when people are not able to make ends meet and feel starvation staring them in the face, they would do anything to survive—especially in our case, where most people lack integrity, loyalty, responsibility, trustworthiness, and so on. Indeed, we have a long way to go.

Author: In terms of all these observations, what can you say about government programs and policies at the moment? Do you think that, the way they are being organized, the country will be able to solve the existing social, economic, political, and educational problems?

Interviewee 1: All I can say is that we have a long way to go. In my opinion, the economic recovery program may not solve all our problems because we have been under the program for almost eleven years to date. Yet not much has changed. At this point in time, I am not sure whether it will. Maybe it is time we reevaluate the program and see where it is lacking. By so doing, we may discover our mistakes and correct them. It is, however, important to find ways and means of using the Ghanaian intelligence as effectively as possible.

Case 2: Social Conditions, Attitude Change, and Education

Author: In your opinion, what is life like in Ghana?

Interviewee 2: Generally, there are difficulties in the country. Economically, goods are there but the money is not there to buy them. Most people are finding it difficult to cope with the rising costs of goods and services. Recently there were massive strike actions and the government responded. People are finding it difficult to make ends meet and are becoming increasingly disappointed. Though many people are working hard every day, they are being paid salaries that are not enough to meet their monthly expenses. Meanwhile, although the government's structural improvement program is in progress, its effect on people's everyday life is not showing clearly. Life is very hard to cope with financially. Although there are some foodstuffs on the market, they are expensive to purchase. Prices are rising every minute in the country. We are not paid in foreign currencies! Yet these currencies determine the value of our cedi. Thus, as currencies such as the dollar and the sterling fluctuate, these fluctuations affect domestic prices directly.

Author: What would you tell somebody who comes to complain to you that there is too much lawlessness in the country—everybody seems to be doing whatever he or she likes?

Interviewee 2: To me, the person's observation is accurate. This is especially glaring when you compare the country when it was under military rule as opposed to our current democracy. Under the military rule, drivers were made to take the required number of passengers, without having to overload their cars and pick-up trucks. However, under the democratic rule, most drivers feel that democracy gives them the mandate to do what they desire even when it is against the law. As such, many of them overload their vehicles with passengers. This is, in fact, lawlessness. These days, unlike what it was like under our military government, when people spoke boldly to challenge those who were engaging themselves in wrong behavior, under democratic rule it is no longer easy for people to rise up and fight against something they see going wrong. Since there are no more guns to be afraid of, corruption is increasing once again. Although the lawlessness is there in the democratic system, one does not know who to report observed wrongdoing to. Some Ghanaians usually engage in many unlawful behaviors and activities just to make ends meet.

Author: Civil servants do not seem to be doing any work in their offices. Could you explain why this seems to be the case in Ghana today? What do you think is missing and what can we do?

Interviewee 2: I think it is a question of lack of integrity, accountability, and responsibility, because if I know the difference between right and wrong, I do not think that I have to wait for someone to force me to do that. Yet this is what people do these days. President Rawlings practices integrity to my understanding. The problem is with those who are surrounding him and the average Ghanaian. Not until you force people to do what is right, although they know it, they will not do it on their own. In my view, you cannot talk about integrity, accountability, and responsibility unless you talk about your faith or religion. I think the problem is a little more spiritual and moral than just economic. Although many people know the right thing, they still go ahead and do the wrong things and feel happy about doing so. Thus, until we start addressing the issue of lack of integrity, accountability, and responsibility in the country, I do not think we have a future as a nation. Without integrity and everything it entails, people will continue to engage themselves in those unlawful activities that have the power to destroy our economy. As a nation, we all need to learn to deal with each other with a great deal of integrity and honesty. It is critical to uphold the truth, live, and defend it. Civil servants also need to realize that they are duty bound to perform their tasks and discharge their duties as expected of them. Yet many will not do so if they lack honesty, integrity, accountability, and responsibility.

Author: Although your observations are quite interesting, the critical question is how you are going to face this issue of lack of integrity. What will be the Ghanaian response?

Interviewee 2: We have to start educating people and we cannot do it without paying attention to religious teachings. As I pointed out earlier, during the military rule, when the gun was there, most people were on good behavior most of the time. This was because they were afraid of the gun. Thus, in this case, people had an external object that drove significant fear into them. Once we came under the democratic rule and the guns went back into the barracks, people continued to engage in corrupt activities and wrong behavior on a larger scale. What this suggests to me is that if people will live a life based on integrity, they will need to have something within them to which they will have to be accountable to for everything they do with their lives. Since I am a Christian, I believe that those who yield the totality of their lives to Jesus Christ must be able to live a life that will help promote social, economic, and political progress in the country. Those who belong to other religious faiths also need to learn to live by the principles of their faith. If we all do so, we will no longer need the guns to force us to learn to live a life of honesty and integrity. In this way, there will be no need for any military revolutions anymore. It is only when we all fail to do so that things begin to get out of hand—and then the soldiers are invited in again and again in the attempt to keep all of us in order and check. But as has been our experience, true integrity cannot be imposed from outside the person. It has to come willingly from within every individual. Maybe we need to learn to use our educational and training programs to prepare the younger generation for this kind of life. We will have everything to gain and nothing to lose in the long term.

Author: You have just mentioned education and pointed out its relevance to preparing people for a life of integrity, accountability, and responsibility. As you are aware, Ghana is currently revamping its education system. Do you think that the new education system will be able to develop integrity and honesty in Ghanaians? If not, what suggestions will you make for helping the system to facilitate the development of integrity in people?

Interviewee 2: Actually, there are some recent improvements in the new education system. Yet there are still many flaws too. We have launched too quickly and too fast into the new education program. The key problems now revolve around the lack of well-educated and trained teachers, teaching materials, and relevant instruments to be used for instruction and practice. I think there is hope in the system because what they are teaching children now will help them to gain practical experience too. The area about cultural practices needs to be reconsidered and revised accordingly because it is not everything that our great grandparents did that was good. We only need to select the good things and leave out the bad. Children should not be introduced to everything because we feel these are part of our culture. We need to focus on issues that will build personal integrity, honesty, and loyalty. There is room for improvement. I must point out, however, that people should not oppose the government's new initiative just because they feel like doing so. They must come out with viable suggestions and alternatives for improvement.

Author: In that case, are you suggesting that the new education system will not develop personal integrity in Ghanaians?

Interviewee 2: Even if it does develop or create integrity, it would not be the type of integrity that I expect of people who want to build the nation. It is going to be a hazy kind of integrity that we can't be very sure of. This is so because when you introduce people to so many things without directing them, they may not be able to make the best choices for their own welfare and the betterment of society— children especially. So there is no guarantee that we can achieve our goal of developing integrity, accountability, and responsibility in the younger generation through the new education structure.

Author: Usually, when someone has done well, we are obliged to give him or her the credit due. Where the same person has done wrong, we must also point out to him or her what wrong has been committed and then rebuke the person. If you were to look back to what has been happening in Ghana for the last ten to thirteen years, what, in your opinion, are some of the greatest achievements of the government in terms of SAPs and SPs? What are some of the evidence you would consider as being substantive?

Interviewee 2: I realize that for the past ten to thirteen years I noticed that the necessary goods and services are there on the market to buy. Previously there were strict controls. As such, even if people had money, they still had difficulties getting the goods. Now, with the free-market system, the goods are there in abundance. If you are able to get money, you can go to the market to get the goods you desire. I think it's better than the former situation of ongoing shortages. Although cheating still exists, the price level is open for bargaining. So, I think that it's an achievement— being able to flood the market with many commodities. Formerly, people found it too difficult to express themselves freely. But now, people are more free to do so. President Rawlings has done very well in many respects.

Author: Do you think the government is really open to listen to people and takes their suggestions into account as it pursues its development agenda.

Interviewee 2: I think that the government has, to a large extent, been willing to listen to people. There is still room for improvement. The opposition parties also need to become more objective and resist the temptation of spreading too many false rumors.

Author: So in terms of infrastructure, what are some of the concrete achievements the government has made in the last ten to thirteen years?

Interviewee 2: Most of the deteriorating major roads have been repaired. The roads were in bad condition. The government came in and did significant rehabilitation and repairs. Electricity has been improved and it is now very easy for many villages to have access to electricity. By the year 2000, it is quite likely that the majority of villages, towns, and cities will get electricity. That's also an effort in the right direction. Many nongovernment organizations, such as World Vision, have also participated in this program. As noted earlier, the education system is also changing.

Author: Coming back to the plight of the urban worker, would you say that he or she is either very happy or somewhat happy or unhappy?

Interviewee 2: They are not very happy. They are somewhat happy because the goods they desire are there on the market. But many are finding it too difficult to pay for their children's school fees and also provide them with decent meals every day. It is not easy to pay their transportation fares and medical bills. The take-home pay is not able to pay for all these things. Those who are hardworking and able to do additional work are able to get by. Others do backyard work and others do trading. People are trying. They are somewhat happy because the commodities are on the market. They are somewhat unhappy because the cash flow isn't sufficient.

Author: What, in your opinion, will it take to change Ghanaian attitudes for the better?

Interviewee 2: It comes back to education. You can teach people to overcome the attitude of continuing lawlessness when you teach them to do the right things. This will, however, take time to happen. People want to have shortcuts. I think that good education and training programs can open our awareness. People can be given continuing intensive awareness messages all across the country. I think one day our eyes will be open if we keep hammering it in. If there are some casualties with practical evidences, eyes will open even further.

PROBLEMS OF HF DECAY AND UNDERDEVELOPMENT

The interviews reveal that the IMF, the World Bank, and the government's collaborative development policies and programs seem to have achieved little long-term progress. This lack of continuing and significant success calls to mind a few relevant questions, including the following: What is the real difficulty being faced by the SAPs and SPs in Ghana? Why have the SAPs and SPs had little temporal impact on Ghanaian well-being? If the Ghanaian economy has actually grown at an average rate of about 3 to 5 percent during the last half of the 1980s and the beginning of the 1990s, who is actually reaping the welfare gains? What can be done to improve the potency and success of these policies and programs?

As is obvious, these questions may be answered neither easily nor perfectly. To provide meaningful answers, several issues must be taken into account. First, it is critical to recognize that in the public sector the quality of work done by government employees is usually below expected standards. Second, all public sector contracts awarded to contractors frequently take too long to complete and the job is often done perfunctorily. Third, trust, integrity, accountability, responsibility, and commitment are often strong missing ingredients in policy implementation and human dealings. As such, the necessary changes required for development to occur in Ghana must include the continuous development of human qualities and the modification of cultural norms, beliefs, and traditions that have been strangleholds on the forces of sustained human-centered development.

As is clear from the interviews, the primary cause of Ghana's problems is HF decay and underdevelopment. In view of this observation, it can be argued that unless the HF is developed, the SAPs and SPs will not achieve any significant and lasting success in Ghana. Progress, however, will be assured when Ghana begins to pursue relevant HF development policies and programs to help the labor force to develop the necessary human qualities and characteristics that are conducive to development.

Any gains achieved by the SAPs and SPs will, therefore, be temporary and definitely fizzle out in the long run. The continuing neglect of HF development in Ghana has led to many problems and hindrances to policy formulation, implementation, and effectiveness. Examples of real-life problems originating from HF decay and underdevelopment in Ghana include ongoing problem accommodation, the continuing age-deflation syndrome, prohibited inner-city hawking by teenagers, growing lawlessness, the misuse of public property, and many others.[1]

AREAS REQUIRING URGENT REFORMS OR ATTITUDE CHANGE

The following is a list of suggestions to improve Ghanaian society by encouraging positive HF development:

1. Education, training, and mentoring to develop the HF is critical to development in Ghana. This will lead to the closure of the incentive gap that encourages negative rent-seeking behavior on the part of Ghanaians, especially, civil servants. The government should educate and train sole proprietors to enter into partnerships.

2. The Ghanaians should create and promote positive action programs to oversee the efficient and continuing operation of essential services in the country (i.e., water, electricity, road rehabilitation, etc.).

3. Effective and efficient law enforcement in such areas as traffic (i.e., enforcing driving regulations and punishing their violations), crime, bribery and corruption, work habits, and schedules for individual employees must be taken seriously. There will be no success in the presence of severe HF decay. It is therefore necessary to develop and implement HF development programs. Success in this regard will encourage people to adhere to sanitation standards and health regulations. These, however, cannot be done effectively without the availability of the HF.

4. Ghanaians must successfully deal with the entrenched palm-greasing culture. There is little business done in Ghana today without having to grease the palms of someone (Adjibolosoo 1995a). Palm greasing has been practiced for many years and has almost become an integral part of everyday business, economic, social, and political activities, regardless of its many varying forms and impacts on the national economy. Almost everybody practices it everywhere—from government offices to the village farmer's office (i.e., under the shady tree on the farm). Because it has become pervasive and widely accepted, those who refuse to practice any form of it usually suffer a lot. That is, they hardly ever get anything done for them. For example, in hospitals those who fail to grease the palms of specific hospital staff members in charge are usually doomed forever. They may not have the opportunity to be seen and treated by the best doctors. In the same manner, they will not acquire the necessary drugs.

5. Ghanaians must create a national vision whose primary goal will be to encourage and draw Ghanaians together to pursue intended goals as specified in development plans, policies, and programs. The success of this also requires the availability of the relevant HF.

6. Ghanaians must organize nationwide seminars and conferences aimed at providing forums for participants to network, exchange ideas, form partnerships, and enter into mutual agreements that can potentially generate growth and continuing human-centered development.

7. Ghanaians must create financial and tax incentives to encourage and promote personal HF development and teamwork to raise both productivity and quality.

8. Ghanaians must make funds available for continuing research into the activities and performance of the sole proprietorship. In addition, they must create materials regarding their problems and how they can be solved using the existing HF.

9. Ghanaians must teach basic principles of business organization and management as they relate to planning, organizing, financing, marketing, personnel, accounting, and so on.

From the HF perspective, therefore, it is my belief that by accomplishing these goals successfully, Ghana will be fully prepared for a development program that has the potential to bring positive changes into the country.

CONCLUSION

Ghana's struggle for development continues. For many decades, very little progress has been achieved, regardless of the magnitude of available foreign financial and technical assistance and expert advice. As such, it is now time to pause for a moment to reevaluate what has been done so far. This reexamination process must be aimed at the discovery of the various factors that have contributed to the current failure. Ghana's development program is not failing to achieve its goals because the leaders have pursued wrong policies. The real source of the problems is HF decay and underdevelopment. Unfortunately, the so-called experts seem to be failing to recognize the real sources of Ghana's economic problems. Until the problems of HF decay and underdevelopment outlined in this chapter are correctly identified and dealt with effectively, the SAPs and SPs will not have any lasting impact on both input productivity and human welfare. By addressing the problem of HF decay, the problems of inequity, injustice, and unfairness will all be minimized.

NOTES

A significant part of this chapter was previously published under the title, "Rethinking the Sources of Economic Underdevelopment in Ghana" (Adjibolosoo 1995b). I am very grateful to the International Institute for Human Factor Development for granting me permission to reproduce parts of that paper here. My research trip to Ghana (June–July 1994) was financed by a grant provided by the Social Sciences and Humanities Research Council of Canada (SSHRC). I gratefully acknowledge the contributions of SSHRC toward the data collection and preparation of this chapter.

1. See a detailed discussion on these problems in Adjibolosoo (1995c, 1–35).

REFERENCES

Adjibolosoo, S. 1995a. *The Human Factor in Developing Africa.* Westport, Conn.: Praeger.

Adjibolosoo, S. 1995b. Rethinking the Sources of Economic Underdevelopment in Ghana. *Review of Human Factor Studies* 1 (2): 1–35.

Adjibolosoo, S. 1995c. The Significance of the Human Factor in African Economic Development. In *The Significance of the Human Factor in African Economic Development,* edited by S. Adjibolosoo. Westport, Conn.: Praeger.

Cornia, G. A., R. Jolly, and F. Stewart. 1987. *Adjustment with a Human Face.* Oxford: Clarendon Press.

Ewusi, K. 1986. *Industrialisation, Employment Generation and Income Distribution in Ghana, 1950–1986.* Accra: Adwensa.

George, S. 1988. *A Fate Worse than Debt: The World Financial Crisis and the Poor.* New York: Grove Weidenfeld.

Kam, T. 1995. After Devaluation, Two African Nations Fare Very Differently: Ivory Coast is Rebounding, Aided by Farm Exports, but Cameroon is Lagging. *Wall Street Journal,* 10 May, A1, A10.

Lipson, C. 1986. Implementing Debt and International Institutions. In *The Politics of International Debt,* edited by M. Kahler. Ithaca: Cornell University Press.

Lipson, C. 1988. The International Organisation of Third World Debt. In *Toward a Political Economy of Development: A Rational Choice Perspective,* edited by R. H. Bates. Berkeley and Los Angeles: University of California Press.

Lungu, G. F., and M. C. Bwalya. 1994. Zambia: Form versus Substance in the One-Party State. In *Policy Reform for Sustainable Development in Africa: The Institutional Imperative,* edited by L. A. Picard and M. Garrity. Boulder, Colo.: Lynne Rienner.

Nelson, J. M. 1990. Introduction: The Politics of Economic Adjustment in Developing Nations. In *Economic Crisis and Policy Choice: The Politics of Adjustment in the Third World,* edited by J. M. Nelson. Princeton: Princeton University Press.

Picard, L. A. 1994. The Challenge of Structural Adjustment. In *Policy Reforms for Sustainable Development in Africa: The Institutional Imperative*, edited by L. A. Picard and M. Garrity. Boulder, Colo.: Lynne Rienner.

Picard, L. A., and M. Garrity, eds. 1994. *Policy Reforms for Sustainable Development in Africa: The Institutional Imperative*. Boulder, Colo.: Lynne Rienner.

Pickett, J., and H. Singer, eds. 1990. *Towards Economic Recovery in Sub-Saharan Africa: Essays in Honour of Robert Gardiner*. New York: Routledge.

Roe, A., H. Schneider, and G. Pyatt. 1992. *Adjustment and Equity in Ghana*. Paris: OECD.

Tarp, F. 1993. *Stabilisation and Structural Adjustment: Macroeconomic Frameworks for Analysing the Crisis in Sub-Saharan Africa*. New York: Routledge.

World Bank. 1994. *Adjustment in Africa: Reforms, Results, and the Road Ahead*. New York: Oxford University Press.

Chapter 7

The Human Factor and the Dilemma of Nigerian Development: A Structural Analysis

Chikwendu Christian Ukaegbu

According to Merton (1968), one of the elements of structural analysis is a focus on the ways in which social structure either constrains or facilitates forms of individual behavior. Social structure itself is the organized set of social relationships in which members of the society or group are variously implicated, and it acts as either a barrier or an open door to the acting out of cultural mandates (Merton 1968). Therefore, the objective of sociological structuralism is to examine a given item of behavior or agent within the larger structured whole (Sztompka 1990). A common path in structural analysis is to examine the effect of social institutions on individual or group behavior. Hence, there tends to be a correspondence between institutional and structural analysis. There is voluminous literature on Nigeria's social institutions. The focus of this literature includes economic development, political processes, education, religion, law, and so on. Very often, analysts have expressed concern in the failures of these institutions which correspondingly translate into developmental failures. This is because effective, efficient, and virile social institutions create avenues for national development.

As in other African countries, Nigeria's developmental failures have been attributed to factors such as colonialism and dependency, the scarcity of modern values, and elite incapacities and perversion. The first factor is synonymous with the view of the dependency school, which posits that the beginnings of Africa's systematic impoverishment were linked to European imperialism.

This brought Africa into the global economy, but did so in a structurally unequal manner. The benefits of the ties formed as a result of colonialism are shared unequally between the core and the periphery in favor of the former and to the detriment of the latter (Dos Santos 1973; Chazan et al. 1992). Therefore, the developmental failures of Africa in general and Nigeria in particular should be blamed on this asymmetrical relationship.

Scarcity of modern values as a constraint to development is the brainchild of the modernization theory. The basic premise of this approach, as Chazan and colleagues (1992) observe, is that African societies are in the process of becoming modern rational entities in which efficiency and scientific logic replace traditional values and belief systems. Modernization was seen as commensurate with mechanization, rapid industrial growth, controlling the political importance of communal identities, political participation, openness to innovation, the presence of a critical mass of people with a high sense of personal efficacy, and many other factors (Inkeles and Smith 1974; Huntington 1971).

One major problem with these two theories is that they deemphasize the autonomy of local actors in the initiation and implementation of development policies and consequently exonerate them from any form of culpability for developmental failures. For instance, the modernization theory presupposes that because African leaders are in nonmodern environments, their well-intentioned policies and practices will not have social receptivity because of the inhibitive traditional values of their target populations and institutions. Therefore, any developmental failures should be blamed not on the failings of the leaders but on the intractable obstacles posed by social institutions.

In the same vein, the dependency approach implies that because the post–colonial society is overwhelmed by various kinds of dependency (economic, cultural, intellectual, political, industrial, technological), leaders cannot be held responsible or accountable for developmental or institutional failures. Events in its thirty-six years of independence have shown that if Nigeria is to develop, the explanatory attention given to modernization and dependency theories must diminish and give way to a national introspective approach in which the society looks inward to identify its strengths and weaknesses, and takes corrective action if the latter is predominantly the case. The negative legacy of colonialism may never be wiped out of Nigeria's historical memory. In fact, one of those legacies, the promotion of ethnic segmentation and tension, is a major part of this chapter. But continuous lamentation over the consequences of colonialism constitutes a diversion that prevents the society from realizing that its destiny rests in its own hands. This is the basic premise of the statist school, on which this chapter is anchored.

In the statist approach to the study of Africa, the state is viewed as a primary motor force behind social and economic occurrence, and state leaders are held responsible for the political and economic deterioration of the early 1980s and after (Chazan et al. 1992). State structures are the key to coming to grips with contemporary African processes. The state is viewed as an actor with interests, capacities, achievements, and frailties, and is autonomous to some extent. Power holders, it is claimed, have created structures of domination that have enabled them to misuse their offices to reap personal gains at the expense of the pressing needs of the bulk of the population (Chazan et al. 1992; Ukaegbu 1994; Diamond 1995). The statist approach is appropriate for this analysis because it is relevant to our structuralist orientation and, at the same time, touches the core of the human factor element in African development. In this chapter, the state is operationally defined as those who govern in military and civilian regimes.

THE IDEA OF THE HUMAN FACTOR

Adjibolosoo (1995c) defines the human factor as "the spectrum of personality characteristics and other dimensions of human performance that enable social, economic, and political institutions to function and remain functional over time." Specific elements of the human factor include integrity, loyalty, accountability, responsibility, motivation, honesty, wisdom dedication, respect for skills, and knowledge (Adjibolosoo 1995c). Therefore, the human factor comprises both personality and human-capital characteristics, with the latter defined as the quantity and quality of skills, knowledge, and capabilities possessed by individuals for the performance of societal roles (Schultz 1961).

The internalization of these attributes are often beyond the control of the individual. Creativity, the product of the interaction between biology and the environment (McNeil 1969; McLemore 1994), is dictated by factors external to the individual. The quality and quantity of knowledge, values, attributes, and behaviors acquired by persons will vary according to the quality and quantity of educational resources, including the nature of impressions made by significant others in various social institutions (Hollander 1981). Therefore, positive institutional experiences are expected to generate positive personality attributes, while negative influences find expression in negative attributes. Hence, we could conceptualize the human factor as a dichotomous variable and thereby make a distinction between positive and negative human factor (Adjibolosoo 1995c).

Positive human factor refers to those personality virtues emphasized by Adjibolosoo (1995b). In contrast, negative human factor means the undesirable personality characteristics which undermine the effective performance of social roles. These include insensitivity to accountability, laziness, lack of integrity, irresponsibility, dishonesty, corruption, lack of dedication and commitment, absence of respect for the rule of law, lack of self-discipline, and so on. The popular belief is that the development process will be accelerated by positive human factor or what Adjibolosoo (1994) refers to as appropriate human factor. By implication, development will be stultified by negative human factor. The latter is what Ezeala-Harrison (1995) referred to as human factor depravity, which he defines as the decay of (positive) human factor.

In this chapter, I argue that the developmental failures of Nigeria derive from human factor depravity, bred, nurtured, and sustained by the political institution. The failings of the political institution in turn rest in the structural antecedent of ethnic segmentation characteristic of the post–colonial state. However, thirty-six years of independence are enough for Nigerians, especially the governing groups, to take responsibility for the condition of the society.

THE STRUCTURAL ANTECEDENT OF NIGERIA'S HUMAN FACTOR PROBLEMS

The Buhari and Idiagbon administration of 1983–1985 observed the preponderance of human factor depravity and instituted the War Against Indiscipline. At that time, many aspects of national life showed conspicuous signs of disorganization. These ranged from simple acts of incivility, such as rush and scramble for services, disregard for queues, and littering the streets, to more serious acts, such as bribery, drug trafficking, oil bunkering, embezzlement, destruction of expensive public infrastructures, arson, armed robbery, disregard for accountability, and a spoils syndrome whereby public office was regarded as an opportunity to plunder the country's wealth (Ukaegbu 1994). According to observers of Nigerian society, the growth of these elements of human factor depravity had a discernible origin in the post–colonial state.

Anthropological literature shows that traditional African societies instilled positive human factor in their populations through their cultural resources. The cultural resources included a ritual system that emphasized immediate retribution for deviance, a political organization which respected hierarchy either by age, achievement, or heredity, a geoethnopolity based on a real or imagined single ancestry, a legal system that was virtually indistinguishable from religion, and family and kinship organizations which emphasized conformity to group norms (Beatie 1964). Defined in Durkheim (1933) terms, traditional African societies may be simple, mechanical, and informal, but they achieved individual commitment, collective consciousness, concern for the public interest, social control, and social order (Beatie 1964). Collective consciousness is the totality of beliefs and sentiments common to average citizens of a society (Durkheim 1933). Quite often, the source of collective consciousness is the real or putative origin of the lineage, clan, or ethnic group. Hence, it could be stated that in much of traditional Africa, ethnic and political boundaries were one and the same thing and the tribe was the world. Embedded in this is the concept of geoethnopolity, which may be defined as the interaction between a group's geographical location, ethnic identification, and political processes. However, colonialism reconstructed the traditional geoethnopolitical boundaries by creating the modern state through the forced unification of disparate ethnic groups and the consequent involuntary participation of these groups in the post–colonial state (Diamond 1995; Glickman 1995; Wiseman 1990; Sklar and Whitaker 1996), where traditional loyalties still remain strong (Essuman 1996).

Collective consciousness can also be equated with the idea of group soul. The post–colonial state in Africa in general and Nigeria in particular lacks group soul. Rather, the state is like a body with many souls claiming different parts. This results in pervasive conflict instead of consensus and accommodation, and detachment from instead of commitment to the public good. In other words, the fundamental structural antecedent of human factor problems in Nigeria and the consequent developmental dilemma is located in the post–colonial state. This is consistent with Diamond (1995), who emphasized that the real causal origins of Nigeria's developmental decay are political and institutional.

According to Diamond, exploitation, cynicism, dishonesty, distrust, and a striking absence of enduring shared commitments to the formal political community and to the nation are pervasive. Diamond (1995) contends further that many of Nigeria's ethnic communities had civic traditions of horizontally bound cooperatives, cultural associations, and mutual aid societies with strong ties of trust and reciprocity. But as Ekeh (1975) observed, these primordial norms and traditions of honesty and reciprocity did not carry over into the arena of the modern state, an alien institution toward which no primordial group feels a sense of ownership or identification. Instead, the modern state is a resource, devoid of moral content or attachment, to be pursued, occupied, milked, and later plundered by the individual politician and his support group (Ekeh 1975). Ekeh's and Diamond's analyses support our earlier argument that traditional African societies had built-in cultural mechanisms for obtaining accountability and other elements of positive human factor through collective consciousness based on primordial identities, a sense of ownership of the community, and a desire to protect that community through a spontaneous concern for the collective good. The absence of these attributes in the post–colonial society creates public-policy obstacles which eventuate in developmental failures. Hence, according to Ohaegbulam (1995), the arbitrary boundaries carved by Europeans have proven to be more of a liability than an asset to the emergent African states.

HUMAN FACTOR PROBLEMS AND PUBLIC POLICY IN THE POST–COLONIAL STATE

Elites in colonial and post–colonial states have always sought and mobilized the support of their primordial or ethnic groups to acquire political power in exchange for the promise of obtaining national resources (Nnoli 1989). The popularly used concept of the national cake implies that the government is an entity whose sole function is to distribute national resources and therefore each ethnic group should strive to secure its own piece of the pie. On its part, the state expends a lot of time and energy trying to balance ethnic claims and demands in order to maintain a semblance of political stability. Hence, public policy in general and development policy in particular are heavily configured in ethnopolitical terms.

Take the case of dispersal of industries for the purpose of balancing political demands. Economic analyses show that the location of industries is primarily based on economic considerations, such as the proximity to raw materials, consumer markets, availability of skilled labor, and easy access to means of communication. When industries are sited far from most of these resources, they lose their advantages. For instance, the steel rolling mills in Oshogbo in Osun State, Katsina in Katsina State, and Jos in Plateau State, are far from the Aladja Steel mill in Delta State, the source of billets for the mills. The billets are transported on land to these far sites at enormous costs. Hence, the rolling mills hardly make adequate returns on their investments (Ukim 1994). Some have also questioned the rationality of a refinery in Kaduna, where there is no crude oil exploration, at least presently. Okigbo (1989) observes a lack of discipline among Nigeria's development planners. This shows up in the infusion of partisan and ethnic politics into the technology of data collection, in the admission of projects into the plan, in the location of government projects, and in the application of policies associated with the plan (Okigbo 1989).

The higher-education sector has witnessed the greatest amount of ethnic rivalry and political exploitation. Thirty-six years after independence, Nigeria has about forty universities and numerous polytechnics and colleges of education (Eribo 1996). The pre-independence premier University of Ibadan aside, it means that universities were established at the rate of 1.08 annually. Since the 1970s, successive governments (federal and state) have used the establishment of universities and other institutions of tertiary education as a tool for acquiring popularity, loyalty, and legitimacy—often a reaction to political pressure fueled by ethnic rivalry. Quite often, new universities are announced and empowered to take off without feasibility studies or the deserved elaborate deliberations about sources and availability of funding (Ukaegbu and Agunwamba 1995).

There appears to be a correlation between the creation of states and the growth in the number of universities. As new states are created, indigenes demand state-owned universities and governors yield in order to obtain popularity. However, this phenomenal, uncontrolled, and uncoordinated growth in the number of universities has not been matched by a corresponding increase in funding (Jega 1996). Instead, universities, polytechnics, and colleges of education are bedeviled by chronic underfunding, deplorable teaching and learning facilities, and brain drain. As Jega aptly notes, virtually every university has become no more than a glorified secondary school.

Presently, the Nigerian university system has lost its intended role as an instrument of intellectual, cultural, and technological innovation and continuity because it has little to bequeath to the next generation. Universities are no longer able to attract the best vocationally committed minds, because the reward system is nonmotivating and materialism has deemphasized excellence in knowledge as an index of success. By implication, the present state of tertiary education renders it incapable of inculcating the appropriate human factor required for national development. This is consistent with the concerns of the World Bank (1991), which laments that the current state of African universities does not afford them the capacity to produce individuals capable of managing development. That is an incalculable handicap for a society seeking economic development in an age when production and distribution are increasingly based on formal knowledge.

State creation is another area of public policy that has been subjected to immense ethnic and political pressure. The first set of states (twelve in number) were created by the federal government in 1967 in response to the secessionist pressures in then Eastern Nigeria (Diamond 1995). As in the case of universities, each administration has used the creation of states as a means of accumulating popularity and legitimacy. Most of the states are not economically viable. Rather, they depend on the federal government to provide all the financial resources for their capital and administrative expenditures. This not only sustains the overconcentration of power in the central government, it also prevents the states from creatively exploiting whatever economic resources are dormant in their environments. This enormous allocative power and responsibility makes the central government (especially the presidency) the focus of constant conflict, either by coups d'etat, as in the case of military governments, or interparty conflicts, ethnic and religious violence, and election malpractice during democratic elections for civilian governments.

More than thirty years ago, even before the first set of states were created, Rothchild (1964) projected that splitting Nigeria into states would produce new minorities and raise the problem of the viability of constituent units, and once the process of state creation commenced it would be difficult to terminate it. The decrees which launch new states do not emphasize the importance of being economically viable. Rather, they focus on administrative convenience, bringing government and development closer to the people, the historical heritage of state indigenes, the preservation of the federal structure, prevention of domination by one state, maintenance of peace and harmony, and minimization of minority problems (Okpu 1983). The responsibility for economic viability and growth is deemphasized, thereby implying that the federal government is the sole provider.

Total dependence on the federal government finds expression in the underexploitation of national economic resources and the underutilization of human creative energies. This is because each state and its citizens place their hopes on federal allocations derived from the resources currently being exploited—in the present case, oil. Whatever other potentially lucrative natural resources may exist in other parts of the country are either ignored or underharnessed, or there is no incentive to search for them.

Therefore, the popular belief and political rhetoric that state creation brings development closer to the people is absolutely false, if development is defined as improvements in living standards—better education, food security, improved health care, more employment opportunities, access to good water, and reliable means of communication. These basic needs can hardly exist without the active participation of citizens in productive activity, which finds expression in improvements in agriculture and industry. According to Nnoli (1989), there is virtually no link between the creation of states and improvement of agriculture or manufacturing in Nigeria. State creation brings about the facelift of the state capital territory and creates opportunities for top bureaucrats, technocrats, and political leaders to plunder public resources, while the adjoining communities and rural areas remain marginalized. Given the abysmal deterioration in living standards and other socioeconomic indicators during the past two decades (1976 to 1996), when most of the states were created, it can be hypothesized that the higher the number of states, the greater the underdevelopment of the country. States are waste pipes because they bring about expansions in the public bureaucracy whose bills they are unable to pay.

It is clear that all of Rothchild's (1964) fears have been proven correct. Many states cannot pay their wage bills, provide municipal service, or complete capital projects. Also, new minorities always emerge whenever new states are created, resulting in culturally distinct communities to redistribute themselves into the opposing categories of "we" and "they" (Akinyele 1996). Even though the number of states has increased from twelve in 1967 to thirty-seven in 1996, agitation for new states continues.

One of the most recent acts of human factor depravity that has hurt Nigeria's development is the arbitrary annulment of the June 12, 1993, presidential election. The results of that election showed that Moshood Abiola, a Yoruba Moslem, had the widest spread of support across the country of any presidential candidate in Nigeria's electoral history (*Africa Confidential* 1993). The vote, according to Lewis (1994), showed a historic merger of Northern and Southern populist interests cutting across ethnic and religious lines. Annulling such a socially integrative election without verifiable reasons is a conspicuous act of human factor depravity.

The annulment deprived Nigerians of the benefit of the services of a prospective incumbent elected by a most popular mandate. That act, coupled with the hurried execution of Ken Saro-Wiwa and nine others after a doubtful judicial process in 1995, have isolated Nigeria from the mainstream of international affairs. Since then, some countries have imposed different forms of restrictions on Nigeria, a situation which has subjected the country's economy and living standards to unprecedented strain. What is more, the annulment of the election resuscitated ethnic divisions which were neutralized by the two-party structure (Ukaegbu 1996; External Service of Radio Ghana 1993). The overall costs of these political actions to the long-term development of Nigeria are incalculable. Apart from the social cost, the transition to civilian rule project, of which the June 12, 1993 election was a part, cost about 35 billion naira of public revenue between 1986 and 1993 (*Nigerian Economist* 1993). For a handful of individuals to dismantle the entire project without good reason shows a striking absence of commitment to the formal political community and a lack of sympathy for the developmental problems of Nigeria.

Human factor depravity has also shown its conspicuous presence in the implementation of public policy in forms such as lack of accountability, embezzlement of huge sums of public funds, illicit awarding of contracts, collusion between government officials and contractors to defraud the government, and lack of commitment to the supervision of government projects. Nnoli (1993) laments that every political office, whether in military or civilian regimes, is subjected to abuse.

For instance, the Okigbo Commission of 1994 (Ukim 1994) reported an alarming level of financial indiscipline and budgetary recklessness by previous governments in general and the administration of General Ibrahim Babangida (1985 to 1993) in particular. The commission found that in the latter administration, a sum of U.S.$12.4 billion earned from petroleum between 1984 and 1994, including the windfall from the Gulf War, was clandestinely spent by Ibrahim Babangida and the then governor of the Central Bank of Nigeria (Okigbo in *Newswatch* 1994). This amount could have paid one-third of Nigeria's external debt at the time and thereby improved the economic fortunes of the country.

In an article titled "The Looting of Nigeria," Mbachu (1993) used statistics from the 1970s to the 1990s to show a stupendous degree of squandermania through stealing of oil, embezzlement, overpricing of contracts, illicit transfer of huge sums of money to foreign banks, and wrong and nonregenerative investments by political elites and their agents in both military and civilian regimes. According to a World Bank report on public expenditure management, between 1973, when the oil boom commenced, and 1990, public investments amounted to U.S.$115 billion (see Mbachu 1993). Out of this sum, 30 percent (about U.S.$70 billion) need not have been spent. Some observers of Nigerian society contend that some private Nigerians own U.S.$33 billion in foreign banks, most of this fortune acquired through corrupt means (*Tell* 1993).

In anticipation of the Failed Parastatals Tribunal, expected to probe the operations of government establishments over a period of time, Adedoyin (1996) investigated some institutions and agencies. About nine projects in sectors strategic to Nigeria's development were said to be candidates for probes involving illicit expenditures of staggering amounts of public funds. The projects include fertilizer, oil, shipping, the Central Bank, steel, telecommunications, housing, rural development, and food storage. If the staggering amounts contained in a series of chronicles were truly illicitly and wastefully spent, Nigeria has lost a golden opportunity for development that is impossible to recapture.[1] In fact, if the totality of this money were to be distributed among the populations, each Nigerian would be a millionaire. Yet those funds have been lost to a few private pockets and uncommitted management of public resources.

In 1981, a ministerial committee found that the cost of implementing projects in Nigeria was much higher than the cost of equivalent projects in Liberia, Ivory Coast, Kenya, and Algeria (Agbese 1993). This high cost is exacerbated by corruption, whereby contractors receive mobilization fees and later abandon the projects, while officials who awarded the contracts, or are expected to supervise them, remain nonchalant because they have been bribed. It is estimated that there are no fewer than 4,000 uncompleted projects in Nigeria, estimated to cost about U.S.$20 billion to complete (Adedoyin 1996). The longer the projects remain uncompleted, the higher the cost of consummating them in the future.

Human factor depravity is not observed in government only. It has also become pervasive in other spheres of society. Behaviors such as negative work ethic (especially in the public sector), drug trafficking, armed robbery, arson, bribery, destruction of public infrastructure, fraudulent business deals, and assassinations have increased in frequency and intensity in the society. The overall condition of disorganization and insecurity discourages local entrepreneurship and private foreign investment. The basic question is why these dimensions of human factor depravity are pervasive.

HUMAN FACTOR DEPRAVITY AND THE THEORY OF DEVIANCE

There are many explanations for human factor depravity (or deviance), two of which are considered here. The biogenic perspective holds that deviants, including criminals, are predetermined or at least predisposed toward deviant behavior by factors within their biological makeup that are transmitted from parents to children (Kratcoski and Kratcoski 1996). The biological model is seriously defective because it assumes that the genetic makeup of Nigerians of the 1960s (when there was a considerably low level of human factor depravity) has changed toward erraticness, attracting uncontrollable behaviors. Besides, many who exhibit various forms of human factor depravity today were members of the society in those years of considerable positive human factor and societal discipline. Granting that genes undergo mutation, it is inconceivable that the genes of the mass of Nigerians simultaneously underwent a metamorphosis that introduced faulty traits.

By contrast, social structural formulations contend that under certain social conditions large numbers of quite normal persons are bombarded by strains, pressures, and deleterious life circumstances which push them into deviance (Merton 1968). According to this viewpoint, individuals are the products of their environments. Therefore, the present high incidence of human factor depravity relative to the past is not a consequence of genetic makeup, but a reaction to the harsh socioeconomic conditions created principally by failures in political and economic governance. Diamond (1995) laments that Nigeria, which was once admired for its grand cultural tradition, rapid educational expansion, and dynamic civil society, is now infamous for its drug trafficking, smuggling, commercial fraud, and endemic corruption. In the same vein, Sklar and Whitaker (1996) express doubts about the future of Nigeria as a viable nation, even though it was the brightest star in the galaxy of new African states at independence in 1960.

Why is the blame for developmental failures placed on the polity? It is common knowledge that, at its inception, the post–colonial state inherited enormous productive, allocative, and distributive power and responsibility. The post–colonial state turned Marx upside down by making the state the infrastructure on which other institutions, including the economy, are built. Therefore, where the state falters, other institutions falter as well. Accounts in this chapter and numerous other sources have noted the pervasive corruption, embezzlement, and lack of commitment among the governing groups of various regimes (see Ukim 1994, 9–14; Mbachu 1993, 12–15; Ige 1996, 8–12). If the huge financial resources that illegitimately filter into private pockets were judiciously invested and the investments managed with commitment, a viable economy would have emerged and improved living standards.

Where the economy is unable to cater for the legitimate desires of the population, the tendency for illegitimate behavior increases. This is exacerbated when public officials brazenly use public resources to service their selfish interests. This results in high incidences of human factor depravity because an undisciplined leadership breeds an undisciplined followership (Nwabueze 1986). This is more so when the sanctions for the abuse of public office are unclear or are ambivalently applied, as has been the case in Nigeria (Diamond 1995).

Further, primordial groups tend to accord tacit as well as overt support of plunder of public resources by their own kin. If an individual in a lucrative public office does not have any wealth to show for his tenure, he is seen as a failure, whereas the one who embezzles experiences no rejection. The primordial group does not accord the same support or recognition to an armed robber, a thief, or a swindler because these are *mala in se*, acts that are inherently evil and traditionally abhorred by the community. This goes back to the beginning of this chapter, where Ekeh argues that the post–colonial state is perceived as an entity to be plundered and milked because there is not a sense of ownership of the state by the various primordial groups.

When individuals are appointed officials of their various village associations, age grades, and town unions, they tend to guard the group's resources with exemplary commitment, care, and diligence. But appoint the same individuals to positions in local government councils or state boards and their commitment, self-discipline, and sense of accountability decline. This is because the agencies are perceived as arms of a distant, anonymous central government, the source of the national cake of which individuals should strive to get their own shares before others finish it. In his "Garden of Eden in Decay," Mazrui (1986) tells a story depicting the cognitive disposition of Africans toward the post–colonial state. A young accountant in a newly independent

Ghanaian government was exasperated by the misuse of public funds by public officials and wanted to do something about it. Upon expressing his concern to his older colleague he was told, "Look young man, Nkurumah has killed an elephant and the meat will be enough for all of us. All you do is to cut your own." According to Mazrui, that elephant was Ghana. What a metaphor for the national-cake syndrome in Nigeria.

DIMENSIONS OF INTERVENTION TO ACHIEVE POSITIVE HUMAN FACTOR

After articulating the discrepancy between commitment to the primordial group and detachment from the formal political community, Diamond (1995) emphatically concluded, "Unless the modern Nigerian State could become the subject of political identification across ethnic groups and communal lines and unless it could impose strong institutional constraints against corrupt behavior in state office, these patterns are bound to intensify over time and shape more and more profoundly patterns of political engagement at all levels." Diamond's apt and emphatic observation does not leave any prescriptions or blueprints as to how crossethnic and crosscommunal political identification could be achieved, but its absence constitutes a fundamental structural obstacle to Nigeria's political and economic development.

Should it be left for time to instill a universalistic orientation in all members of the different ethnic groups, or should there be a conscious effort to manipulate the existing geoethnopolitical structure to suit the demands of an ethnically segmented society? According to Horowitz's (1985) highly sophisticated proposition, a bloody phenomenon cannot be explained by a bloodless theory. By implication, a structurally induced problem cannot be solved without a conscious manipulation or adjustment of the structure. Therefore, the optimism held by modernization theory—that as more and more Nigerians secure formal education, cosmopolitan outlook will submerge localism and primordialism and therefore elevate the national spirit and create a collective national soul—may be a false one. After all, the history of Nigeria shows that the educated, who have been at the forefront of governance, have exacerbated ethnic consciousness in their quest for local support for power.

Concerned about the problems caused by political centralization within ethnic segmentation that culminates in false nationhood in Africa, Adjibolosoo (1995b) finds the answer in administrative decentralization and notes, "In a decentralized system, people will feel more responsible for their actions. If they embezzle funds, it will be those of their own local communities, not of a distant and anonymous state. If a local official embezzles funds allocated to the building of a school or a hospital, the people of that village will certainly not be indifferent. . . . This will pave the way for a real democratic system, democracy at the grassroots level, and easier to organize."

Decentralization takes various forms, one of which is deconcentration. Deconcentration refers to the delegation of authority to employees of a central government agency who are situated outside the headquarters. An example would be delegation of authority from the Director General of a ministry to his State Directors (Hyden 1983). This is a case of administrative decentralization. According to Wunsch (1991), deconcentration typically fails to alter prevailing patterns of control and decision making or to produce fundamental improvements in service delivery performance in outlying areas.

Devolution, by contrast, means the legal conferment of powers upon formally constituted local authorities to discharge specified or residual functions, as in the case of powers given to a local council to administer primary education (Hyden 1983). The difference between deconcentration and devolution, Hyden maintains, is that the former describes an intraorganizational pattern of power relationships, while the latter refers to an interorganizational transfer of power to geographic units of local government lying outside the command structure of the central government. Devolution therefore implies separateness or diversity of structures within the political system.

These two forms of decentralization have been tried on certain institutions at various points in Nigerian development, yet the developmental process in general and the performance of specific agencies in particular have not improved. For instance, devolution, a more profound process (Koehn and Ojo 1996), was tried in 1991, when the Babangida administration shifted the responsibility for primary education to the local governments (Ekpu 1993). This led to frequent strikes by teachers, who asked the federal government to reassume responsibility for primary education. If devolution is the most extreme form of decentralization, as Rondinelli (1981) claims, it has not worked in this case.

Also, according to Ekeh (1975) and Diamond (1995), if the post–colonial state is perceived as an alien institution toward which no primordial group feels a sense of ownership or identification, both deconcentration and devolution will prove impotent because they have no primordial content. The bulk of resources, policies, and implementation guidelines still comes from the anonymous, distant central government which must be milked and plundered (Ekeh 1975).

In this regard, we turn to the current experiment in Ethiopia, which Koehn and Ojo (1996) have classified as ethnic decentralization, an experiment deliberately patterned along nationality lines. According to Koehn and Ojo, all the new regional boundaries created under Article 1 of Proclamation No. 7 of 1992, with the exception of the capital (Addis Ababa), explicitly followed the geographic distribution of Ethiopia's population by nationality. The Transitional Charter also affirmed the right of nationalities and peoples to determine their own affairs by themselves, and Ethiopia's 1994 Constitution grants each region the right to determine its official language (Koehn and Ojo 1996). This experiment tends to have a primordial content from which political, economic, administrative, and managerial actors can develop a sense of collective destiny through the invocation of common or collectively agreed upon cultural resources. Because state creation in Nigeria does not accord as much rights and autonomy to states, it is merely a form of administrative decentralization where states operate under the watchful eye of the central government.

The Ethiopian experiment fits neither the case of deconcentration nor devolution as defined by Hyden (1983). It also cannot be described as a form of administrative decentralization. Rather, it is a case of ethnopolitical decentralization because a modicum of the right of ethnic self-determination is involved. From Koehn and Ojo's (1996) description, the Ethiopian experiment is close to corporate pluralism or confederacy and a bold step toward the reconfiguration of the post–colonial state to suit local conditions. However, the potential efficacy of this experiment rests on what segment of the new configuration controls the bulk of regional resources. If the central government remains the custodian, allocator, and distributor of the bulk of national resources, the new configuration will still experience constrictions similar to the old order. But if the right of nationalities and peoples includes the right to extract, invest, and allocate many of the resources around them (i.e., create their own wealth), primordialism may have the capacity to release both the creative and moral abilities of citizens to nurture and sustain these new rights. It is under this form of decentralization that Adjibolosoo's (1995b) insights, cited earlier, will have efficacy.

In the Nigerian context, ethnic decentralization may instill a positive moral content into the development endeavors of various ethnic groups. But in a country with more than 250 ethnic and linguistic groups, some populous and others tiny, it is a Herculean task and perhaps purile political engineering to decentralize on strictly ethnolinguistic lines. To correct this geoethnopolitical structural defect caused by colonialism, it may be appropriate to decentralize along zonal lines so that zones can determine their own bases of moral consensus. The presumption is that it will be easier to construct a moral consensus within smaller ethnozonal spaces than within the larger and more complex ethnoreligious environment. Nmoma (1995) observes that the regional divisions in Nigeria run deeper than rivalry between ethnic groups because the competing identities of the Muslim and Christian cultures fuel the tensions between the three major ethnic groups (Hausa-Fulani, Yoruba, and Igbo). Nigeria has witnessed a great deal of religious tension, conflict, and violence since independence.

Another important question is whether ethnic decentralization will instigate and facilitate balkanization of the country, as has always been feared by the Organization of African Unity (OAU). It depends on the national charter governing the process. An important aspect of the charter should emphasize that any attempt by one group or a collection of groups to excise themselves from the union will not receive the support of others. This is the same principle embedded in the OAU.

Placing the bulk of the blame for Nigeria's developmental failures on the geoethnopolitical structure sounds like an oversimplification of the problem. Does the country have the quantity and quality of skills to foster development? Is it not possible that the development process has been impaired by the absence of skilled manpower rather than the failures of the political institution? The astronomical expansion of tertiary education since independence (Eribo 1996) shows that quantity of manpower is not one of Nigeria's problems. The conspicuous contributions and effective participation of Nigerians in many fields of knowledge around the world, including positions involving intricate technical knowledge, also indicates that the problem is not quality. Furthermore, numerous analyses of the Nigerian civil war, when technological innovation flourished in secessionist Biafra, demonstrates that the critical factor is not the quantity or extraordinary quality of manpower, but the political motivation that can free and tap the creative energies of the existing pool of human resources.

The Nigerian civil war, otherwise known as the Nigeria–Biafra conflict, clearly demonstrated that Nigerian scientists and engineers can be socially relevant through the application of their skills and knowledge to the solution of societal problems. Under the auspices of an agency known as Research and Production (RAP), Biafran scientists, engineers, and technicians produced petrol and petroleum products, arms and ammunition, and refined and packaged edibles to the point that illiterate populations in the society were aware of the relevance of their activities (Biersteker 1978). By those activities, RAP contributed to sustain the war for three years, 1967 to 1970. Further, those scientists, engineers, and technicians exhibited an unprecedented degree of vision, loyalty, diligence, dedication, commitment, motivation, hard work, and sacrifice (i.e., the appropriate human factor characteristics).

The Biafran experience challenges the argument made by dependency theory that the content of Western scientific and technological education received by African scientists and engineers is far removed from the problems of their countries. This is because most, if not all, of the Biafran scientists and engineers were first-generation professionals trained in Euro-American and first-generation indigenous universities that had a strong Western influence. Arguments which emphasize other factors, such as the dearth of research and development institutions, a weak base of indigenous science and technology, and absence of a capital-goods production sector as constraints to technological development, also beg the question. All these seemingly debilitating conditions existed in Biafra in addition to a military blockade, yet scientists and engineers were able to make a remarkable achievement in society.

At the end of the war, the Project Development Agency (PRODA) was established by the Nigerian government to continue and perhaps improve upon the achievements of the Biafran RAP. In fact, PRODA was expected to be a replica of RAP because a significant number of its pioneer staff and management were drawn from the latter. Though some breakthroughs have been made by PRODA, it is not an overstatement to say that its twenty-five years of existence have not achieved the amount of social relevance recorded by RAP in three short years of secessionist Biafra.[2] That Nigerian scientists and engineers complain of underutilization of their skills and capabilities may not be as much a function of human factor depravity among them as it is a result of macro-institutional problems (Ukaegbu 1995). Members of RAP were Nigerians before they became Biafrans, and became Nigerians once again after the war. It could be argued that the technological breakthroughs in secessionist Biafra were a reaction to the war situation, which motivated individuals to work to survive at all costs, but the poverty, destitution, ignorance, disease, and deprivation which the majority of the population have experienced in peacetime Nigeria should have triggered the kind of motivation, commitment, and struggle characteristic of a society confronted with a real war situation. It is only a developmentally sensitive governing group that can draw such a parallel.

The reality is that the geoethnopolity of Nigeria as presently constituted is entrepreneurially constrictive and motivationally inhibitive. It stultifies the creativity of different nationalities because the 96-percent national revenue from a single commodity (oil) is the sole economic basis of national life in the midst of other vast natural resources. Hence, a significant segment of the population is excluded from a vigorous involvement in the creation of national wealth. In short, the present structure constitutes what may be called a geoethnopolity of antiprogress.

However, some observers have expressed optimism that the intention of the present Abacha regime to probe public officials through the proposed Failed Parastatals Tribunal will introduce accountability to national life. Provided that the findings and reports of that tribunal are not treated with ambivalence and double standards, as happened in previous regimes, the probe may return sanity to the country and pave the way for national development. In other words, and as Diamond (1995) maintains, the probe should impose strong institutional constraints against corrupt behavior in state offices.

Over the years, Nigerian policy makers have invoked several social psychological and persuasive measures in an effort to obtain societal discipline and instill positive human factor. These include movements and agencies such as Ethical Reorientation, War Against Indiscipline, the Directorate of Social Mobilization, Self-Reliance and Economic Recovery (MAMSER), the Bureau of Public Complaints, and the National Orientation Agency (the agency currently charged with achieving positive attitudinal and behavioral transformations among Nigerians.) The popular strategy used by these agencies is to preach to the public in order to elicit behavior modification in the direction of positive human factor. But as Okigbo (1989) noted, jingles and slogans may tickle the ear, but they cannot by themselves fill the stomach.

Since the mid-1980s, government has sloganized development by promising the society food security, housing, good water, health care, education, transportation, and so forth for all by the year 2000. That magic year is at the doorstep and none of the problems prompting these promises has been scratched. If anything, they have deepened. It is ironic that the officials who made these promises in their public speeches helped derail their realization through corruption and mismanagement. To revisit the problem, in 1996, the Abacha regime inaugurated Vision 2010 (borrowed from China and Malaysia), another magic year when Nigeria will achieve an economy strong enough to launch the society in the path of development. If the history of target 2000 repeats itself, Vision 2010 will expire as one of those political jingles that tickled the ear but could not by itself fill the stomach.

Most often, the persuasive attention of behavior-modification agencies focuses on peripheral populations such as market women, students, labor unions, cooperative societies, professional associations, farmers, and traders. The governing group, the architects of Nigeria's disorganization, are usually left out. If the persuasive strategy as an instrument of behavior modification is at all efficacious, it should emphasize a philosophy of top-centered intervention. Consequently, the National Orientation Agency should constantly organize reorientation seminars on human factor issues for the head of state/president and his ministers, the ruling council (if a military regime), governors, their commissioners and director generals, senators and assemblymen and assemblywomen, local council chairpersons, their councillors, and other high political, administrative, and managerial officials. These officials should be made to realize and accept that the anomic human factor depravity that presently exists in Nigerian society is primarily a function of political misgovernance. Otherwise, efforts and resources will be dissipated on attempting to correct the human factor depravity of the powerless while the depravity of the powerful is the real cankerworm that undermines national development.

COMPETING CHOICES

The foregoing analysis shows that there are several competing political choices for the solution to Nigeria's human factor decay and developmental problems. These include a political decentralization that constructs new bases of moral consensus within new segments in a Nigeria of interdependent units, a leadership that can show good examples and impose strong institutional constraints against human factor depravity in a centralized political organization, and the use of persuasive mechanisms to obtain conformity to public norms within a centralized political organization. In its thirty-six years of independence, Nigeria has tried the last two strategies (though oftentimes with ambivalence), but problems of human factor decay and developmental failures continue. Even if an honest, dedicated, committed, and universalistic-oriented leader emerges at some point, will members of his or her primordial group and other ethnic groups support his or her praxis of development?

It could be argued that the lack of leadership firmness in the imposition of institutional constraints against corrupt behavior in public office and the impotence of the persuasive mechanism over the years is a result of the absence of a collective moral commitment to the post–colonial state. After all, if a bloody phenomenon cannot be explained by a bloodless theory, a structural problem likewise cannot be solved by a psychosocial prescription.

Common sense therefore suggests that a decentralization akin to the current Ethiopian experiment, that has a primordial content and makes primordial groups or a collection of primordial groups masters of their own destinies, be tried. This is consistent with Azevedo (1995), who suggested that some measure of regional autonomy or a degree of decentralization must become serious alternatives to the present ethnic and political challenges confronting African states. In order for this strategy to succeed in constructing positive human factor characteristics for development, action should be based on negotiated agreements by groups rather than on arbitrary divisions by a few. The resultant corporate pluralism has demonstrated the capacity to absorb the fallout of primordialism in Canada, Switzerland, Belgium, Malaysia, and the Netherlands, the tragic case of Yugoslavia notwithstanding (Edwards and Shearn 1987; Marger 1994).

But, as was observed earlier, the two-party structure of the annulled 1993 presidential election unprecedentedly attempted to neutralize the disparate bases of moral consensus that existed among ethnic groups under multiparty politics. That means multipartyism was vulnerable to parochialism and ethnic segmentation. Ethnic decentralization may encourage the balkanization of the country, especially if the constituent units are unfaithful to the agreements. It may therefore be worthwhile to institutionalize the two-party structure within a federal system and hope that through the process of sustained democratic political succession ethnic political thinking will be blurred and future developmental endeavors will benefit from the resultant cosmopolitanism and nationalistic thinking. Equally critically important is a constitutional redefinition of citizenship to make every Nigerian a de facto citizen in whatever part of the country he or she resides. The current indigenization formula, which excludes nonindigents of states from employment and postemployment security in state jobs and other resources, is not only a contradiction of the demands of balanced federalism, it is also a double standard in political interaction. It makes individuals strangers in their own country, heightens cognitive and physical attachment to primordial attractions, sustains the physical separation of ethnic groups, encourages ethnic consciousness, and consequently precludes individual commitment to the formal political community. If it is true (as sociological structuralism suggests) that individuals are the products of their environments, then the environment has to be adjusted in such a way as to produce the desired kinds of individuals and social outcomes. One thing is clear: The solution to Nigeria's human factor decay and development dilemma rests heavily on the governing group making an appropriate choice.

NOTES

I thank Stephanie Silsby and Amanda Hill of the Department of Sociology, University of Wyoming, for their secretarial help.

1. See details in *Theweek* (Adedoyin 1996; Agboroko 1996; Age 1996); *Newswatch* (Agbese 1993); *African Guardian* (Mbachu 1993).

2. This observation is based on the author's inside experience of wartime RAP and a longitudinal study of peacetime PRODA and other research institutes in the country.

REFERENCES

Adedoyin, A. 1996. Nemesis Is Here. *Theweek* (11 November): 8–13.

Adjibolosoo, S. 1994. The Human Factor and the Failure of Economic Development Policies in Africa. In *Perspectives on Economic Development in Africa*, edited by F. Ezeala-Harrison and S. Adjibolosoo. Westport, Conn.: Praeger.

Adjibolosoo, S. 1995a. Africa Must Chart a New Course. *Dunenyo* 1 (3): 1–2.

Adjibolosoo, S. 1995b. *The Human Factor in Developing Africa*. Westport, Conn.: Praeger.

Adjibolosoo, S. 1995c. The Significance of the Human Factor in African Economic Development. In *The Significance of the Human Factor in African Economic Development*, edited by S. Adjibolosoo. Westport, Conn.: Praeger.

Africa Confidential. 1993. July, 2.

Agbese, D. 1993. Polar Opposites: Frequent Policy Shifts Put a Cog in the Wheel of Development. *Newswatch* (4 October): 22–25.

Agboroko, G. 1996. Waiting for the Judge. *Theweek* (2 September): 10–15.

Akinyele, R. T. 1996. States Creation in Nigeria: The Willink Report in Retrospect. *African Studies Review* 39 (2): 71–94.

Azevedo, M. 1995. Ethnicity and Democratization: Cameroon and Gabon. In *Ethnic Conflict and Democratization in Africa*, edited by H. Glickman. Atlanta: African Studies Association Press.

Beatie, J. 1964. *Other Cultures*. New York: The Free Press.

Biersteker, T. 1978. *Distortion or Development: Contending Perspectives on the Multinational Corporation*. Cambridge: MIT Press.

Chazan, N., R. Mortimer, J. Ravenhill, and D. Rothchild. 1992. *Politics and Society in Contemporary Africa*. Boulder, Colo.: Lynne Rienner.

Diamond, L. 1995. Nigeria: The Uncivic Society and the Descent into Praetorianism. In *Politics in Developing Countries: Comparing Experiences with Democracy*, edited by L. Diamond, J. J. Linz, and S. M. Lipset. Boulder, Colo.: Lynne Rienner.

Dos Santos, T. 1973. The Structure of Dependence. In *The Political Economy of Development and Underdevelopment*, edited by C. K. Wilber. New York: Random House.

Durkheim, E. 1933. *The Division of Labor in Society*. New York: Macmillan.

Edwards, J., and C. Shearn. 1987. Language and Identity in Belgium: Perceptions of French and Flemish Students. *Ethnic and Racial Studies* 10 (2): 135–148.

Ekeh, P. 1975. Colonialism and the Two Publics: A Theoretical Statement. *Comparative Studies in Society and History* 17: 91–112.

Ekpu, R. 1993. Dreams, Shattered Dreams. *Newswatch* (4 October): 19–21.

Eribo, F. 1996. Higher Education in Nigeria: Decades of Development and Decline. *Issue* 24 (1): 64–67.

Essuman, J. 1996. The Human Factor: A Neglected Variable in Africa's Structural Adjustment Program. *Review of Human Factor Studies* 2 (1): 93–108.

External Service of Radio Ghana. 1993. July.

Ezeala-Harrison, F. 1995. Human Factor Issues in the History of Economic Underdevelopment. *Review of Human Factor Studies* 1 (1): 1–25.

Glickman, H. 1995. Issues in the Analysis of Ethnic Conflict and Democratization Processes in Africa Today. In *Ethnic Conflict and Democratization in Africa*, edited by H. Glickman. Atlanta: African Studies Association Press.

Hollander, E. P. 1981. *Principles and Methods of Social Psychology*. New York: Oxford University Press.

Horowitz, D. 1985. *Ethnic Groups in Conflict*. Berkeley and Los Angeles: University of California Press.

Huntington, S. 1971. The Change to Change: Modernization, Development and Politics. *Comparative Politics* 4 (3): 55–79.

Hyden, G. 1983. *No Shortcuts to Progress*. Berkeley and Los Angeles: University of California Press.

Ige, T. 1996. A Call to Account. *Theweek* (23 September): 8–12.

Inkeles, A., and D. Smith. 1974. *Becoming Modern: Individual Modernity in Six Developing Countries*. Cambridge: Harvard University Press.

Jega, A. 1996. Manufacturing Ignorance: The Nigerian Regime and ASUU. *Africa Now* (August). Information from *Naijnet* (11 September).

Kratcoski, P. C., and L. D. Kratcoski. 1996. *Juvenile Delinquency*. Upper Saddle River, N.J.: Prentice-Hall.

Koehn, P., and O. Ojo. 1996. Decentralization and Socioeconomic Development in Nigeria, Ethiopia, and Eritrea: Current Directions and Future Prospects. Paper presented to the Conference on Philosophy, Politics, and Development in Africa, Binghamton University, 7-9 June, Binghamton, New York.

Lewis, P. 1994. Endgame in Nigeria: The Politics of a Failed Democratic Transition. *African Affairs* 93 (72): 323–342.

Marger, M. 1994. *Race and Ethnic Relations*. Belmont, Calif.: Wadsworth.

Mazrui, A. 1986. "Garden of Eden in Decay." Television Documentary, Cassette #7 of *The Africans: A Triple Heritage*, sponsored by the Annenberg CPB Project.

Mbachu, D. 1993. The Looting of Nigeria. *The African Guardian* (1 November): 12–15.

McLemore, S. 1994. *Race and Ethnic Relations*. Boston: Allyn and Bacon.

McNeil, E. B. 1969. *Human Socialization*. Belmont, Calif.: Brooks/Cole.

Merton, R. 1968. *Social Theory and Social Structure*. New York: The Free Press.

Nigerian Economist. 1993. July, 20–21.

Nmoma, V. 1995. Ethnic Conflict, Constitutional Engineering and Democracy in Nigeria. In *Ethnic Conflict and Democratization in Africa*, edited by H. Glickman. Atlanta: African Studies Association Press.

Nnoli, O. 1989. *Ethnic Politics in Africa*. Ibadan, Nigeria: Vantage.

Nnoli, O. 1993. Nigeria: The Failure of a Neo-Colonial Society. In *Dead-End to Nigerian Development*, edited by O. Nnoli. Dakar: CODESRIA.

Nwabueze, B. 1986. Nigeria: In Search of a Future. In *Nigeria In Search of a Future*, edited by G. Ofomata and C. Ukaegbu. Nsukka: University of Nigeria Faculty of the Social Sciences.

Ohaegbulam, U. 1995. The Dynamics of the State Boundaries in Post–Colonial Africa: The Prospects for the Future. In *State and Society in Africa*, edited by F. Shams. New York: University Press of America.

Okigbo, P. 1989. *National Development Planning in Nigeria: 1900–92*. London: James Currey.

Okigbo, P. 1994. Cited in *Newswatch*, 24 October.

Okpu, U. 1983. Nigeria's Dilemma: Development or New States. *Africa Roma* 38 (2): 183–203.

Rondinelli, D. 1981. Government Decentralization in Comparative Perspective: Theory and Practice in Developing Countries. *International Review of Administrative Sciences* 47 (2): 133–145.

Rothchild, D. 1964. Safeguarding Nigeria's Minorities. *Duquesne Review* 8 (Spring): 35–51.

Schultz, T. 1961. Investment in Human Capital. *American Economic Review* 51 (1): 1–17.

Sklar, R., and C. Whitaker. 1996. *Nigeria: Rivers of Oil, Trails of Blood, Prospects for Unity and Democracy*. Washington, D.C.: Center for Strategic and International Studies, 1–8.

Sztompka, P. 1990. R. K. Merton's Theoretical System: An Overview. In *R. K. Merton: Consensus and Controversy*, edited by J. Clark, C. Modgil, and S. Modgil. New York: Falmer Press.

Tell. 1993. 22 November, 14.

Ukaegbu, C. 1994. Indiscipline in Nigeria: Causes, Patterns, Interventions and Implications for National Development. Paper presented at the National Workshop on Attitudinal Adjustments, Nike Lake Hotel, 23–25 August, Enugu, Nigeria.

Ukaegbu, C. 1995. The Constraining Factors that Undermine Technological Development and Effective Utilization of Scientific Manpower. *Review of Human Factor Studies* 1 (2): 36–59.

Ukaegbu, C. 1996. Ethnicity and Electoral Politics in Nigeria: Voter Behavior at the June 12, 1993 Presidential Election. *International Journal of Group Tensions* 26 (2): 73–107.

Ukaegbu, C., and C. Agunwamba. 1995. Structural Adjustment and Manpower Utilization: The Case of Nigerian Scientists and Engineers. In *The Significance of the Human Factor in African Economic Development*, edited by S. Adjibolosoo. Westport, Conn.: Praeger.

Ukim, U. 1994. Where Is the Money?: Where Does Nigeria's Oil Money Go To? *Newswatch* (24 October): 9–4.

Wiseman, J. 1990. *Democracy in Black Africa: Survival and Renewal*. New York: Paragon House.

World Bank. 1991. *The African Capacity Building Initiative: Toward Improved Policy Analysis and Development Management*. Washington, D.C.: IBRD.

World Bank. 1993. *African Guardian*, 1 November, 12–15.

Wunsch, J. 1991. Sustaining Third World Infrastructure Investments: Decentralization and Alternative Strategies. *Public Administration and Development* 11 (1): 431–451.

_____

Chapter 8

Culture and the Human Factor in Chile's Economic "Miracle"

David E. Hojman

The Chilean economy is Latin America's star performer (Hojman 1990, 1993, 1994, 1995a). This chapter examines the role played by culture (the human factor) in Chile's economic "miracle," and explores some of the multiple ways in which culture and institutions have contributed to shape each other.[1] The chapter is concerned with what aspects of national culture, if any, made Chileans different from other Latin Americans, in that Chile adopted free-market, open-economy policies (FMOEP) before other countries in the region, persevered with these policies even when the risk of failure seemed high, and eventually converted these FMOEP into the source of dramatic economic and political success.

The "Hispanic capitalism" (Loveman 1988) brought to Chile by the Spanish conquest in the sixteenth century was a society of extreme income and wealth inequalities.[2] The country that was born out of these violent contradictions only managed to overcome them very slowly. Rather than a Chilean culture, for centuries it made more sense to talk about two parallel subcultures: that of the Conquistadores and their descendants and that of those defeated by the conquest and their own children and grandchildren. Today, Chile's healthy civil society and democratic politics are largely the result of the development of middle sectors and their own subculture. Most progressive elements in contemporary Chilean culture come from this particular subculture of the middle sectors.

The *New Shorter Oxford English Dictionary* defines "culture" as "the distinctive customs, achievements, products, outlook, etc., of a society or group; the way of life of a society or group." The *Encyclopaedia Britannica* provides a fuller but otherwise similar definition:"The integrated pattern of human knowledge, belief and behavior. Culture thus defined consists of language, ideas, beliefs, customs, taboos, codes, institutions, tools, techniques, works of art, rituals, ceremonies, and other related components; and the development of culture depends upon people's capacity to learn and to transmit knowledge to succeeding generations." This chapter concentrates on those aspects of Chilean culture which have had a substantial impact, either positive or negative, on the pace of economic growth in the 1980s and 1990s, and which are likely to have a similar impact in the future.[3]

Writing about Chile, Constable and Valenzuela (1991) take a rather negative view of the country's culture before the 1973 military coup. Their impression of national culture under the 1973–1990 military regime is even more negative.[4] In the view of Constable and Valenzuela, by the time of the restoration of democratic government in 1990, "Chilean society had evolved enormously since 1973 [in some respects]; it was more worldly, more skeptical of the state, and more aggressive in pursuing its ambitions. . . . There was a new appreciation for the values of moderation and compromise that had once been bitterly discarded—and a firm rejection of the utopian visions that had inspired and scarred a generation" (p. 319).

While there are undeniable elements of truth in Constable and Valenzuela's (1991) description of Chilean culture both before and during the Pinochet military regime, their picture is far from complete. Moreover, it is not possible to understand the extremely positive elements that Constable and Valenzuela observe after 1990, in particular the successful marriage of the most favorable aspects of the pre- and the post-1973 cultures, without accepting that at least some of the seeds for these highly positive developments were sown both before (in some cases long before) 1973, and between 1973 and 1990.

CHILEAN CULTURE IS DIFFERENT FROM OTHER LATIN AMERICAN CULTURES

The formation of a national self-image by Chileans came long before the same process affected neighboring countries (Loveman 1988; Bethell 1993; Collier and Sater 1996). The speed of formation of a national self-image, in people of different social classes as members of the same nation, may be at least partly related to the depth of the country's inequalities.[5]

A strong feeling of national identity was reinforced by geographical isolation. Between the Andes and the Pacific Ocean, the Atacama desert and the Antarctic, Chile is probably one of the most isolated countries on earth. The last time Chile was invaded by a foreign power was in the 1540s. The country's natural frontiers and remoteness not only discouraged potential invasions from neighboring countries, but also European immigration. Between 1850 and 1895, Chile received only 34,000 European emigrants, as compared with Argentina, which received 1.5 million (Subercaseaux 1988, 98). European immigration to Chile peaked at 11,000 in 1890, but for most of the period between 1851 and 1906 the number was less than 100 persons per year (Bizzarro 1987, 249). Chileans are often proud of their isolation.[6]

Ethnically, the Chilean population is not homogeneous. There are no well-defined ethnic cleavages, but rather a continuous range of ethnic types, from European to indigenous. Chile is not a multiethnic society. Practically the whole of the population is of mixed race, *mestizos*.[7] For the purposes of this discussion, what is important is that the absence of any well-defined ethnic cleavages prevented the formation of castes, and with them the creation of unbreachable cultural cleavages.[8] Today, there are still gaps between the subcultures of different social classes, but no independent gaps between the subcultures of different ethnic groups.

During the Spanish conquest and the early stages of the colonial period, Chile was different from, for example, Peru or Mexico, in that in Chile there was little gold or silver. In that sense, Chile offered good opportunities for farmers, but not for plunderers. A similar difference has been noted by Harrison (1985) between Costa Rica and Nicaragua. Armed resistance to Spanish (and criollo) rule by the Araucarian Indians during the whole of the colonial period made Chilean society a "frontier" society and a comparatively poor military society.

In some important respects, Chilean culture is different from Mexican Ibero-Catholic culture, as described, for example, by Octavio Paz (quoted in Harrison 1985, 1992). Chilean men are less affected than Mexican men by any pathological feelings of *machismo*. Possible reasons for this difference range widely, from the absence of a *Malinche* myth in Chile to a completely different history of relations with the United States.

According to a recent statement by the Archbishop of Santiago, 77 percent of Chileans define themselves as Catholic, but only 6 percent go to mass (*El Mercurio* 1996, 5). Economic expansion during the nineteenth century, especially during its second half, was presided over by politicians who tended to object to the Church's attempts to interfere in political matters. The University of Chile, founded in 1842, was largely controlled by agnostics and freemasons. The influence of the Catholic Church before 1973 had been declining in Chile for more than a century. Under the 1973–1990 Pinochet military regime, the Church recovered some of its old prestige by engaging in brave attempts at protecting the human rights of the victims of political persecution. However, the Catholic hierarchy has been unable to stop the expansion of Protestantism (Bothner 1994; Vargas Llosa 1996).

The influence of organized religion was never as widespread as in other nominally Catholic societies. Unlike in Spanish history, Chilean history has never seen a strong association of Catholicism with totalitarianism, and therefore there has never been a popular (or a national) reaction against the Church, linked to an antitotalitarian struggle. In the Chilean version of the Spanish language there are no instances of swearing with an anti-Catholic or antireligious content. The Spanish word *hostia*, for example, is not used with its peninsular blasphemous meaning. When a Spaniard uses this word with a swearing intention, Chileans simply do not understand.[9]

Most Chileans are proud of their country's democratic traditions. In general, Chileans have traditionally seen themselves as different from (and often better than) the rest of Latin America. Chileans love to think that they are "the English of South America." They see Chile as "less tropical" and "more boring" than the rest of the region, more civilized, more democratic (despite almost seventeen years of Pinochet military rule), showing more respect for the rule of law, and less prone to corruption. Chileans believe that there is more realism in their country, and less "magical realism." The subcultures of all Chilean social classes are full of isolationist and nationalistic mythologies (Larrain 1994). Possibly the only (partial) exceptions to this feeling of regional superiority have been the love affair that left-wing Chileans developed for Fidel Castro's Cuba in the 1960s, and a secular ambivalence in relation to Argentina.

The absence of corruption (relatively speaking) is periodically confirmed by reports from, for instance, the Economist Intelligence Unit. A 1996 report by Transparency International cited Chile as the least corrupt country in Latin America, though only twenty-first in their world ranking, followed (after a long gap) by Argentina, at thirty-fifth (Norman 1996). For a long time, the Chilean middle sectors have been more urbanized, economically stronger, and politically more influential than elsewhere in the region.

Unfortunately, a particular area in which traditional Chilean society from the sixteenth to the twentieth centuries was no different from the rest of Latin America was the negative attitude of people of Spanish origin towards Indians or *mestizos*. This was, of course, also a negative attitude of those with greater wealth toward those further down the social pyramid. The Spanish historian Gonzalo Fernandez de Oviedo in the sixteenth century described the indigenous peoples as "naturally lazy and vicious, melancholic, cowardly, and in general a lying, shifty people. . . . Their marriages are not a sacrament but a sacrilege. They are idolatrous, libidinous and commit sodomy. Their chief desire is to eat, drink, worship heathen idols, and commit bestial obscenities" (quoted in Veliz 1980, 53). This dismissive and damaging tendency of the upper class was still there 400 years later. According to Loveman (1988, 113), "This propensity to disparage the mental and technical capabilities of the working classes endured into the twentieth century. . . . Over and over again [the Chilean historian Francisco] Encina bemoaned the debilitating effects of miscegenation . . . [and] emphasized the *precious gift of European blood* which the resident foreign merchants contributed to the *Chilean race*" (italics in original).

To summarize, Chilean culture has been, and is today, different in many respects from Ibero-Catholic Latin American culture. However, the traditional subculture of the Chilean upper classes was as divisive and contemptuous of the lower social strata as elsewhere in the region.

HISTORICAL ROOTS OF FREE TRADE, BEFORE AND AFTER INDEPENDENCE

The purpose of this section is to show that when FMOEP were introduced (or, rather, reintroduced) in Chile in the mid-1970s, they were not a foreign import, the product of an alien doctrine invented in the University of Chicago's Economics Department. Far from it: Free trade had made positive contributions to Chile's progress over centuries, precisely during those periods when this progress was most dynamic. This is a good example of historical institutions contributing to create a particular pro-free-trade and pro-exports subculture, a subculture which itself supported FMOEP and related institutions when they were reintroduced in 1973 after an absence of about forty or fifty years.

In the eighteenth and nineteenth centuries (i.e., both before and after the country's independence from the Spanish crown), Chile experienced considerable economic progress thanks to (relatively) free trade and exports (De Ramon and Larrain 1982; Fontaine 1982; Larrain 1982).[10] During the War of Independence (1810–1818), the cause of free trade enjoyed the support of convincing advocates, such as Anselmo de la Cruz (De la Cruz 1982). The prospect of free, or freer, trade was deliberately used in order to enlist popular support for the cause of national independence. As Bernardo O'Higgins, the founding father of the Chilean nationality, once explained, "I was emphatic in that two measures were needed, in order to push the people away from their indifference and to make them interested in the revolution: the election of a Congress and the establishment of free trade" (quoted in Fontaine 1982, 52).[11]

In the nineteenth century, it was precisely free trade that made Chile powerful (Mamalakis 1976; Loveman 1988; Bethell 1993; Collier and Sater 1996). Free trade and exports made Chile an important regional power. They made victory possible in the War of the Pacific against Peru and Bolivia (1879–1883). Here there is another substantive difference between Chile, on the one hand, and Peru and Bolivia on the other, and possibly also between Chile and the rest of Latin America. In the nineteenth century, openness to international trade made Chile powerful, economically, industrially, and militarily, and three times victorious in wars against Peru (twice against Bolivia).[12] It is not surprising that nineteenth-century Chilean historians and intellectuals developed a positive view of free trade (Farina and Huerta 1991), and that, on the contrary, Peruvian and Bolivian historians and intellectuals reached a negative conclusion about free trade (which was also in practice in their own countries) during the same period. This may also be at least part of the reason why continent-wide Latin American or Latin-Americanist historical approaches and interpretations fail to explain nineteenth-century Chile adequately.

From early on in the twentieth century, many solid arguments were put forward against the excesses of protection to domestic manufacturing, both before and during application of the import-substitution development strategy (Ahumada 1958; Baklanoff 1959; Mamalakis 1965; Johnson 1967; Carey 1989). However, these sensible arguments were not listened to.[13]

To summarize, when FMOEP were reintroduced in the mid-1970s, these policies were not new or alien to Chile. On the contrary, free trade had made substantial contributions to Chilean economic progress in the eighteenth and nineteenth centuries. In the 1950s, 1960s, and early 1970s, new converts to FMOEP were won as many people had become disillusioned with the excesses and failures of, and corruption associated with, protection to domestic manufacturing during the import-substitution period (i.e., between the 1930s and 1973).[14] By 1973, there was a free-trade subculture in Chile, itself the result of the evolution of historical institutions, which was prepared to at least give FMOEP the benefit of the doubt. Over the long term, the causality relationship had worked both ways: Historical developments and institutions contributed to create a free-trade and pro-exports subculture, and this subculture supported FMOEP and related new institutions in the 1970s and 1980s.

THE BASQUES IN CHILE:
CULTURE SHAPING INSTITUTIONS

It has been argued that one of the most important factors contributing to Chilean culture being different from that of the rest of Latin America is the presence of a relatively large population of Basque origin in Chile. This was the view, for example, of Francisco Encina (1948) and the writer Miguel de Unamuno (1965, 1968, 1996). The Basques were not part of the initial wave of Conquistadores. The first Basque immigrants arrived in the seventeenth and eighteenth centuries, when they constituted about 45 percent of the admittedly small immigrant population (Bizzarro 1987, 55–56). They made their fortunes in commerce, rather than as soldiers, *hacendados*, or *encomenderos*. The argument is that, unlike other Spaniards, Basques were more interested in hard work than in social prestige.[15]

Basque culture was different from that of Castile and the rest of Spain. In their native country, most Basques were fiercely independent small farmers. Jose de Cos Iriberri, a writer who contributed some ideas to the intellectual melting pot that eventually led to Chilean independence, argued in 1799 that

The countries in which agricultural land is more widely distributed are precisely the countries with the best customs ['costumbres']. . . . In Spain itself, significant differences can be observed between the customs of the people of the provinces of Alava, Guipuzcoa and Vizcaya [i.e., the Basque country], where, either because of direct ownership or tenancies in perpetuity, rural land is more evenly distributed, on the one hand, and the customs in those provinces where the number of landowners is smaller, on the other hand. (Villalobos 1971, 135)

About three-quarters of the names associated with the struggle for independence in the period from 1810 to 1818 came from Basque families (Willems 1971, 450). We may choose to interpret this either as proof that the Basques had a greater love for political freedom or for freedom from Madrid, or, alternatively, that because they were engaged in commerce they had more to gain from the destruction of monopolies granted by the Spanish crown and from the establishment of free trade. Maybe these explanations are not in contradiction with each other and all of them are true.[16]

Eventually, rich Basques became part of the *clase alta* (upper class). A hundred years after independence, by the beginning of the twentieth century, "23 percent of the most valuable land was owned by Chilean Basques, and 529 out of the 2,498 wealthiest families in Chile were Basque (21 percent)" (Bizzarro 1987, 56).[17] It may be argued that 21 or 23 percent is quite a large share to be controlled by a single ethnic group. However, it may also be argued that 21 or 23 percent is not enough to make a significant difference, especially considering that a Basque surname in Chile in the twentieth century is not really a guarantee of either being ethnically Basque or of belonging to a particularly Basque culture. This raises the question of "who is a Basque in Chile after two or three hundred years of intermarriage" (Loveman 1988). Basques, Spaniards from other peninsular regions, and non-Spanish Europeans had been mixing with each other since the seventeenth and eighteenth centuries, not to mention the racial mixing between all Europeans, but Spaniards in particular, and the indigenous population.[18]

Moreover, it would be a mistake to assume that the culture and attitudes of the Basque immigrants to Chile in the seventeenth and eighteenth centuries and their descendants have remained unaltered, generation after generation. Three-quarters of the patriots during the War of Independence had Basque surnames, but what about after that? During the decades of the Conservative Republic (i.e., between the 1830s and 1870s), casual empiricism suggests that people with Basque surnames were more or less equally distributed among supporters of the conservative establishment and supporters of the liberal opposition. Later on, during the 1891 Civil War, those with Basque surnames overwhelmingly supported the Congress side. Supporters of the Balmaceda side were often chided and dismissed as social climbers or *parvenus* ("*siuticos*," Subercaseaux 1988). The most prominent Balmaceda supporters (which to a large extent belonged to the new middle sectors) did not have Basque surnames: Banados Espinoza, Frias Collao, Del Rio, Barbosa, Cotapos, Godoy, Valderrama, Ballesteros, Chacon, Eastman, and Mackenna. However, there were exceptions (see Note 16), and the surname Balmaceda is itself Basque. But the general trend was that, in a matter of about 100 years, snobbery, from being anti-Basque, had become pro-Basque (see Notes 15 and 17). To the extent that snobbery always discourages entrepreneurial attitudes, pro-Basque snobbery had become a racist, paternalistic, and reactionary barrier to economic development.

Possibly Basque culture made a positive difference to Chile. Basque influence could have been favorable, especially when the Basques represented a progressive force in commerce and politics in the eighteenth and nineteenth centuries. Both then and later, Basque participation may have contributed to making the Chilean upper class more open and better disposed to receive and include talented people coming from other social classes and immigrants from other ethnic origins. Basque participation may also have contributed to making the upper class more frugal and less keen on external signs of social prestige (a pattern already observed in the frontier society of earlier colonial times). Even if all this is true, it does not follow that the presence of Basques was either a necessary or a sufficient condition for Chilean economic success in the 1980s and 1990s. The concentration of Basques in Santiago de Chile today is not greater than that in Buenos Aires or Mexico City (Bizzarro 1987).[19]

Why should the Basques have made such an important contribution to Chile's progress, a pattern that was not repeated in either Buenos Aires or Mexico City? There are three reasons. First, the Basques arrived in Chile during the eighteenth century; that is, much earlier than they arrived in Argentina and Mexico (most Basque emigration to Mexico followed the end of the Spanish Civil War in 1939). They arrived in Chile early, and in relatively large numbers. The Basques brought a culture of hard work to Chile, which they had been developing in Europe for generations as proud and independent small-family farmers. Quite a lot of this culture had been lost in the Basque homeland by the 1930s. Second, when the Basques arrived in Chile, conditions there were already favorable. Chile's frontier society was poor and unpretentious. A permanent state of war against the local Indians had created conditions that encouraged savings and discouraged conspicuous consumption. Clearly, these special circumstances were not present in either Argentina or Mexico. Third, the Basques arrived in Chile at the most favorable moment for them to eventually become a middle class, which until then had not existed in Chile.

THE MIDDLE SECTORS, EDUCATION, SAVINGS, AND ECONOMISTS

The gradual development of middle sectors, with their own subcultures, since the mid-nineteenth century, contributed to reducing the harshness of a society originally divided into the few who owned everything and the many who owned nothing (see Note 2). Many of the most positive aspects of Chilean culture today, in the political, economic, and social arenas, come from this subculture of the middle sectors. This includes virtues such as tolerance, compromise, political democracy, and the moderation of extreme inequalities by the state (Hojman 1993; Collier and Sater 1996). The Basque immigrants, with their own Basque culture in the late eighteenth and early nineteenth centuries, did represent a progressive influence, to a large extent precisely because they were the middle sectors of that time. The Basques constituted a bridge over the immense gap between the inheritors of the Conquistadores and the children of the vanquished. Initially, many Basques in Chile were small shopkeepers, socially and economically halfway between the *hacendados* and their landless laborers.

Tolerance and compromise are typical of Chile's middle sectors, not only because of ideological reasons or because these sectors were initially weak, numerically and politically. They are also a result of the fact that the middle sectors have very diverse origins (Boyle and Hojman 1985, 1993). In the nineteenth century, these origins were both rural and urban, in retail trade, in craft production, in white-collar employment in the public and private sectors, in school teaching, in the professions, in the military, in administration of rural properties, in small farms, and in small and medium-scale mining.[20] During the twentieth century, the ranks of the middle sectors continued to grow from all of these sources, plus employment and ownership in manufacturing, and, after the 1970s, expansion of financial services.[21] Foreign immigrants have always joined the ranks of the middle sectors. It was their heterogeneity which made the middle sectors open, tolerant, capable of compromise, and democratic.

From early on, the middle sectors were avid consumers of education and information. In order to respond to their demand, the number of places in primary education increased 3.6 times between 1865 and 1895. The number of places in secondary education increased 3.4 times. The University of Chile was founded. During the 1890s, Santiago, with one-quarter of a million inhabitants, of whom only one-third could read, had seven daily or weekly newspapers, with a total circulation of over 50,000 (Subercaseaux 1988, 120–121).

·From a long-term perspective, the size, economic importance, and political power of the middle sectors has been increasing all the time, despite some short-term fluctuations. Sometimes the progress of the middle sectors has been at the expense of those at the top of the income-distribution pyramid, sometimes at the expense of those at the bottom, and sometimes simply the result of economic expansion from which all gained. Between 1938 and 1950, the purchasing power of the average white-collar salary increased from 1.1 to 1.9 times the purchasing power of the average factory wage. Between 1954 and 1968, the share of national income of the middle 70 percent of the population (i.e., excluding the richest 10% and the poorest 20%) increased from 50 to 60 percent (Bethell 1993, 119, 138). Between 1989 and 1992, the share of national income of the middle 60 percent (excluding the top 20% and the bottom 20%) increased from 33 to 36 percent (Hojman 1996).

Different countries put a different degree of emphasis on investment in human capital, depending, at least partly, on national cultural attitudes. For a long time, Chilean society and Chilean families, especially from the middle sectors, have been keener on investment in human capital than other societies and families in the region. This may be yet another way in which the particular characteristics of Chilean culture contributed to economic success.

Investment in human capital by families can be seen as a substitute for savings. Until the introduction of privately run pension funds in the 1980s, Chilean domestic savings were very small (except for those who could save in U.S. dollars in Miami, London, or Switzerland). Families did not save because high inflation made saving suboptimal (or even suicidal), and because the financial institutions were primitive and unreliable. Instead, upper- and middle-income families—indeed, anyone who could afford it—preferred to invest in the education of their children (this is possibly a good example of institutions affecting culture). The recent introduction of new institutions, such as pension funds and competent financial regulatory bodies, has increased the rate of domestic savings to East Asian levels. Contributions to pension funds are compulsory, but this has not prevented families from continuing to invest in the education of their children as enthusiastically as ever.

If we accept that economic success depends at least partly on good policies, the presence of highly qualified economists, or "economic technocrats," possibly increases the probability of these policies being implemented (the expression "technocrat" is not given a pejorative meaning here).[22] The number of economic technocrats is itself the result of many years of investment in human capital by a country and by individual households. The number of highly qualified economists in Chile is increasing all the time. The design and implementation of FMOEP under both Pinochet and his successors has largely been the result of the work of economic technocrats (Fontaine 1988; Valdes 1989; Montecinos 1993; Puryear 1994).

There is no precise information as to the number of economic technocrats in each Latin American country, or as to who should be described as an economic technocrat. The annual Latin American Meetings of the Econometric Society (LAMES) is the most important venue of the technocrats in the region (see Note 18). The number of LAMES participants from each country is possibly a good indicator of the total number of highly qualified economists in that country. Information for 1992, 1993, and 1994 is presented in Table 8.1, together with GDP data and the Human Development Index (HDI). According to these data, by the early 1990s Chile possibly had, in relation to its national output, about six times more highly qualified economists than Argentina or Brazil, and about ten times more than Mexico. A crossnational multiple regression exercise was performed to test for the impact of Gross Domestic Product (GDP) and of the number of technocrats on HDI. The conclusion is that both GDP and the number of technocrats have independent, statistically significant, positive effects on human development (see Table 8.1).[23]

The subculture of Chile's middle sectors is more favorable to the nation's social and political integration and to the development of civil society than the traditional subcultures of those at the top (and at the bottom) of the social pyramid.[24] The middle sectors' subculture is also more favorable to economic growth in a direct way, since it emphasizes education. Until the 1980s, institutional limitations made savings by households impossible, but the middle sectors responded by increasing their rates of investment in human capital. A corollary of high human-capital investment is that Chile today has a large number of highly qualified specialists in many disciplines, including professional economists who have contributed to the design and implementation of sound economic policies.

Table 8.1
GDP, LAMES Participation, and Human Development

Country	GDP	PART	P/G	HDI
Argentina	169	93	2.0	0.853
Bolivia	16	3	1.9	0.530
Brazil	807	135	1.7	0.756
Chile	95	112	11.8	0.848
Colombia	182	17	0.9	0.813
Costa Rica	16	19	11.9	0.848
Dominican Republic	23	1	0.4	0.638
El Salvador	11	3	2.7	0.543
Guatemala	31	1	0.3	0.564
Honduras	10	1	1.0	0.524
Mexico	632	104	1.1	0.804
Peru	70	28	4.0	0.642
Uruguay	21	31	14.8	0.859
Venezuela	164	32	0.7	0.820

Sources: UNDP (1994); *Econometrica* (1993, 1994, 1995).

Key: GDP: Total real GDP, billion PPP dollars, 1991; PART: Total number of participants in the three meetings (the same name in the three meetings is counted three times); P/G: Ratio between the number of participants and GDP. The value indicates the number of participants (after correcting for "excessive" participation by the respective nationals in Mexico City, Tucuman, and Caracas) for every $10 billion of GDP; HDI: Human Development Index, 1992.

CULTURAL CHANGE (AND CONTINUITY) IN THE 1970s AND 1980s

It is difficult to say whether any particular aspect of contemporary Chilean culture developed before or after 1973. A national culture is changing all the time, especially in the presence of fast economic and social change. This section concentrates on institutional change after 1973, and on possible ways in which such change has contributed to modify national culture.

Since 1973, there have been important changes in economic policy, including market liberalization and privatization (Hojman 1990, 1993). The pattern of international trade has changed by making the economy more open. Changes in the financial sector have brought inflation under control, established privately run pension funds, and created active regulatory agencies. The labor market has been changed by the introduction of more jobs for women: The number of these jobs has increased in both absolute and relative terms. Changes in education include further concentration of state resources towards the bottom of the education (and income) pyramid, an increase in the number of prebasic places, and direct payment of university fees by families with some support from grants and soft loans (Hojman 1995b). It may be argued that it is too early to see any cultural changes that may have been provoked by post-1973 institutional change. However, as mentioned, families, and especially middle-income families, are saving more than before. This is apparent once their (compulsory) contributions to pension funds are added to their (voluntary) out-of-pocket expenditure in education.

Another important area of cultural change that was possibly provoked by institutional change is the attitudes of women, working-class women in particular. Following severe economic recessions in 1975–1976 and 1982–1983, many working-class men, who were the primary breadwinners in their families, lost their jobs. Expectations of finding another job in the near future were poor, and many women were forced to look for jobs for the first time. In some cases, a demand for female labor had been created by new economic activities, such as export agriculture (Boyle 1986; Serrano 1988; Bradshaw 1990; Vogel 1995). The number of places in prebasic education experienced a large increase, giving young mothers more freedom. Household expenditure patterns changed, as women now had a greater say on how to spend income that had been earned with their own direct effort. Both men's and women's cultural attitudes changed. Women eventually became used to the additional income and freedom, and they do not seem to be prepared to become housewives again. Male household heads and other male partners were forced to reconsider their attitudes to women's work and to the sexual division of labor.

There have been substantial cultural changes in relation to previously held isolationist and nationalistic myths and inferiority and superiority complexes that were previously experienced toward neighboring (but unknown) and other countries. A typical age-old myth had it that Chilean wine was the best, or at least among the best, in the world (Larrain 1994). Today, Chileans know that they can make, market, and sell wine that may not be the best in the world, but is highly successful among an increasingly large number of consumers everywhere. The reality is similar to the myth, but not identical. Reality is less glamorous but financially more profitable, and possibly also intellectually more satisfying. Chilean self-confidence and assertiveness have also been boosted by other successes, such as the international acclaim received by the Chilean system of privately run pension funds.

Another good example of cultural change which has resulted from the introduction of FMOEP after 1973 is the cultural attitudes toward the national institution of the *cuna* (literally, "wedge"). Having a *cuna* is knowing, on a personal level, someone who is in a position of power or influence and can dispense a petty favor. This is typically a relative or a friend who is also an official. This official will, for example, allow the lucky beneficiary to jump a queue. The Spanish word for brother-in-law is *cunado*, and the two words may be related through the implication of nepotism.

But FMOEP since 1973 have led to the privatization of state enterprises and to the liberalization of practically all markets. Queues are less frequent and shorter than before. The public sector is smaller and there is less need for ordinary people to meet government officials. Free markets mean that prices are no longer controlled and no goods are rationed, so all these particular queues disappeared. Having a *cuna* is still useful, but it is a lot less useful than before. If they have not done it already, eventually Chileans will change their attitude toward *cunas*, simply because having one is less important than before. Cultural attitudes are possibly exposed to a process of natural selection. Those attitudes which no longer perform a useful role tend to become extinct (Basu 1995).

Sowell (1993) has argued that some of the most spectacular experiences of fast economic development have been preceded by the end of international isolation. This may be exactly what happened to Chile. Opening the economy to the rest of the world in the 1970s and 1980s was a real trauma. Even exile was part of this trauma, and it helped, by exposing left-wing Chileans to worlds they knew only from books.[25]

Just as a relatively exogenous change in institutions can eventually alter cultural attitudes, a more or less exogenous cultural change can eventually lead to institutional change. This is a chicken-and-egg problem. The post-1973 Chilean experience seems to suggest that it is easier or faster to change institutions than culture. The Chicago-trained economic advisers to the military regime did not attempt to change popular or national culture. Instead, they addressed their efforts to changing General Pinochet's views. However, such a reading of the Chilean case may be partial and misleading. Pinochet and many other Chileans changed their views, and the FMOEP experiment became a success, because many essential cultural conditions were either already present or were eventually introduced.

It is not antidemocratic to admit that in a nondemocratic society it may be easier to reach the ear of the dictator than to change the whole of that society's culture. It is not particularly elitist to admit that, in some cases, it may be easier and more productive to change the culture of the elites than the culture of the masses. However, this may be a false dilemma. Elite and mass cultures are different, and both of them, as well as the institutions, need to change.

Possibly the most important contribution by the Chicago-trained economic advisors was that their policy recommendations of price stabilization, the liberalization of markets, and openness to international trade succeeded in taking power away from several special interest groups (Olson 1982). This put many ordinary Chileans in control of their own lives for the first time. These ordinary Chileans had many qualities which up to then had not been fully used because the required institutional conditions were not present. These qualities—insightfulness, the ability to articulate and solve problems, vision and perception, responsibility, accountability, commitment, knowledge, integrity, and so on—contributed to transforming these ordinary Chileans into hard-working and successful small- and medium-scale entrepreneurs and nontraditional exporters.

FMOEP were introduced, and institutions were changed accordingly, only after 1973. Following these policy and institutional changes, several instances of changes in culture, attitudes, and behavior became apparent by the 1980s and 1990s. These include a higher savings rate, greater expenditure in education, a more balanced approach towards neighboring countries, and, especially, a marked increase in women's participation in the labor force and in their readiness to spend their new income according to their own priorities.

CONCLUSION

In order to assess the role played by the human factor in Chile's economic success, this chapter has explored differences and similarities between Chilean and other Latin American cultures and looked at several aspects of the interaction between culture and institutions. The historical origins of free trade in Chile is relevant because, far from being an alien import invented in Chicago, free trade has deep roots in Chilean culture. Rather than a foreign imposition, adoption of FMOEP in the 1970s and 1980s is a good example of culture (and history) contributing to shape institutions. The Basque presence in Chile offers another perspective on culture shaping institutions. This theme was further developed by looking at the middle sectors, savings, investment in human capital, education, and professional economists. Historically, the middle sectors were prevented from saving by high inflation and institutional deformations. They responded by investing in education. A particularly favorable consequence of this was a large supply of highly skilled labor, which itself contributed to economic growth. This assessment of cultural change and continuity in the 1970s and 1980s emphasizes the role of new policies and institutions in inducing cultural change after 1973.

Economic development is always the same everywhere because it has to do with economic growth and economic efficiency. However, it is also unique (maybe, paradoxically, unique everywhere), because it requires the successful matching of economic growth and economic efficiency, on the one hand, with the development of a new national culture, on the other. A national culture that is functional to fast economic development is like *un traje hecho a medida*.[26] Culture can change institutions and can itself be modified by institutional change. Thus, the circle is completed. If the new institutions are favorable to economic development and the new cultural attitudes are favorable to the new institutions, this becomes a virtuous circle. Chilean culture is changing all the time. There are positive and negative aspects in Chilean culture, in the sense of how functional they are to economic growth and development. There are aspects of Chilean culture that are no different from those in traditional Ibero-Catholic Latin American culture, and there are other aspects which are extremely different. Many of the negative aspects are no different from the rest of the region. Many of the positive aspects are exclusively Chilean.

It is appropriate to close this chapter with a quotation from the site manager of a salmon farming plant on the island of Chiloe in Southern Chile. In the late 1980s and early 1990s, salmon farming became a huge success, with Chiloe-based shipments making Chile the second exporter in the world after Norway. In the view of the site manager, "It's more a question of reeducating the people. Rather than earning well for one week out of three, and frittering away that one week's pay on drink, the Chilote [i.e., the Chiloe inhabitant] has had to be reeducated. He has had to learn how to work for four weeks in a row and manage his salary" (Provan 1996, 35). Part of this quotation is as patronizing, racist, and misleading as those quotes from Fernandez de Oviedo in the sixteenth century and Encina early in the twentieth century, mentioned before. But there is also something new. The difference is that our site manager is now saying that the Chilotes have actually changed for the better.

How should the site manager's negative and positive words be interpreted? A first possibility is that he is right. Institutional change after 1973 would have changed the Chilotes' attitudes. A second possibility is that it is the site manager who has in fact really changed. Maybe he has just learned that the Chilotes are efficient workers. The Chilotes would have always been efficient workers, but the site manager would have only realized it just now (thus, the site manager's negative assessment would be wrong). There is even a third possibility, namely, that the site manager's positive assessment is a lie. He has learned that openly disparaging your own workers is very unwise as a marketing strategy in the quality-food export business.

It would be difficult to say whether it was the recent introduction of salmon farming that changed the Chilotes' cultural attitudes, or, alternatively, the Chilotes' attitudes (their new ones, rather than their alleged traditional ones) that made salmon farming successful. It is an interesting question for further research. In any case (and there may be other possibilities), the change in the Chilotes' cultural attitudes (if there has been any), and the change in the site manager's cultural attitudes (if there has been any), are, for different reasons and in different ways, good for industrial relations, for output, and for exports, and therefore good for economic development.

APPENDIX: THE RELATIONSHIP BETWEEN TECHNOCRATS AND HDI

$$HDI = 0.61 + 0.02 \ P/G + 0.0003 \ GDP$$

$$(13.3) \quad (2.8) \quad\quad (2.2)$$

Adjusted R^2: 0.38

$N = 14$

(t statistics are in parentheses)

This regression represents only a first approximation to the relationship between the number of technocrats and HDI. Possibly a more accurate link should be nonlinear (a U-curve or a J-curve). The respective parameters are possibly country-specific.

NOTES

1. The word "miracle" is used here in quotes, not to suggest that the miracle will be short-lived, but, on the contrary, because, given the many conditions favorable to economic development that have been converging in Chile for a relatively long period of time, the real miracle would have been that Chile had failed to succeed. For general discussions of the relationship between national culture and economic development, see Freedman (1960), Eisenstadt (1972), Harrison (1985, 1992), Lowenberg and Yu (1992), Sowell (1993), Greif (1994), Cornell and Kalt (1995), and Olson (1982).

2. The sixteenth-century colonial official Hernando de Santillan describes how the Spaniards "killed, maimed and set dogs upon the Indians, cut off feet, hands, noses and teats, stole their lands, raped their women and daughters, chained them up and used them as beasts of burden, burned their houses and settlements and laid waste their fields" (quoted in Loveman 1988, 60). Loveman concludes that "The authoritarian politics of conquest had already created in Chile the foundations of a highly stratified class society" (p. 70).

3. Possibly in every country, the collective self-image is first learned at school. See Frias (1990) for an indicator of what Chilean children learn of their country's history at school, and any of the multiple editions of the novel by Alberto Blest Gana, *Martin Rivas*, that they are supposed to read.

4. According to Constable and Valenzuela (1991), before 1973, "Chile had long been divided by enclaves of clan, class, and party, but it had masked these divisions with a veneer of civility. Within their circles, people were generous and gracious, making social rituals of visits to grandparents and hospitalized friends. But Chilean society was also ingrown and insecure. Even successful people were quick to dismiss others' merits, and individuals were marked for life by family names and party affiliations. It was a country of parallel subcultures that never touched, of parochial worlds whose members rarely ventured beyond their familiar, if often claustrophobic, confines" (p. 141). On what happened during the years of the military regime, Constable and Valenzuela have this to say: "While genteel Chileans kept a discreet distance from dictatorship, less scrupulous social climbers gravitated towards the new centers of power. Mediocre figures who would never have risen in a democracy were named judges, deans, and may-

ors. . . . The arrogance of power made petty tyrants of minor bureaucrats and created a new culture of authoritarian privilege. Narrow access to the top exacerbated the old tendency to discredit and criticize" (p. 145).

5. As a Chilean boy who grew up in the 1950s, the author of this chapter was often treated by older relatives who had traveled to Peru (and who by no stretch of the imagination could be described as left-wing), to stories of the appalling poverty and the huge gap between the rich and the poor in that country. Even if these stories were exaggerated, their impact on Chilean children was likely to be substantial. For a comparison of income-distribution patterns and quality-of-life indicators between Chile and other Latin American countries, including Peru, see Hojman (1996).

6. A good recent example are the negotiations on Chile becoming an associate member (not a full member) of Mercado Comun de America del Sur (South America's common market), which culminated in June 1996.

7. During the colonial period, the absence of indigenous blood was a source of social prestige, so many *mestizos* tried to hide their origins. At the beginning of the seventeenth century, there were about 10,000 Europeans in Chile. By the 1830s, the country's population was about 1.1 million (Bizzarro 1987, 249, 403). Given the natural rate of population growth during the period, plus a modest stream of European immigration, it is possible to argue that, ethnically, Chileans in the 1830s may have been completely European. However, this would be wrong. Despite the fact that European immigration increased during the nineteenth century, a stroll down any street in Santiago de Chile today will confirm that people look very different from people in Madrid, Bilbao, or Santiago de Compostela. According to the historian Rolando Mellafe, "white mestizos" already outnumbered Europeans and *criollos* by a ratio of four to one as early as 1620 (Loveman 1988, 40).

8. However, the Spanish word *castas* was used during the colonial period to refer to the different ethnic mixes of Spanish, Indian, and Black bloods.

9. Between the early 1950s and the mid-1960s, the Chilean middle sectors effortlessly shifted their all-important electoral support from the anticlerical Radical Party to the (informally) Catholic Christian Democratic Party. The reasons for the shift had nothing to do with religious questions, but with political, economic, and social issues.

10. The first export boom occurred at the end of the seventeenth century.

11. It must be emphasized that free trade in the late eighteenth and early nineteenth centuries was very different from today's free trade. During the late colonial period it simply meant the legal authorization to engage in trade, though export duties and import tariffs could be (and often were) very high. The merchant classes in Chile, both European and *criollos*, were against even this limited version of free trade, possibly because they had comfortable links with the Peruvian monopolies and they may also have been engaged in smuggling (see Veliz 1980, 119–136). Paradoxically by contemporary standards, free trade would have increased fiscal revenue from export and import taxes, and therefore it would have made the need to tax local activities less pressing.

12. After their victory in the War of the Pacific, a Chilean army occupied the Peruvian capital, Lima, for the third time during the nineteenth century. Previous occupations had followed the War of Independence (1820) and the war against the Peru–Bolivia Confederation (1836–1839). Of course, victory in these wars also contributed to strengthen a feeling of national identity among all Chileans.

13. The most influential pressure group favoring protection to domestic manufacturing, the Industrialists' Association (*Sociedad de Fomento Fabril*), had been founded in 1883.

14. For some evidence of corruption after the beginning of the Parliamentary period in 1891 and more recently, see Jobet (1971, 397–398).

15. An interesting example of anti-Basque snobbery in 1790 is presented in a study by Vial (1971, 87). Spanish law used to give parents the right to challenge in court the marital choice of their sons or daughters (this right was used by racist parents to avoid "contamination" by non-white blood). A young woman, in support of her intention to marry the man she loves, offers as exhibit a letter from her sister. In the letter, the sister describes the behavior of another man, a Basque, who is also their father's choice as husband for the first daughter: "The Biscayan pest has been looking at our rural properties and nothing escapes his eye. He has become greedy. He gave Dad six young cows, thus convincing Dad to take him to Santiago with a view to marrying you. So be prepared. . . . Dad does not want you to marry a real gentleman" (my translation). For evidence of Basque hard work and entrepreneurial attitudes elsewhere in colonial Spanish America, see Ugalde (1994).

16. There were exceptions. In 1788, one of the most vociferous opponents of free trade was a merchant called Francisco Javier de Errazuriz (Veliz 1980, 127–128). Errazuriz is a typical Basque surname.

17. In a study which used sources from the 1950s (mostly membership lists of prestigious clubs), Willems (1971) identified 319 surnames as those of Chile's *clase alta*. He concluded that 101 of the 319 surnames (32%) were Basque. However, his results are not very helpful in terms of identifying wealth or political power, since the study included an undisclosed number of "impoverished" members of the upper class. But these results are extremely useful in terms of identifying snobbery. The strongest claim of some of these people to be accepted as members of the upper class did not rest on their wealth but on their surnames. This is of course highly compatible with the Constable and Valenzuela (1991) observations for the pre-1973 period (see Note 4).

18. What about Chilean Basques (or Chileans with Basque surnames) in the 1990s? The lists of participants in the annual Latin American Meetings of the Econometric Society (LAMES) provide a helpful guide. For a Chilean economist, participation in LAMES indicates excellent academic training, possibly to the postgraduate level, and it suggests a high probability of an active role, either present or future, in national policy making. Out of fifty-two Chileans who participated in LAMES 1992 (Mexico City), LAMES 1993 (Tucuman), or LAMES 1994 (Caracas), one-quarter had Basque surnames, more than one-third had Castilian and other Spanish surnames (including Catalonian), and more than one-third had non-Spanish surnames (including German, Italian, English, French, Irish, Yugoslav, Askenazi Jewish, Arabic, and others). If participation in LAMES toward the end of the twentieth century is as accurate an indicator of the political power, social standing, and wealth of different Chilean ethnic groups as land ownership was at the beginning of the century, then the position of Chilean Basques has changed very little.

19. It is also realistic to assume that culture and attitudes have changed in the Basque country itself, from those of small farmers in a highly competitive capitalist system in the seventeenth and eighteenth centuries to the culture of those who were defeated by (or sided with) Franco during the Spanish Civil War to that of Basques considering emigration to South America in the era of international capitalism and globalization in the late twentieth century. The culture and attitudes that Basque immigrants brought to Chile also depend on the historical period when migration took place.

20. Between 1865 and 1895, as the country's population increased by about 50 percent, the number of urban white-collar employees increased by more than 400 percent, and that of professionals and shopkeepers by more than 300 percent. Between 1880 and 1900, the number of officials in the Ministry of Justice, Religious Affairs, and Education increased from less than 900 to more than 5,900 (Subercaseaux 1988, 91, 93).

21. It is interesting to contrast the origins of state-fostered industrialization in Chile and Brazil. In Chile, industrialization was pushed by civilian policy makers and technocrats, mostly civil engineers, working for the Development Corporation (CORFO). CORFO was the creation of civilian middle-class Radical governments. In Brazil, industrial development was encouraged by military governments and opposed by civilian oligarchies (Martins 1995, 141). This makes the links between industrialization, the urban middle sectors, and civilian and democratic politics much stronger in Chile. It also helps to explain why adopting FMOEP was more difficult for the Brazilian than the Chilean military.

22. Economic development results from the contribution of many forms of skilled labor. This chaper focuses on economists, but equally valid contributions are made by members of other professions, including sociologists, political scientists, anthropologists, human geographers, civil engineers, medical doctors, historians, and so on.

23. Possibly suggesting broader aspects of cultural change, both the prestige attached to economics and the public profile of many individual economists in Chile have increased since the 1960s.

24. Maybe it is unfair to argue that the subculture of the popular classes is dysfunctional to economic growth and development. In any case, these popular classes lack the political power to impose their own solution. For some of the views held by the middle and popular sectors, see Halpern and Bousquet (1991), Irarrazaval (1991), and Larrain (1994).

25. Chileans had suffered previous traumas: the 1891 Civil War, the Ibanez dictatorship (1927–1931), and the Great Depression. But they were not followed by the opening of the economy and society to the rest of the world and by rapid economic expansion. The last trauma which was followed by opening and growth was independence from Spain in 1810.

26. This metaphor was suggested by Juan Jose Sobrado.

REFERENCES

Ahumada, J. 1958. *En vez de la miseria*. Santiago: Editorial del Pacifico.

Baklanoff, E. N. 1959. Model for Economic Stagnation: The Chilean Experience with Multiple Exchange Rates. *Inter-American Economic Affairs* 13 (1): 58–82.

Basu, K. 1995. Civil Institutions and Evolution: Concepts, Critique and Models. *Journal of Development Economics* 46: 19–33.

Bethell, L., ed. 1993. *Chile since Independence*. Cambridge: Cambridge University Press.

Bizzarro, S. 1987. *Historical Dictionary of Chile*. 2d ed. London: Scarecrow.

Blest Gana, A. 1965. *Martin Rivas*. Buenos Aires: Andina.

Bothner, M. S. 1994. El soplo del espiritu: Perspectivas sobre el movimiento pentecostal en Chile. *Estudios publicos* 55: 261–296.

Boyle, C. 1986. Images of Women in Contemporary Chilean Theatre. *Bulletin of Latin American Research* 5 (2): 81–96.

Boyle, C. M., and D. E. Hojman. 1985. Economic Policies and Political Strategies: Middle Sectors in Contemporary Chile. *Boletin de estudios latino americanos y del Caribe* 38: 15–45.

Boyle, C. M., and D. E. Hojman. 1993. The Middle Sectors. In *Chile: The Political Economy of Development and Democracy in the 1990s*, edited by D. Hojman. London: Macmillan.

Bradshaw, S. 1990. Women in Chilean Rural Society. In *Neoliberal Agriculture in Rural Chile*, edited by D. E. Hojman. London: Macmillan.

Carey, G. 1989. *Chile Sin UF.* Santiago: Zig-Zag.

Collier, S., and W. F. Sater. 1996. *A History of Chile, 1808–1994.* Cambridge: Cambridge University Press.

Constable, P., and A. Valenzuela. 1991. *A Nation of Enemies: Chile under Pinochet.* New York: Norton.

Cornell, S., and J. P. Kalt. 1995. Where Does Economic Development Really Come From? Constitutional Rule among the Contemporary Sioux and Apache. *Economic Inquiry* 33: 402–426.

De la Cruz, A. 1982. Balanza de comercio que conviene al reino de Chile. *Estudios publicos* 7: 131–140.

De Ramon, A., and J. M. Larrain. 1982. *Origenes de la vida economica chilena: 1659–1808.* Santiago: CEP.

Econometrica. 1993, 1994, 1995. Pp. 61, 2; 62, 2; 63, 2.

Eisenstadt, S. N. 1972. Intellectuals and Tradition. *Daedalus* 101: 1–19.

El Mercurio. 1996. 23–29 May, international edition. Santiago: Empresa Editora El Mercurio S.A.P.

Farina, C., and A. Huerta. 1991. El liberalismo chileno en sus origenes: una aproximacion a sus tesis. *Estudios publicos* 43: 427–452.

Fontaine, A. 1982. Economia libre y seguridad nacional en Chile: una vision historica. *Estudios publicos* 7: 49–60.

Fontaine, A. 1988. *Los economistas y el Presidente Pinochet.* Santiago: Zig-Zag.

Frias, F. 1990. *Manual de historia de Chile.* Santiago: Zig-Zag.

Friedmann, J. 1960. Intellectuals in Developing Societies. *Kyklos* 13: 513–541.

Godoy, H. 1971. *Estructura social de Chile.* Santiago: Universitaria.

Greif, A. 1994. Cultural Beliefs and the Organisation of Society: A Historical and Theoretical Reflection on Collectivist and Individualist Societies. *Journal of Political Economy* 102 (5): 912–950.

Harrison, L. E. 1985. *Underdevelopment Is a State of Mind: The Latin American Case.* Lanham, Md.: University Press of America.

Harrison, L. E. 1992. *Who Prospers? How Cultural Values Shape Economic and Political Success.* New York: Basic Books.

Hojman, D. E. 1990. Chile after Pinochet: Aylwin's Christian Democrat Economic Policies for the Nineties. *Bulletin of Latin American Research* 9 (1): 25–47.

Hojman, D. E. 1993. *Chile: The Political Economy of Development and Democracy in the 1990s.* London: Macmillan.

Hojman, D. E. 1994. The Political Economy of Recent Conversions to Market Economics in Latin America. *Journal of Latin American Studies* 26 (1): 191–219.

Hojman, D. E. 1995a. Chile under Frei (Again): The First Latin American Tiger—or Just Another Cat? *Bulletin of Latin American Research* 14 (2): 127–142.

Hojman, D. E. 1995b. Educational Standards and Neoliberal Ideology in a Free-Market, Open-Economy Development Model. In *Neoliberalism with a Human Face? The Politics and Economics of the Chilean Model*, edited by D. E. Hojman. Liverpool: University of Liverpool, Institute of Latin American Studies.

Hojman, D. E. 1996. Poverty and Inequality in Chile: Are Democratic Politics and Neoliberal Economics Good for You? *Journal of Interamerican Studies and World Affairs* 38 (2 & 3): 73–96.

Jobet, J. C. 1971. La desmoralizacion nacional. In *Estructura social de Chile*, edited by H. Godoy. Santiago: Universitaria.

Johnson, L. J. 1967. Problems of Import Substitution: The Chilean Automobile Industry. *Economic Development and Cultural Change* 15: 202–216.

Larrain, F. 1982. Proteccionismo y desarrollo economico. *Estudios publicos* 7: 61–75.

Larrain, R. 1994. *Intervencion de Ricardo Larrain, in Cultura y sociedad: encuentros y desencuentros*. Valparaiso: University of Valparaiso Press.

Loveman, B. 1988. *Chile: The Legacy of Hispanic Capitalism*. New York: Oxford University Press.

Lowenberg, A. D., and B. T. Yu. 1992. The Role of the Intellectual in Economic Development: A Constitutional Perspective. *World Development* 20 (9): 1261–1277.

Mamalakis, M. J. 1965. Public Policy and Sectoral Development: A Case Study of Chile 1940–1958. In *Essays on the Chilean Economy*, edited by M. J. Mamalakis and C. W. Reynolds. Homewood, Ill.: Richard D. Irwin.

Mamalakis, M. J. 1976. *The Growth and Structure of the Chilean Economy*. New Haven: Yale University Press.

Martins, J. de S. 1995. The Alliance between Capital and Property in Brazil: The Trend to Backwardness. In *Growth and Development in Brazil: Cardoso's "Real" Challenge*, edited by M. D'A. Kinzo and V. Bulmer-Thomas. London: Institute of Latin American Studies.

Montecinos, V. 1993. Economic Policy Elites and Democratisation. *Studies in Comparative International Development* 28 (1): 25–53.

Norman, P. 1996. New Zealand "Least Corrupt Country." *Financial Times* (3 June): 5.

Olson, M. 1982. *The Rise and Decline of Nations*. New Haven: Yale University Press.

Provan, S. 1996. Chile's Islanders Net an Aquatic Earner. *Financial Times* (28 February): 35.

Puryear, J. M. 1994. *Thinking Politics: Intellectuals and Democracy in Chile, 1973–1988*. Baltimore: Johns Hopkins University Press.

Serrano, C. 1988. Mujeres: sobrevivencia y cambio cultural. In *Chile en el umbral de los noventa*, edited by J. Gazmuri. Santiago: Planeta.

Sowell, T. 1993. Diversidad cultural: una perspectiva universal. *Estudios publicos* 49: 227–241.

Subercaseaux, B. 1988. *Fin de siglo: la epoca de Balmaceda*. Santiago: Aconcagua.

Ugalde, L. 1994. *Appreciation of Productive Work*. Caracas: Sivensa Foundation Academic Program.

United Nations Development Program (UNDP). 1994. *Human Development Report*. New York: UNDP.

Valdes, J. G. 1989. *La escuela de Chicago: Operacion Chile*. Buenos Aires: Grupo Zeta.

Vargas Llosa, M. 1996. El Evangelio segun La Pintana. *El Pais* (14 January): 15–16.

Veliz, C. 1980. *The Centralist Tradition of Latin America*. Princeton: Princeton University Press.

Vial, G. 1971. Los prejuicios sociales en Chile al terminar el siglo XVIII. In *Estructura social de Chile*, edited by H. Godoy. Santiago: Universitaria.

Villalobos, S. 1971. El bajo pueblo en el pensamiento de los precursores de 1810. In *Estructura social de Chile*, edited by H. Godoy. Santiago: Universitaria.

Vogel, I. 1995. Gender and the Labour Market: Women's Experiences of Labour Force Participation in Chile. In *Neoliberalism with a Human Face? The Politics and Economics of the Chilean Model*, edited by D. E. Hojman. Liverpool: University of Liverpool, Institute of Latin American Studies.

Willems, E. 1971. La clase alta chilena. In *Estructura social de Chile*, edited by H. Godoy. Santiago: Universitaria.

Chapter 9 _____

Human Development in India:
A Macro Perspective

Shekhar Chaudhuri and Sunil Kumar

During the 1950s and 1960s the concept of development ignored the social dimension. However, during the last three decades, several new concepts have emerged concerning development at the national and global levels (Galtung 1982). Today, the human factor is a central concern in development. Development here means the development of people. This approach to understanding development is different from earlier concepts, which treated economic growth and development synonymously. Economic growth and human development may not move hand in hand. As is well-known, higher per capita income alone cannot ensure better living conditions. It is, therefore, imperative that if human well-being is considered important, the development strategy must view people as a central concern of the development agenda. In view of these observations, the primary objective of this chapter is to discuss some key aspects of the process of Human Factor Development (HFD) in India with a focus on the post-independence period and the various factors that influence it.

The organizing framework for this chapter is illustrated in Figure 9.1. HFD is influenced directly as well as indirectly by the economic conditions and institutional environment. The interaction between economic environment, the HFD process, and Institutional Environment (IE) is complex. Economic conditions (EC) influence HFD in a variety of ways. The economy provides opportunities for employment and utilization of available skills. Economic conditions influence standard of living, skill formation, and knowledge acqui-

Figure 9.1
The Human Factor Development System

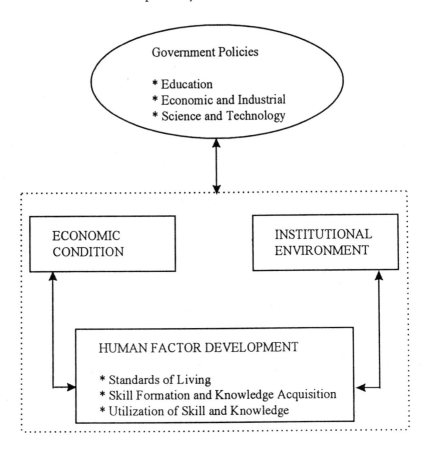

sition. They also influence the institutional environment through the creation of new institutions and the sustenance of existing institutions through supply of funds and creating demand for the activities of these institutions. The institutional environment as conceptualized in this chapter comprises the higher-level educational and research institutions, and plays a major role by providing facilities for the development of people's knowledge and skills. Another role played by the institutional environment is that of providing employment opportunities to research workers and academicians. The institutional environment is influenced by HFD as well as EC. Figure 9.1, however, also shows arrows from EC and IE toward HFD. In this chapter, the attempt is made to explore this interactive process in detail.

The other variables shown in Figure 9.1 are government policies, which are specified outside the rectangular box. The government, indeed, plays essentially four roles: catalytic, regulatory, entrepreneurial, and supportive. It can catalyze the creation of institutions, regulate their functioning, set up institutions owned by the state, and support various institutions by providing them with funds, technical assistance, and other kinds of support. In what follows, government policies related to education, science and technology, economic planning, and industry and their impact on HFD in India have been explored further.

THE GENERAL STATE OF THE INDIAN ECONOMY

Adjibolosoo (1995) provides a comprehensive definition for the human factor. To Adjibolosoo, the HF is essential for superior performance of firms engaged in global competition. The HF comprises six unique dimensions: spiritual capital, moral capital, aesthetic capital, human capital, human abilities, and human potentials. Adjibolosoo maintains that it is the availability of the relevant HF that provides the necessary leadership qualities for achieving higher productivity goals and quality standards. Our analytical framework is based on this definition of the HF.

We have analyzed HFD on the basis of four dimensions that we believe capture the essential features of the HF definition provided by Adjibolosoo (1993, 1994, 1995). The four dimensions are: standard of living, skill formation and knowledge acquisition, the utilization of skills and knowledge, and human values and ethics. The standard of living has been assessed on the basis of economic conditions, health, and status of child labor. Skill formation and knowledge acquisition are also dealt with at three levels: elementary and secondary education, adult education, and higher education. The utilization of skills is assessed at the macrolevel by using data on applications from live register-of-employment exchanges as a surrogate. Values and ethics are assessed broadly on the dimensions of justice, honesty, sensitivity toward others, and fairness. Due to their nature, it is difficult to quantify these dimensions. We describe traditional values briefly and comment on the contemporary scene with a special reference to the professional class and the political leadership.

Standard of Living

The concept of standard of living has been interpreted in a variety of ways and, as such, it has been measured in very many ways. Some of the macromeasures most commonly used to ascertain the standard of living for different countries include per capita income, per capita electricity generation, per capita availability of food grains and milk, and so on (Clark and Roy 1994; Moon 1991). Morris (1979) argued that the satisfaction of the basic human needs of a people must be used to measure the standard of living. He suggested that life expectancy, infant mortality rates, and literacy rates are better measures of a people's standard of living. In order to have a better understanding of the standard of living in India, one has to consider three main dimensions: economic (measured by per capita net national product [NNP]), health (measured by child mortality rate and life expectancy at birth), and status of child labor.

Economic Environment

India's per capita NNP nearly doubled during the period from 1950 to 1994 (see details in Table 9.1). However, the level of economic well-being in India is very low compared to world standards. The Human Development Report of 1994 placed India in seventy-second place among developing nations in terms of per capita gross national product (World Bank 1994a). Per capita NNP has grown at an average rate of 1.7 percent per year at factor cost (1980 prices) since independence. However, there have been some fluctuations. While per capita NNP declined by a record 8.2 percent during 1979–1980, it improved by 8.3 percent in 1988–1989. On a year-to-year basis from 1951 to 1994, India recorded a continuing decline in its per capita NNP (Agarwal and Varma 1996).

Table 9.1
Net National Product at Factor Cost (1980–1981 Prices)

Year	Total (Rs Crore)	Per Capita	Index Number of NNP per capita
1950 - 51	40450	1127	100.0
1955 - 56	48288	1229	109.0
1960 - 61	58602	1350	119.8
1965 - 66	65734	1355	120.3
1970 - 71	82211	1520	134.9
1975 - 76	95433	1572	139.5
1980 - 81	110685	1630	144.7
1985 - 86	139025	1841	163.6
1990 - 91	185683	2213	197.2
1991 - 92	185503	2167	193.2
1992 - 93	193222	2216	197.5
1993 - 94	202670	2202	197.0

Sources: Manpower Profile India Yearbook (1995); Agarwal and Varma (1996).

Trends in the sectoral share in GDP over the years broadly indicate the nature of demand for skilled people. The share of manufacturing in GDP has slowly increased from 11.4 percent in 1950–1951 to 19.2 percent in 1993–1994. Moreover, the growth rate of the manufacturing sector has fluctuated on a year-to-year basis. Growth rate was maximum at 11.1 percent in 1978–1979 and minimum at −1.85 percent in the next year. Part of this fluctuation is explained by fluctuations in agriculture. Moreover, the contribution of manufacturing to the growth of GDP has been declining in recent years. In 1992, the industrial sector's contribution to GDP growth was 0.6 percent compared to 0.9 percent in 1972. These fluctuations and the low share of the manufacturing sector in GDP is reflected in the fluctuating demand pattern for skilled labor in the country.

The level of per capita Gross Domestic Investment (GDI) does not reveal a healthy picture of the Indian economy. In the last twenty years, per capita GDI increased by 60 percent from U.S.$50 to U.S.$80 at 1987 U.S. prices. India's performance has been far from satisfactory in comparison with other rapidly developing Asian countries. Indeed, the slow rate of growth in per capita GDI in India is another explanation for the slow overall growth of demand for skilled labor.

Slow and irregular rates of growth of per capita NNP are coupled with uneven income distribution. This is reflected in the high level of poverty in India. Though the percentage of population below the poverty line of Rs. 101.80 for rural areas and Rs.117.50 for urban areas (at 1983–1984 prices) has declined during the last five decades since independence, only a marginal decline has occurred in the absolute number of people below the poverty line. Regional and communal disparity is another characteristic of the pattern of poverty in the country. Poverty among scheduled castes and scheduled tribes is more than 50 percent and 57 percent, respectively (CMIC 1988). In 1987–1988, the Punjab had only 7.2 percent of its population below the poverty line, the lowest in the country, while Orissa had the highest incidence of poverty at 44.7 percent.

Health

Child and infant mortality rates reflect the basic human need for survival and are considered strong measures of standard of living. There has been significant improvements in India's infant mortality rate, from 173 per 1,000 in 1955–1956 to 88 during 1990–1995. The child mortality rate has also declined, from 152 to 46 in the same period. Still, India's economic performance is below average. India was sixty-fourth among developing nations on the basis of infant mortality rate according to the *Human Development Report* (World Bank 1994a). Improved health conditions are also reflected in improved life expectancy at birth. Life expectancy of females at birth improved from 40.6 years in 1960–1961 to 58.7 years in 1990–1991 (Agarwal and Varma

1996). This is a reflection of improved pre- and post-natal care. In 1990–1991, the life expectancy of a female child at birth stood higher than that of a male child. This perhaps is an indicator of change in attitudes in India toward the nutritional needs of the female child. However, the life expectancy of female children in India is much lower than the average life expectancy of 64.5 years for all developing countries. The 1994 *World Development Report* (World Bank 1994b) placed India in the fifty-second position among developing nations in terms of life expectancy at birth.

Unlike economic indicators, health indicators have shown continuous improvement in India. India's development experience indicates strong negative correlation (−0.9788 with a significance level of .001) between per capita NNP and infant mortality rate. This apparent paradox may be explained by the impact of a population growth rate of more than 2 percent per year. India achieved a gross domestic product growth rate of more than 4 percent since independence versus only 1.2 percent in the pre-independence period (1900–1947). But the problem of poverty continues because of the high population growth rate.

Child Labor

The use of child labor continues in India even after five decades of independence. This phenomenon is an indication of the poor standard of living in the country. The data presented in Table 9.2 show that from 1961 through 1981 the number of children employed in hazardous processes has increased considerably. Reasons for using child labor include poverty, illiteracy, and parental ignorance. Child labor results in educational backwardness. Students drop out from their schools very early to take up certain jobs. One of the authors had an opportunity to visit glass units in Firozabad (a small city in north India) and carpet-making firms in Bhadoi and Mirzapur in north central India. The author found that children were employed by the glass industry for low wages, and in the carpet industry they were employed mainly for making fine quality

Table 9.2
Child Labor in India

Year	Number of children in banned and hazardous processes (millions).	Total number of children in child labor (millions)
1961	0.308	14.5
1971	0.374	10.7
1981	0.671	13.6

Source: Government of India (1961, 1971, 1981).

carpets because their thin and tender fingers enabled them to achieve higher productivity and better products. International pressure on the government has forced it to take steps to ensure that children are not exploited. The government has begun issuing *Kaleen* certificates for carpets made without child labor. The implementation of such schemes, however, is difficult, as the carpet industry is spread all over the country and is generally in the informal sector. The problem of child labor is likely to continue until the economic status of the poorer strata of the society is improved.

ECONOMIC PLANNING AND INDUSTRIAL POLICY

In the immediate post–colonial period, India lacked the basic infrastructure and skilled people for rapid economic growth. There were shortages of raw materials and food. National planners faced the challenge of achieving goals of economic development and social justice with very limited resources. Resource scarcity required a synergy of efforts by different organizations and departments of the government. The five-year national planning process was adopted to synchronize the efforts of different departments by clearly stating the objectives and direction for growth and development (Government of India 1957). This enabled the country to invest its resources in a well-defined direction.

The stated objectives of these plans may be classified into three broad categories: poverty alleviation, socialistic pattern of development, and self-reliance (Government of India 1952, 1957, 1986, 1988, 1990; Chaudhuri 1995). The poverty alleviation objective is evident from the following statement in the first five-year plan:

The central objective of planning in India at the present is to initiate a process of development which will raise living standards and open out to the people new opportunities for a richer and more varied life. . . . The urge to economic and social change . . . comes from the fact of poverty and of inequalities of income, wealth and opportunity. . . . The elimination of poverty cannot, obviously, be achieved merely by redistributing existing wealth. Nor can a program aiming only at raising production remove existing inequalities. The two have to be considered together. (Government of India 1952, 7–8)

India's planners thought that poverty could be eliminated by increasing production, as it would result in a larger national cake for all. In the first three five-year development plans, the primary focus was on economic growth to reduce both unemployment and poverty. However, the benefits of increases in production did not trickle down to the poor automatically. As a result, by the end of the fourth plan the issue of equity and social justice got special attention from national planners. The fifth plan drew up a clear strategy for poverty eradication. Various employment-generating schemes like *Jawahar Rojgar Yojana*, Integrated Rural Development Programs, were initiated. To a large extent, however, the benefits of these schemes have accrued to well-to-do people owing to their better access to power centers. The siphoning off of substantial parts of the resources from various schemes by intermediaries, lack of communication resulting in lack of awareness about various schemes among target groups, lack of organized efforts on the part of the target groups to press their demands, and fragmentation of schemes and lack of coordination among them are some of the significant problems that have plagued poverty alleviation programs (Vaidyanathan 1995). It is no wonder that the unemployment rate is more than 20 percent.

The objectives of the socialistic pattern of development and self-reliance influenced the adoption of the mixed economy model of development in India. Deliberate intervention by the state in planning for development was considered necessary to reduce the gap between India and other developed nations. The private sector was not willing to invest in long-gestation, low-return, and high-investment capital-intensive basic industries. Hence, the government considered it necessary to intervene by taking over the role of entrepreneur in capital-intensive fields. The public sector has played an important role in the development of the country since then. It accounted for more than 71 percent of total employment in the organized sector in 1994 versus 58 percent in 1961 (DGET Report 1994). The mixed economy model and protection of domestic firms through an import substitution policy had some adverse impacts on the economy. The policy of protection created barriers for the entry of foreign firms into the country. Without exposure to international products, Indian consumers were less demanding. As such, industries did not have much incentive to be more efficient and effective through technological and managerial innovations. Indian firms entered into collaborations with foreign firms to import technology, but the technology imported by Indian firms was generally obsolete.

Though considerable product and process adaptations have been made in India, a large gap continues to exist between the technological standards of the developed nations and that of India. This technology gap is between ten to fifteen years after nearly five decades of independence. India's position as an industrialized nation has slid down from the tenth position in 1950 to twenty-sixth currently (Agarwal and Varma 1996). The worsening industrial position of the country is partly explained by continued technological backwardness in most industries. We believe that the technological gap has also contributed to the problem of migration of highly skilled people to the West. The skill and knowledge of graduates from the premier technological institutes (the Indian Institutes of Technology [IITs] and others) is comparable to the best anywhere. However, it is estimated that in some years close to 60 or 70 percent of the graduates from some of the IITs in certain disciplines have gone to the United States and other developed countries to look for greener pastures.

Though lack of utilization of the skills and knowledge of India's best engineers has contributed to their migration to the West, the lack of recognition and importance accorded to the engineering, manufacturing, design, and research functions by local firms is responsible for the migration of some of the best engineers residing in the country to lucrative managerial careers. Every year there is literally an exodus of IIT graduates from the Indian Institutes of Management (IIMs), the elite management schools of the country.

SCIENCE AND TECHNOLOGY POLICY

Science and Technology (S&T) in India has the distinct imprint of the country's first Prime Minister, Jawaharlal Nehru, who established the basic framework for its development. He assumed charge of the Presidency of the Council of Scientific and Industrial Research (CSIR) in 1947. His government backed up this involvement with financial support. In the early years, the central government provided almost all the financial requirements of the Indian Council of Medical Research, the Indian Council of Agriculture Research, CSIR, and the Atomic Energy Commission.

On March 4, 1958, the government adopted a Scientific Policy Resolution (SPR) which articulated and further elaborated on the ideas and efforts of the previous years. India's SPR was considered by many developing nations as a historic landmark. It committed the country wholeheartedly to the scientific approach to development. Another important landmark in the sphere of S&T in India was the announcement of the Technology Policy Statement in 1983 by the central government.

What have been the achievements and failings of the scientific and technological efforts of the country since independence in relation to human factor development? About 50 percent of the country's production is based on imported technology. Of the remaining 50 percent, the major chunk is based on adopted and indigenized technology. It is estimated that approximately 5 percent of the country's industrial production is based on indigenous R&D ("We Get Left-Over Technology" 1991). These views have been echoed by Lavkare and Gulati (1989), Jain and Uberoy (1993), Patel (1989), Bhattacharya (1988), and Parthasarthy (1994), among others. The fact that 45 percent of industrial production is based on imported technology which has been indigenized and adapted to local conditions is by itself no mean achievement. The ability to scale down plants and adapt processes to locally available materials in the engineering industry is quite common (Chaudhuri 1986; Chaudhuri and Moulik 1986; Desai 1984). Even in process industries, this has been achieved to a considerable degree. Parthasarthi (1994) noted that there are currently at least forty major professional systems or products in the areas of telecommunications, television and radio broadcasting, civil aviation, industrial electronics and control systems, and so on, under commercial production which are based on domestic technology supported or promoted by the central government's department of electronics. Several notable technological innovations have been achieved by laboratories under the Ministry of Defense and CSIR.

Our purpose is not to develop an inventory of all the technological achievements of the country, but to develop an understanding of how the government's

S&T policies influenced HFD in India. The widely perceived weakness of the S&T system is the low level of utilization of research conducted at the national R&D laboratories. A variety of reasons are believed to be responsible for the present state of affairs. Preference for imported technology by manufacturing firms and their lack of commitment to R&D, poor communication between industry and research institutions, and the propensity of scientists in the latter to undertake basic research rather than applied research that has potential for industrial applications are some of the oft-mentioned reasons. Part of the problem lies in the process of training and developing the country's scientific and technical person power. The elite institutions' reference groups are scientists and technologists in the West. Their work is inspired by research conducted in the West which, in most cases, is only remotely connected to the problems existing in the country. Part of the problem also lies in the predicted environment in which industry has been operating these last five decades. Without competitive pressures there was no incentive for firms to invest in R&D in major ways for product or process innovations.

SKILL AND KNOWLEDGE ACQUISITION THROUGH EDUCATION

The Institutional Environment

Independent India inherited a system of higher education patterned after the British model (*India 2001* 1995). Unlike British universities, however, Indian universities have been under the administrative control of the Indian government. As a result, bureaucracy has crept into the system and Indian universities have lost the dynamism that was once the characteristic of the better known ones. In view of this, Jawaharlal Nehru, the first Prime Minister of India, felt the need to reorganize the educational system to reflect the emerging needs of a newly independent nation. The setting up of the University Education Commission under Sarvepalli Radhakrishnan (1948–1949), the Committee on Elementary Education (1950–1952), and the Secondary Education Commission (1952–1953) were steps in this direction. A national policy on education was evolved on the basis of the comprehensive report of the Kothari Commission in 1966. The national policy of 1968 adopted many of the recommendations laid down by the Kothari Commission. The objectives of the policy were (1) free and compulsory education until the age of fourteen; (2) improved status, emoluments, and education of teachers; (3) a three-language formula and development of regional languages; (4) equalization of educational opportunities, science, and research; (5) development of education for agriculture and industry; (6) improvement in quality and production of inexpensive textbooks; and (7) investment of 6 percent of national income on education (*India 2001* 1995).

In 1986, the National Policy on Education (NPE) was enacted by parliament. The NPE highlighted the need for setting up *Navodaya Vidyalayas* in each district of the country for talented children to develop their full talents.

Two hundred and eighty such schools were set up by 1991–1992 to provide free education. In 1992, the central government initiated further action. The Program of Action of 1992 provided for the development of open universities. The Indira Gandhi National Open University of India is the second largest of its kind in the world (*India 2001* 1995).

The share of elementary education in the budget has been varying from 45 to 50 percent over the years since independence. The share of technical and other higher education in the budget has been declining since 1992–1993. Reduction in the budget of higher education is directed toward the share of adult education and other special education in the country. The central government has accorded high priority to adult education in the eighth plan (1992–1997). The national stock of educated people power has gone up from less than 4 million in 1951 to about 48 million in 1996. Educational facilities have not only increased, but also diversified at all levels and in different subjects. The country's sizeable educated population is one of the largest in the world.

The objectives of various educational policies, however, have not been fully achieved. Though the Indian government has increased expenditures on education over the years, it has not been able to achieve the target set by the Kothari Commission in 1968. While only 1.27 percent of GDP was spent on education in 1951, it rose to 4.06 percent of GDP in 1991. India's expenditure on education is extremely low compared to international trends. For example, Australia spends more than 9 percent, South Korea spends 16.8 percent, and Malaysia spends more than 20 percent of their overall expenditure on education versus 2.2 percent of such expenditure by the Indian government in 1993 (World Bank 1995).

Though quality varies, the best among the educated are on par with the best anywhere (*India 2001* 1995). However, the content of different courses at various levels, especially at the higher levels of education, lacks ethical considerations. Education in all the IIMs, the premier management institutes of the country, is not geared toward whole-person development. Holistic, real-life management problems face utter neglect (Chakraborty 1995). Management neglects the development of holistic consciousness in the labor force. There has been impressive growth in the educational and research institution infrastructure in the country since independence. The number of degree-granting engineering colleges grew from 53 in 1951 to 354 in 1992. The number of diploma engineering colleges increased from 89 to 911 and the number of medical colleges went up from 32 to 185 in the same period.

Elementary and Secondary Education

Improvement in elementary and secondary education since independence has been rather slow. The number of middle schools increased from 49,663 in 1961 to 155,707 in 1994. Primary schools increased from 330,399 to 572,923 in the same period. However, India's population nearly doubled in the same period. Hence, the growth rate of primary schools was less than the population growth rate, resulting in overcrowding in primary schools, particularly in urban areas. Another significant feature of primary education is the drop-out rate. Though the enrollment in primary schools has increased by more than 200 percent in the last thirty-five years, more than 60 percent of the schooling population drops out after six years of education (Agarwal and Varma 1996, 301). These drop outs are mostly girls. While 104.5 percent of boys in the relevant age groups are enrolled in middle schools, the percentage of girls drops down to 79.3 percent. Moreover, a large part of the Indian population that did not receive formal education during childhood remains illiterate after five decades of independence.

Adult Education

The literacy rate was abysmally low (16.6%) at the time of independence. Different schemes for adult education have significantly improved the literacy rate since independence. India achieved a literacy rate of a little over 50 percent by 1991. In 1994, India was in the seventy-first position among all developing nations, as reported in the *Human Development Report* (World Bank 1994a). The female literacy rate in the age group of fifteen to twenty-four years is low, at 40 percent versus an average of 67 percent among developing nations.

Higher Education: Engineering and Medical

There has been impressive growth in the number of skilled engineers and doctors in India. The level of enrollment in engineering and medical colleges went up from 48,000 and 40,000, respectively, in 1961 to more than 270,000 and more than 138,000, respectively, in 1994. Availability of doctors increased from seventeen per 100,000 persons in 1951 to forty-eight in 1992 (Agarwal and Varma 1996).

A similar pattern can be observed in the field of general higher education. Enrollment in first-degree and higher-level courses increased significantly between 1967 and 1994 (*Manpower Profile India Yearbook* 1995). Improvement in enrollment has increased the number of engineers and doctors in the country. The number of engineering graduates increased by 17.2 percent from 1961 to 1971—the highest rate. The number of graduate doctors experienced the highest rate of growth from 1971 to 1981. The growth rate in the previous period was also high. The decade of the 1980s and the early years of the 1990s, however, exhibit a slowdown in the growth rate of the number.

The impressive increase in the stock of doctors and engineers, however, is not reflected in per capita availability because of the high population growth rate. As a result, India compares unfavorably with other developing nations. India has a density of 3.5 scientists and technicians per 1,000 persons against 49.5 scientists and technicians per 1,000 persons in the Republic of Korea and 29.5 in Brazil (World Bank 1994a).

Utilization of Available Skills and Knowledge

Efforts to improve the technological, social, and other skills and knowledge of the population would be meaningless without equally effective programs aimed at their utilization. Its measurement is difficult because of its inherently subjective nature, but the distribution of applicants on the live register of employment exchanges may be used as a surrogate measure of skills and knowledge utilization. The data presented in Table 9.3 indicate that the level of utilization of the available skills in the country has declined sharply in the recent past. The number of engineering graduates who have registered with employment exchanges increased from 38,300 in 1986 to 137,500 in 1992. In the field of medicine, the number of registered graduates with employment exchanges increased from 3,800 in 1971 to 28,100 in 1992. In 1992, 3,700 post-graduate engineers and 3,200 post-graduate doctors were registered with employment exchanges. It is estimated that the number of engineers in the working age group is more than 587,300 (IAMR 1995).

The Indian labor market exhibits two important characteristics. On an aggregate basis, India's population is characterized by low levels of skill and knowledge. But there exists a small proportion of the population which possesses high levels of skills and knowledge. The higher levels of skill and knowledge of the latter, however, have not been fully utilized.

Other than engineering and medical colleges, various types of institutions relating to higher education and research have come up since independence. These include institutes of national importance and advanced research institutes. The institutes of national importance include six Indian Institutes of Technology; five Indian Institutes of Management; the All India Institute of Medical Sciences, New Delhi; the Post-Graduate Institute of Medicine and Research, Chandigarh; and the Indian Statistical Institute, Calcutta. More than forty research laboratories have been set up in the country under the auspices of the Council of Scientific and Industrial Research. The Indian Institute of Public Administration in New Delhi, the Center for Policy Research in New Delhi, and the Indian Institute of Education in Pune were established during this period. The research laboratories do not award degrees, but some of them have strong doctoral programs in affiliation with collaborating universities. The Ministries of Agriculture, Health, and Industries and Commerce have also set up research institutes which operate under their purview.

Such institutions have helped in the development of a strong base of highly skilled and knowledgeable people in a variety of fields. The percentage of scientists, engineers, and technicians engaged in R&D activities has gone up from 3.37 percent in 1978 to 5.85 percent in 1990 (*Manpower Profile India Yearbook* 1995, 204). However, the country has not been able to fully utilize the skills and knowledge of the persons trained by these institutes. A large proportion of people trained at these elite institutions migrate to developed countries for better career opportunities. According to estimates, 30.8 percent

Table 9.3
Distribution of Applicants on Live Register of Employment Exchanges by
Educational Level (in Thousands)

Educational Level	1971	1976	1981	1986	1991	1992
Matriculates	1296.8	2828.6	5878.1	8682.0	13110.9	13528.5
Undergraduates	605.2	1255.2	2325.5	3806.0	5516.4	5572.7
Graduates	354.4	926.2	1542.9	2306.6	3387.5	3450.1
Arts	147.0	416.3	751.8	1066.7	1398.3	1367.7
Science	99.2	241.3	337.2	467.6	659.9	690.4
Commerce	52.2	137.0	251.6	429.1	611.3	607.2
Engineering	18.6	18.1	19.9	38.3	124.3	137.5
Medicine	3.8	8.2	15.6	23.8	30.8	28.1
Agriculture	7.3	8.3	13.0	24.9	31.7	29.7
Education	22.7	85.9	127.1	225.6	442.4	486.5
Others	3.6	11.1	26.7	30.4	88.8	103.0
Postgraduates	39.2	94.8	141.9	293.1	419.7	455.0
Arts	18.9	52.6	81.8	162.9	213.5	228.5
Science	10.1	24.6	28.0	57.4	90.9	94.3
Commerce	2.9	9.5	17.8	36.1	57.3	61.7
Engineering	0.4	0.3	1.6	0.7	4.1	3.7
Medicine	0.1	0.3	0.8	1.9	2.9	3.2
Agriculture	0.7	0.9	0.9	1.5	2.7	3.9
Education	4.7	4.8	7.3	22.8	31.5	34.1
Others	1.4	1.8	3.7	9.9	16.8	25.6
Total	**2295.6**	**5104.8**	**9888.4**	**15087.7**	**22434.5**	**23006.3**

Source: Manpower Profile India Yearbook (1995).

of the graduates of IIT in Bombay from 1973 to 1977, and 24.7 percent of the
graduates of IIT in Madras from 1964 to 1986 settled abroad (*Manpower Profile India Yearbook* 1995).

The Socio–Politico–Cultural Environment

The socio–politico–cultural environment is an important factor that has
influenced the process of people development in India. Contemporary Indian

society is not significantly different from what it was in the past on many essential features. It is characterized by constraint, credulity, status, authority, bigotry, and blind fatalism. The popular beliefs and customs of people in the country still show signs of magic, animism, and superstition.

India has seen the confluence of diverse religions and cultures, brought in by invaders and developed by indigenous peoples. The contemporary human values and ethical beliefs are a result of this intermingling process. A variety of factors, such as technology, income and social status, language, racial stock, and economic conditions, have influenced the value and ethical development process. As such, there are regional variations in the values and customs of the people of India. It is no wonder, therefore, that it is widely believed that it would be meaningless to think about something that can be called "Indian culture" or "Indian values." On the other hand, any outsider visiting different cities and regions would easily discern significant commonalities in behavior patterns among individuals, depending on relationships, religious and social customs, conception of the individual's purpose in life, duties, and rights. Chakraborty (1995, 3) noted, "Besides the indigenous Vedantic, Buddhist, Jaina and Sikh traditions, Indian culture has absorbed numerous enriching strands from Islamic, Christian and Parsi traditions. And yet even within this great diversity of outward forms of culture, e.g., crafts, music, architecture, dress, painting, food and so on, we detect also numerous significant commonalities constituting a distinct class when compared to non-Indian cultures."

Hinduism is the dominant religion in the country, with approximately 85 percent of the population as adherents. Many customs and traditions have been influenced by the values espoused by this dominant group. According to Indian tradition, the two main goals of human beings are _abhyudaya_ (prosperity) and _nihsreyasha_ (ultimate consummation). _Abhudaya_ is composed of three aspects: _dharma_ (rectitude and righteousness), _artha_ (money and wealth), and _kama_ (desires and needs). _Nisreyasha_ (ultimate consummation) refers to the end state of all human beings which results in the liberation of the spirit. Most people attain this state over a long period of time, though a few may consciously pursue this goal and achieve it in a shorter period. An important aspect of the Indian ethos is _nishkama-karma_ (desireless work or _karmayoga_). The advice given by the scriptures is that one can become more effective and efficient in work when it is done in all humility as an offering to God and not out of the compulsions of egoistic vital drives (Chakraborty 1995). Great leaders like the Buddha, Vivekananda, and Gandhi lived by these values and tried to disseminate them through their personal examples. They lived in simplicity and self-denial.

It should be noted that, in the past, though these values were strongly ingrained in the Indian psyche, they did not get in the way of economic development in a general sense. This is borne out by history. Throughout the centuries, India has been the favorite target of invaders from the north as well as sea-faring traders from Europe because of her wealth (see details in Aurobindo 1975). The wealth of India was created alongside achievements in the field of culture: architecture, music, dance, literature, sculpture, painting, and so on. Distribution of wealth and conservation, the values sought to be created by the teachings of seers of yore, were also given emphasis as borne out by travelogues of ancient travelers who wrote about trust, openness, absence of theft, absence of famine, and ecological denudation. According to Chakraborty, wealth creation and cultural development was possible because these were inspired by the concept of *nishkama-karma* (i.e., work done as an offering to the Supreme Being). Adjibolosoo (1995) emphasized the significance of the spiritual and moral aspect of the HF in development. According to him, the HF, through the commitment and integrity it creates, directs and motivates people to achieve higher productivity objectives and quality standards.

PERTINENT PROBLEMS AND EVIDENCE OF HUMAN FACTOR DECAY

Over the years, there has been considerable dilution in traditional values in India, which is apparent from the numerous scams unearthed recently. Today's professional class is driven predominantly by mercenary goals. Chowdhury (1990) echoes this view on the basis of a survey. A recent newspaper report mentioned that the board of directors of the national airlines of the country passed a resolution conferring on themselves free passes to travel abroad with their families for their entire lifetimes. Chakraborty (1995), on the basis of an opinion poll from a group of junior and middle-level executives in a program on values, concluded that almost 85 percent of the group (age range from twenty-five to fifty) had a poor and negative perception of work life within the organizations in general. Meanness, pettiness, and smallness seemed to be the dominant attributes of organizations.

In the preliberalized economy, the grabbing of industrial liscences by influencing administrators, bureaucrats, and other people in positions of trust and power was an important ingredient of corporate success. For example, Indian managers find nothing wrong in hiring employees away from competitors to pirate their technology (Monappa 1977). Of course, Western nations and Japan have gone through this phase of development in the past. The manager of today is primarily appraised on the basis of his economic contribution or profit generation. His own values and ethical considerations are subordinate to the company's values and company loyalty.

Economic liberalization has only changed the spectrum of dishonest practices. The quantum of these practices, however, has not changed. The trend is not any different from those common in the political arena. The charges of corruption and misuse of power are increasing against the political leaders of the country. People use and adopt unfair means to wield power and try to use that power for their personal benefit. There is growing concern in the country regarding whether trade union leaders are concerned about the welfare of employees.

The laws of the country are complex on even simple matters. These laws exist primarily to put restrictions on unfair practices in business and other walks of life. Yet they do not seem to provide any long-term solutions to the problem of corruption. Dishonest people are always able to find loopholes in every rule. The solution to this problem perhaps lies in coordinated efforts by the government, judiciary, industry, academia, media, and administrative system. Both political and religious leaders also have a role to play.

CONCLUSION

Our analysis of HFD in India reveals a mixed picture. In spite of the per capita NNP doubling during the period from 1950 to 1994, India is seventy-second among developing nations. Though the percentage of population below the poverty line has come down significantly during the post-independence era, the absolute number of persons below the poverty line has only been reduced marginally. There are significant regional and communal variations in the incidence of poverty. Though the child mortality rate has come down considerably, it is still very high compared to that of many other developing nations. The life expectancy of female children has gone up significantly, but is still behind that of many developing nations. Despite the government's efforts to improve the educational infrastructure, the school drop-out rate is high and so is the incidence of child labor. Adult literacy in India has improved greatly in the post-independence period, but is still low compared to that of many developing nations.

Paradoxically, India has a large population of qualified scientific, technical, and medical persons, a significant part of which is unemployed or inappropriately employed. A significant proportion of the country's elite engineers migrate to the West every year in search of better opportunities. This problem of brain drain is compounded by the migration of the well-trained engineers remaining within the country to commercial careers. Indian managers are considered good at process innovation. They are quick to adopt any process to suit their business environment, but they are poor at product innovation. The tradition of original R&D activities needs to be developed. For this, a close coordination between relevant research institutions, industry, academia, policy-making bodies, and implementing agencies is required. A widely perceived weakness of the S&T system in the country is its lack of linkage with industry. Lack of practical orientation of scientists and engineers in the national R&D institutions, absence of proper incentives for undertaking R&D for product and process innovations in industry, and the overly theoretical education in the national technological institutes inspired by Western models are some of the important reasons for this state of affairs.

India's education system, particularly at the higher levels, fails to impart ethical and moral values to students. This is partly responsible for the deteriorating value standards in the country. There is a need to integrate ethical and holistic learning at all levels of education in the country. Political and religious leaders of the country need to adhere to ethical standards in their activities and create an environment of trust, openness, and honesty to support the efforts of educators. It is time to reflect and bring ethical orientation into the political system of the country. Indeed, any programs put in place to develop the human factor in India on a continuing basis will enhance the efficiency and effectiveness of India's future development programs. The policy of divide and rule pursued by political leaders needs immediate replacement by democratic principles and a concern for the welfare of all. Yet this cannot happen successfully without having developed the human factor (Adjibolosoo 1995). The judicial system, media, and intellectual thinkers of the country need to pay immediate attention to this problem.

Significant improvements in NNP, health facilities, and technical infrastructure over the years have been neutralized by a growing population and imbalances between the demand and supply sides of the HFD system. While our analysis, being very macro in nature, does not allow us to make detailed and specific recommendations for improving the HFD system, we wish to reiterate that HFD must be made a central focus of India's economic development program. The economic growth of the country cannot by itself ensure HFD. Sensitivity to wider ramifications resulting from the interdependent nature of the subsystems within the overall HFD system is essential. Better coordination between several interdependent subsystems is essential for effective human development. When India is successful in developing and implementing programs aimed at human factor development, it will place itself in a position whereby it can effectively pursue sustained human-centered development in the years ahead.

REFERENCES

Adjibolosoo, S. 1993. The Human Factor in Development. *The Scandinavian Journal of Development Alternatives* 12 (4): 139–149.

Adjibolosoo, S. 1994. The Human Factor and the Failure of Economic Development and Policies in Africa. In *Perspectives on Economic Development in Africa*, edited by F. Ezeala-Harrison and S. Adjibolosoo. Westport, Conn.: Praeger.

Adjibolosoo, S. 1995. Human Factor Engineering: The Integrating Core of Productivity and Quality Education. In *Productivity and Quality Management Frontiers*, edited by D. J. Sumanth, J. A. Edosomwan, R. Poupart, and C. G. Thor. Norcross, Ga.: Institute of Industrial Engineers.

Agarwal, A. N., and H. O. Varma. 1996. *India: Economic Information Yearbook 1996.* Delhi: National Publishing House.

Aurobindo, S. A. 1975. *The Foundations of Indian Culture*, 63. Pondicherry: Sri Aurobindo Ashram. Quoted in S. K. Chakraborty, 1995, *Ethics in Management: Vedantic Perspectives* (New Delhi: Oxford University Press).

Bhattacharya, U. K. 1988. Engineering Research Institutes, Technology Development and Economic Growth: A Case Study. *Economic and Political Weekly*, 4 June.

Center for Monitoring Indian Economy (CMIE). 1988. *Standard of Living of Indian People.* Bombay: CMIE.

Chakraborty, S. K. 1995. *Ethics in Management: Vedantic Perspectives.* New Delhi: Oxford University Press.

Chaudhuri, P. 1995. Economic Planning in India. In *Industry and Agriculture in India since Independence,* edited by T. V. Satyamurthy. New Delhi: Oxford University Press.

Chaudhuri, S. 1986. Technological Innovation in a Research Laboratory in India: A Case Study. *Research Policy* 15: 89–103.

Chaudhuri, S., and T. K. Moulik. 1986. Learning by Doing. *Economic and Political Weekly,* February.

Chowdhury, S. 1990. Changing Values for Changing Times. *Economic Times,* June.

Clark, C., and K. C. Roy. 1994. *Comparing Development Patterns in South and East Asia: Challenges to Neoclassical Economics.* Boulder, Colo.: Lynne Rienner.

Desai, A. V. 1984. India's Technological Capability: An Analysis of its Achievements and Limits. *Research Policy* 13: 303–310.

Galtung, J. 1982. *Different Theories and Practices of Development.* Paris: United Nations Educational, Scientific and Cultural Organization.

Government of India. 1952. *The First Five Year Plan.* New Delhi: Planning Commission, Government of India.

Government of India. 1957. *Review of First Five Year Plan.* New Delhi: Planning Commission, Government of India.

Government of India. 1961. *Census of India.* New Delhi: Government of India.

Government of India. 1971. *Census of India.* New Delhi: Government of India.

Government of India. 1981. *Census of India.* New Delhi: Government of India.

Government of India. 1986. *Program of Action: National Policy on Education 1986.* New Delhi: Ministry of HRD, Government of India.

Government of India. 1988. *Research and Development Statistics 1986–87.* New Delhi: Department of Science and Technology, Government of India.

Government of India. 1990. *Research and Development Statistics 1988–89.* New Delhi: Department of Science and Technology, Government of India.

India 2001. 1995. Banglore: Indmark.

Jain, A., and A. Uberoy. 1993. Science and Technology Policies: A Comparative Study of the Japanese and Indian Experiences. *Journal of Scientific and Industrial Research* 52: 717–727.

Lavakare, P. J., and R. R. Gulati. 1989. India Moves Ahead in Technology. *Yojana,* 15 August, 55–73.

Manpower Profile India Yearbook. 1995. New Delhi: Institute of Applied Manpower Research.

Monappa, A. 1977. *Ethical Attitudes of Indian Managers.* New Delhi: All India Management Association.

Moon, B. E. 1991. *The Political Economy of Basic Human Needs.* Ithaca: Cornell University Press.

Morris, M. D. 1979. *Measuring the Condition of the World's Poor: The Physical Quality of Life Index.* New York: Pergamon.

Parthasarthi, A. 1994. Acquisition and Development of Technology: The Indian Experiences. In *Problems of India's Development,* edited by R. C. Dutt. New Delhi: India International Centre.

Patel, S. J. 1989. Main Elements in Shaping Future Technology Policies for India. *Economic and Political Weekly* (4 March): 463–466.

Vaidyanathan, A. 1995. The Political Economy of the Evolution of Anti-Poverty Programs. In *Industry and Agriculture in India since Independence*, edited by T.V. Satyamurthy. New Delhi: Oxford University Press.

"We Get Left-Over Technology—An Interview with Dr. R. A. Mashelkar." 1991. *Economic Times*.

World Bank. 1994a. *Human Development Report*. Washington, D.C.: World Bank.

World Bank. 1994b. *World Development Report*. New York: Oxford University Press.

World Bank. 1995. *World Development Report*. New York: Oxford University Press.

The Human Factor and
Underdevelopment in Mexico

Senyo B-S. K. Adjibolosoo

Present-day Mexicans were known as the Aztecs in the ancient past. The Aztecs lived in an area that was rich in minerals. They were a people who attained a high level of civilization that rivaled that of Egypt. They built pyramids and engaged themselves in other activities that not only provided their livelihood, but also shaped their lives. These people made their living from agriculture, cultivating yellow maize and, later, growing wheat and other grains brought by the Europeans (Prescott 1843, 32). The Aztecs were a people given to architecture, art, and culture. They built wonderful palaces, monuments, and other structures. Prescott (1843, 37–38) observed that the Mexicans came to their current location

from the remote regions of the North—the populous hive of nations in the new world, as it has been in the old. They arrived on the borders of Anahuac, towards the beginning of the thirteenth century, some time after the occupation of the land by kindred races. For a long time they did not establish themselves in any permanent residence; but continued shifting their quarters to different parts of the Mexican Valley, enduring all the casualties and hardships of a migratory life. On one occasion, they were enslaved by a more powerful tribe; but their ferocity soon made them formidable to their masters. After a series of wanderings and adventures, which need not shrink from comparison with the most extravagant legends of the heroic ages of antiquity, they at length halted on the southwestern borders of the principal lake, in the year 1325.

They stopped in this area and made a home here.[1] There were, however, different types of rivalry among the groups. A segment of the group seceded from the main body and created its own new area of location. The Mexicans had divided into factions. They were a group of strong, warlike, and hard-working people. Their presence was felt and their reputation spread very quickly throughout the whole valley (Prescott 1843, 38).

In 1971, the population of Mexico was 48,313,438. This population was made up of 70 percent *mestizo* and 28 percent Indian. In 1970, the total population of Mexico City alone was 7,005,855. The main language is Spanish and the Mexican population is predominantly Catholic. The estimated population for 1978 was 66,944,000. This was made up of 55 percent *mestizo* and 29 percent Indian. The estimated population of Mexico City was 8,988,200 in 1978.

The people of Mexico have committed themselves to discovering the path to development. Yet all their attempts in the past did not yield any significant results.

This chapter is aimed at explaining why Mexico has been less successful in its development program. The chapter briefly reviews the history of Mexico and discusses the pertinent social, economic, political, and educational problems. Certain traditional views and policies put forward to deal with these problems are discussed. Approaching the Mexican problem from the human factor perspective, the chapter concludes that the primary foundation of Mexico's problems is HF decay and underdevelopment (Adjibolosoo 1993, 1994, 1995a, 1995b). Thus, until the HF is properly developed, Mexicans cannot expect to achieve social progress, economic development, and political emancipation (Adjibolosoo 1996).

SOCIAL CONDITIONS IN MEXICO, 1900–1910

In 1906, at the Third Mexican Catholic and First Ecumenical Congress, the participants, who engaged themselves in detailed discussions regarding the existing social conditions in Mexico at that time, observed the following: "If we look at the views referring to the family, we find that depopulation, divorces, illegitimate births, infanticides, crimes of adolescents, abandonment of infants, and suicides of minors are increasing every day. With regard to customs, we constantly find an alarming increase of the traffic in immorality, pornography, scandal, crime, suicides, prostitution, and drunkenness. In social relations, pauperism, capitalism, strikes, financial panics, speculation, speculation with public funds, etc., etc. [are increasing]" (quoted in Callcott 1965, 178). They also noted that "Crime increases in proportion to the progress of lay education, as statistics show; and the general upheaval of society is the bitter and putrid fruit of the atheistic school" (quoted in Callcott 1965, 183).

To deal effectively with these problems, the Catholic Mission in Mexico was concerned with and solely committed to moral education. Sunday school programs and activities were used to provide religious instructions aimed at teaching office boys and servants how to do their duties. Laborers were taught and trained to love work and shun any activities that could destroy their lives. Sports, music, and theatrical programs that had moral underpinnings were used to educate the young people in morality.

Mexicans were brought into debt servitude by the Spanish colonizers. They were forced to work for the colonial masters and lived in perpetual bondage. Those who could not pay the cash advances made out to them by their Spanish employers worked for them permanently. Alcoholism was a significant problem for the native Indians. These people drank a great deal and worked very little. They were discouraged about life and never believed that they could improve and enhance their well-being. About 53 percent of all cases of insanity were diagnosed as being the result of alcoholism (Callcott 1965, 192). Therefore, these people did not care very well for their children. People engaged themselves in various types of antisocial activities and behavior. Prostitution and thievery were rampant, indolence was common, and people failed to work hard. Child abuse in its many forms was a common feature of Mexican life. Associated with all these problems were excessive pauperism, criminal activities, immorality, and suicide (Callcott 1965, 178).

Mexico was still impoverished even after 1821, when it became a sovereign nation. Its level of poverty created continuing political difficulties (Cline 1968). As such, Mexico began to look abroad for financial resources to develop. Cline observed, "A vicious circle of deterioration was characteristic: forced to look abroad for capital and loans to rebuild a shattered economy and run their affairs, governments found their credit sinking lower and lower as default upon default made financial aid to them more and more risky; the ruinous rates of interest left smaller and smaller amounts of principal available" (p. 40).

Indeed, the pursuit of progress in Mexico was not an easy one. The Mexican development program was infested with enormous social, economic, political, and educational problems. To add insult to injury, Mexico suffered from a huge debt load. The vicious cycle of poverty led to a continuing decline in personal disposable incomes. The economy was therefore dragged into a trap of economic underdevelopment.

EDUCATIONAL AND SOCIAL DEVELOPMENT

Thompson (1992, 36–52) discusses the development of schools in Mexico in the eighteenth and nineteenth centuries, and concentrates her detailed discussions on the expansion of opportunities for the lower classes and women. She notes that there were approximately 55,000 people in the city of Guanajuato and 400,000 in the whole province in 1792. A royal Spanish decree was ordered in 1790 for the establishment of free access to schools for everyone. To accomplish the requirements of this order, public schools were to be instituted in all communities and these schools were required to offer free education to all poor children of school-going age. During this time period, there were different types of schooling systems developed and used in Mexico.

For example, the *amiga* was a kind of private school system whose program compared closely with what we label today as nursery schools. In this school system, children were taught in the house of the *amiga* (i.e., the teacher). The primary curriculum focused on the memorization of catechism. Teachers were not necessarily expected to be literate before they could serve as *amiga*. Parents were asked to pay some money to defray the cost of the education given to their children. Children could enroll in this program as early as age three. This system of education operated in many small towns until the 1830s (Thompson 1992).

There were also private schools. Most people who taught in these schools were members of a teachers guild. Parents had to pay school fees to have their children enroll in the private school programs all across Mexico. As noted by Thompson, by the close of the eighteenth century there were many private schools that served about 100 boys in the Guanajuato area.

There were public schools as well. The Guanajuato area began to engage itself in the provision and development of secular public primary schools for boys in the 1790s. There was another schooling system usually referred to as the *escuela pia*. There were also free primary day schools which were funded by both towns and parishes. These schools were usually conducted in parishes or convents. As such, the classes were taught by both priests and nuns. In addition to the teaching of a religious curriculum that involved the memorization of the catechism, children were helped to learn to read and write. Moral education regarding how to conduct oneself properly was an integral part of this curriculum. These schools served the Mexican population through to 1810. By the year 1813, six schools were publicly funded to serve more than 500 children in the city. In distribution, there were two secular schools for boys, two for girls, and two *escuelas pias* for boys only (Thompson 1992).

As observed by Thompson (1992, 22), the curriculum used in all schools placed significant emphasis on religious instruction. The primary objective was to train the children to acquire personality characteristics that would help them develop good manners and be good citizens. As noted, children were taught reading, writing, and spelling. By the year 1810, civics was added to the school curriculum. In most cases, the curriculum was gender based, in that girls learned needlework, drawing, music, and home economics in the private schools and boys were taught calligraphy, grammar, mathematics, history, and art (Thompson 1992). The regular day school activities were conducted between eight o'clock and eleven o'clock in the morning and the second section of the school's activities happened between two o'clock and five o'clock in the afternoon—five days a week. In some cases, children attended classes on Saturday mornings. There were no regular school activities on holy days.

Since those who crafted the educational program believed that personally acquired skills were relevant to one's effective performance in society, work-related training and apprenticeship were added to the school curriculum after 1805. In most cases, it was students who had already graduated that enrolled themselves in apprenticeship programs of their own choices. As has been the case in most places all over the world, most girls discontinued schooling after the age of ten or twelve. In a few cases, those girls who continued their schooling programs either went to attend special colleges or convent schools (Thompson 1992, 23). On the other hand, boys continued their schooling programs and attended Latin grammar schools, colleges, seminaries or convent schools, or the military academy.

Teaching in the eighteenth century carried certain risks, in that teachers sometimes never got paid on time. For example, Thompson (1992, 25) noted that, in 1791, the town council was ordered to pay a primary school teacher, Gregorio Rodriguez, his salary. This order was, however, not carried out until two months later. In a similar case, Doroteo Romero, the director of a boys primary school, was not paid any salary for a period of three years.

After having declared its independence from Spain in 1821, Mexican authorities revised and reorganized the structure and administration of formal education. The local government in Guanajuato continued to give strong leadership to its own educational program. However, in other areas, such as Mexico City, both private and church influence was still significantly strong. In 1826, using a combination of the contents of the 1812 Spanish and the 1824 Mexican Constitutions, the state of Guanajuato made sure that public schools were jointly administered and funded by municipalities and the state, with the state determining the curriculum and its contents. By 1815, the educational curriculum was highly secularized, to such a point that the clergy were not allowed to teach in the public schools of the city of Guanajuato. Thompson (1992, 27) notes, "The state constitution of 1826 and, later, legislation by the state congress mandated all towns and villages to establish public primary schools for the purpose of teaching children to be religious, patriotic, and useful citizens."

To promote the primary education program, Mexico used the Lancasterian method in the nineteenth century. This method was developed by Joseph Lancaster in the latter half of the eighteenth century. This method used the more mature students to provide instructions to the younger ones. The procedure provided the opportunity for many children to be instructed at the same time. Indeed, it has been noted that the method created the environment for continuing discipline through ongoing surveillance, monitors, and rules. These created the environment for the development of obedient citizens. The Lancasterian method was used in Guanajuato after the town council voted for its adoption in June 1827. Opposition against the use of this methodology was, however, based on the view that its use was not compatible with Catholicism. Though the primary curriculum stressed religious instruction and behavior, the Guanajuato leadership did its best to diminish the influence of the clergy in the school system (see details in Thompson 1992, 26–31).

Vaughan (1994, 105) observed that three decades after the overthrow of Porfirio Diaz, the Mexican government tried to promote social change in the country. Rural schools were to provide the kind of education that encouraged literacy and ongoing learning. This program, however promoted modernization and forced the peasants to crave an urban lifestyle. According to Vaughan (1994, 106), the desire of the post-1910 Mexican revolution reformers was to transform, through educational reform, the peasants, who they believed to be a "mass of sickly, lethargic, superstitious pariahs," into "literate, sober, clean, scientific, market-oriented, and patriotic farmers." They promoted the teaching of practical skills such as farming, beekeeping, health care, child rearing, and many others. Between 1920 and 1940, Mexican educational policy was aimed at the transformation of the behavior of the rural people (Vaughan 1994, 108).

Socialist education was introduced in December 1934. The primary objective of this introduction was to destroy the religious and superstitious aspects of education and to remove clerical power. Many people, however, questioned the value of socialist education in Mexico at the time. Those who did not believe in the usefulness of socialist education argued that it produced totalitarianism and incompetence. President Lazaro Cardenas purged the educational system of the growing antireligious sentiments in 1936. Those who believed in socialist education always argued that it provided a significant platform through which teachers could fight against social injustice and hence promote national progress. The adherents of the socialist philosophy believed that it would promote land reform, trade union rights, cooperative marketing, sanitation, science, and modern agriculture (Vaughan 1994, 109). In recent years, various Mexican governments have engaged themselves in programs aimed at the promotion of basic education, adult education and training, preparatory schools, and institutions of higher learning. However, regardless of what has been done to refocus education throughout the years, the Mexican education system failed to develop the HF in the national labor force. This failure has had a devastating impact on the Mexican economy.

THE STATE OF THE MEXICAN ECONOMY

Regardless of the usual uncertainties associated with elections, the 1970 election year in Mexico was a relatively peaceful one. The Mexican economy continued to grow at almost the same pace as it had in the 1960s. For example, the gross national product experienced a 6.4-percent real growth rate. During the 1960s, Mexico's per capita income rose by 46 percent in real terms. This rate of growth was significantly different from what it was in previous decades (i.e., 39% in the 1940s and 26% in the 1950s).

While public expenditure was excessively high before the 1970 election, when Diaz Ordaz was elected into power in 1970 he significantly reduced public spending. Diaz's primary objective for doing so was "to keep in reserve a number of large projects that might have had to be activated if a persistent economic recession in the U.S. had spilled over into Mexico" (*Britannica Book of the Year* 1971, 510). A significant proportion of public expenditure was channeled into public works, in addition to the building of the underground railway of Mexico City in the second half of the 1970s. During this same period, the growing consumer demand led to continuing growth in business investment. This demand was due to increases in minimum wages (minimum wages increased by 15% for urban workers and 16% for rural dwellers). Imported inflation, however, created price instability in Mexico in 1969. The official cost-of-living index rose by 3.5 percent in 1959. When the prices of such items as steel, newspapers, textiles, restaurant charges, and building materials continued to increase, the general price level in Mexico continued its upward trend. By the middle of the 1970s, the wholesale price index had risen by 6.4 percent. It was at this point that the government began to take steps to control the growing rate of inflation in the country. As an initial step toward the attainment of this objective, credit conditions became difficult in the latter part of the 1970s.

Indeed, the Mexican economy experienced tremendous expansion between 1972 and 1973. There were huge increases in the production and sale of different industrial items. Gross domestic product was estimated to have declined slightly, from 7.3 percent in 1973 to 7 percent in 1974. While inflation was rising, the external balance of trade was also plummeting significantly. Certain factors identified as the key causes of continuing increases in the retail price index included the rising costs of imported items, excess internal demand for goods and services, and increases in the prices of petroleum products (*Britannica Book of the Year* 1975, 481–482).

However, between 1978 and 1981, the growth rate of the Mexican economy continued to decline further. In 1982, Mexico's economic growth rate was only 0.2 percent. The huge foreign debt had finally taken its toll. Inflation was about 100 percent. Capital flight escalated, and Mexico's export earnings declined significantly because of the huge oil glut on the world market. The rate of growth of the Mexican economy continued to decline from about 4.5 percent in 1990 to 3.5 percent in 1991, to 2.6 percent in 1992. This trend of continuing decline in the economic growth rate persisted. Yet, Mexico ranks very high among petroleum producers.

The government attempted to stimulate exports in 1970, and exports increased by 15.7 percent. Though the government controlled imports, they increased by about 5.9 percent. This created a trade deficit that was $70.2 million less than what it was in 1968 (*Britannica Book of the Year* 1971, 510). The continuing growth in imports led to ongoing deficits, even though tourism boomed during this period. For example, the total number of tourists visiting Mexico in 1969 increased by 11.5 percent.

Mexico is excessively rich in oil and natural gas. A significant amount of Mexican gas was sold to the United States in the late 1970s. Mexico signed agreements to sell oil to France, Spain, Canada, Japan, Sweden, and Brazil from the 1980s onward. Mexico signed trade agreements with Spain, Czechoslovakia, France, and Sweden for technical cooperation. Yet, regardless of these activities, the Mexican economy remained in perpetual shambles, and such problems as growing external debt, increasing unemployment, inflation, poverty, low incomes, and so on were rampant.

MEXICAN PROBLEMS AND THEIR
PERCEIVED ORIGINS

A haze of smog is usually trapped over Mexico City twenty-four hours a day because of the mountains and hills that surround the city. Mexico City is populated by sprawling slums and shanty towns. By mid-1979, the estimated number of people dwelling in Mexico City was 14.2 million. Inmigration from other parts of the country has contributed significantly to the continuing growth of Mexico City. Usually, as noted by Sarmiento (1980), the men migrate into Mexico City first. They are then followed later by their wives, children, and other relatives. This second phase happens after the migrant men have found jobs and places to live. For these migrants, life is very difficult most of the time. Most of the work available to them is hard physical labor. Since such jobs are usually located further away from the residential areas of the working class, it is not uncommon for these migrant laborers to spend five to six hours traveling in overcrowded buses and subway trains to and from work (Sarmiento 1980, 528). Once in the city, most migrant labor never returns to the countryside—whether they have jobs or not.

This problem has been compounded because Mexico's agrarian reform failed to provide the peasants with lands for cultivation. Lack of land and viable economic opportunities in the rural areas promoted hopelessness in the countryside. Thus, most people left for the city to look for jobs that are usually nonexistent. The ongoing inmigration of men, women, and children from rural to urban areas led to the creation of highly depressed slums and squatter areas. The way of life and the mood of such people are excessively depressing. Drugs, prostitution, teenage pregnancies, and so on are common. Under these conditions, most people hardly ever have a reason to live. As such, both hopelessness and helplessness reign supreme in Mexican social, economic, and political life.

Mexico City is not only polluted, it is also noisy. The processing of food is most often accomplished under unsanitary conditions. About 50 percent of the city dwellers are said to suffer from gastrointestinal, respiratory, or nervous problems (Sarmiento 1980, 528). Traffic congestion in Mexico City is beyond description. A few hours of being caught in such traffic conditions is horrifying, and the frustration this creates increases tensions among motorists and pedestrians alike. Indeed, such experiences usually create ongoing emotional problems and antagonisms. They also lead to the loss of vital work hours and hence loss of output, reduce personal efficiency, and encourage indolence because of the fatigue produced in the labor force. The thought of being caught in traffic also diminishes employee desire to get on crowded buses and trains to go to work. As is usually the case, diminished desire for work produces low employee productivity.

The sources of Mexico's problems are as varied as the number of scholars who write about these problems. Many scholars who have taken a detailed look at Mexico's problems have come out with conclusions suggesting that the problems come as results of the absence of representative democracy, continuing human rights violations, excessive discrimination against indigenous populations, injustice, inequity, unfairness, poverty, and so on. Castaneda (1995, 3), for example, observed

Among my ideas that ran counter to the received wisdom of the day were the conclusion that the absence of democracy in Mexico was not just a political drawback but one of the principal causes of the glaring social inequities that plague Mexico; that cold-turkey, free-market policies would not solve Mexico's economic dilemmas; that only a combination of state and market, trade liberalization and protectionism, redistribution and integration with the United States could place Mexico back on the path of economic growth; and that better and more constructive relationship with the United States could not be based on doing whatever Washington desired or mistaking Mexico's interests for those of its northern neighbor.

Many scholars have pointed out, quite correctly, that Mexico has suffered from continuing financial mismanagement. The excessive mismanagement of the Mexican economy has created serious balance-of-payments problems since 1992. Political turmoil reached its peak during the reign of Carlos Salinas. Subsequently, Mexico experienced negative growth in its per capita income. Corruption and other types of illegal activities reached their apogee under Carlos Salinas's administration. To add insult to injury, the Mexican drug trade advanced to higher levels. Political assassinations were common in the country. Those who engaged in criminal behavior and activities did not allow anybody to stand in their way.

Between 1993 and 1995, Mexico experienced significantly higher levels of unemployment. For example, among Mexico City's most economically active, the unemployment rate was estimated as 6.3 percent in mid-1979 (Sarmiento 1980, 528). Many skilled and unskilled labor suffered from severe unemployment and its attendant problems. The lack of critical skills was a result of the inability to attend and complete schooling. In Mexico, education is only compulsory up to grade six. For this reason, many children drop out of school at about age twelve and join the labor force to make a living or make income to supplement the family budget. Since most children usually lack critical skills because they drop out of school too early, they are very often unable to find decent jobs. As such, most of them engage themselves in such activities as car washing, shoe shining, selling of assorted manufactured items, and so on. For some women (including young girls), prostitution is the primary means by which they make a living. It is not easy for these people to find good rental homes in Mexico City because rent is usually excessively high and the income they generate from such illegal activities is excessively low. Criminal activities have become part and parcel of most street children's lives in Mexico City, especially in the dwelling areas of the working classes. Similarly, those who engage themselves in domestic services hardly ever make enough money to care properly for themselves. The best of all Mexican labor usually migrates elsewhere. These individuals travel far and wide looking for employment opportunities in which they can utilize their acquired skills. Such opportunities provide them with higher incomes with which they acquire the basic necessities of life. The bulk of this labor force heads for the United States.

While national exports plummeted in 1988, imports increased in magnitude. From this time period to 1992, Mexico's current account deficit ballooned. For example, Mexico's trade balance worsened from $4.3 billion in 1990 to $20 billion in 1992 (see details in Castaneda 1995, 52). What worsened the debt situation was the excessively high Mexican taste for imported goods and services. Since Mexicans have come to believe that what was manufactured elsewhere (i.e., in the United States) was better than those items produced in Mexico, they preferred to purchase foreign items as opposed to those manufactured within the country. It seems to be the case that most people believe that the use of foreign commodities is a status symbol. Those who purchase and use imported items usually view themselves as being better off than others who consume items made in Mexico. Yet the irony is that most of the so-called "Made in the U.S." items have actually been manufactured in Mexico. In most cases, these items are manufactured in Mexico, later labeled in the United States, and then exported back to the Mexican market and sold at exorbitant prices. Thus, because of the low demand for locally manufactured items, the Mexican economy has always experienced significantly low levels of economic growth. Coupled with these difficulties, high oil prices led to a continued worsening of Mexico's balance-of-payments position. Since the magnitude of Mexico's international debt is huge, higher interest rates created further external debt problems. The continuing economic problems led to currency devaluations in 1976, 1983, and 1987, and the rising unemployment rate continues to lead to ongoing social decay in Mexico.

Castaneda (1995, 5) believing that Mexico's problems go beyond the factors discussed so far, observed the following:

The blame for the debacle itself, however, lies elsewhere. It must first of all be placed squarely on the lack of democratic reform in Mexico under Salinas. Economic mistakes, political abuses, and the dramatic increase in inequality in what was already one of the world's most unjust societies might not have been entirely avoided through democratic rule and authentic accountability, but they were absolutely inevitable in the absence of representative democracy. Without it, overcoming the weight of tradition, corruption, and triumphalism (often fanned from abroad) was simply impossible. It was not just a pity, however, that Salinas did not practice glasnost along with his supposed—and failed—perestroiker [sic]; the lack of the former condemned the latter to dogmatic zeal and ultimate failure. The restraints that democratic politics would have imposed on Salinas's "modernization" drive and economic reforms would have allowed Mexico to achieve the right mix of change and stability, modernity and tradition, competitiveness and justice.

To say the least, Mexico's problems are numerous. Though scholars usually agree on what the problems are, they hardly ever agree on what the actual causes are and how to deal successfully with these problems. The problem, however, is that policies based on orthodox development theorizing, policy formulation, and implementation have all failed to bring long-lasting relief to Mexico. In what follows, it is argued that Mexico's problems have their origin in HF decay and underdevelopment (Adjibolosoo 1993, 1994, 1995a, 1995b).

HUMAN FACTOR DECAY: THE PRIMARY SOURCE OF MEXICAN PROBLEMS

Mexico's problems are usually viewed as being either social, economic, or political, or all three combined. As such, policies pursued for many decades have usually aimed at dealing with observed social, economic, political, and educational problems. However, regardless of the magnitude of the number of plans, policies, programs, and projects that have been used to deal with Mexico's numerous problems, this nation seems to be sinking deeper and deeper into much more serious social, economic, political, and educational problems. This being the case, if policies being pursued currently were focused on dealing with the real causes of Mexico's problems, the amount of policy failure being experienced in Mexico should diminish in size, because Mexico's ongoing problems go deeper than have been perceived by traditional development theorizing. In view of this observation, the critical question is as follows: What is the primary source or foundation of Mexico's inherent social, economic, political, and educational problems?

To answer this question appropriately, it is important to note that the Mexican educational program, though it has been very successful in helping people to acquire significant amounts of human capital, has not been that successful in preparing people for a life of service to themselves and to the Mexican society at large. Indeed, Mexican education and training activities are continuously failing to help Mexicans acquire the requisite HF characteristics that make development happen (Adjibolosoo 1995a). The Mexican education system does not have a specific program of activities that would lead students to acquire such qualities as integrity, responsibility, accountability, commitment, trustworthiness, loyalty, and the like. In reality, many Mexicans have come to view education as a basic means of getting out of poverty. As such, when Mexicans go to school, the primary concern of most students is what to study in order to work in one of the most prestigious professions so as to make a significant amount of money on which to live.

Teachers are usually not well paid for their commitment and work. As such, there is little incentive for such teachers to give their best in preparing the youth for a life of service to all humanity. Though the catechism is learned in most schools, it is but a mere rote memory learning process. In many regards,

Mexican education programs are no more than the government's way of attempting to indoctrinate people to do what is expected of them. In many cases, materials being used in Mexican schools are outdated, have contents that are hardly ever relevant to Mexican society, or both. Teacher education requires a significant overhaul to prepare teachers for the task of educating, training, and mentoring of youth to be responsible citizens and leaders of Mexican society in the future. Indeed, teachers need to be helped to perceive that productive education must always go beyond the basic view in Mexican society that education is merely a key for personal survival in a difficult society or a route through which one can buy oneself out of poverty. That is, to the Mexican, formal education is nothing more than a process whereby people obtain certificates that serve later as excellent meal tickets (see details in Adjibolosoo 1996).

Mexico, like many other developing countries, is not only stuck in traditions and archaic cultural practices, but also many Mexicans are extremely unwilling to embrace positive change. They are servants to their culture. As things stand today, though a significant number of Mexicans are excessively creative in their own areas of expertise, they lack personal and group industry. Many Mexicans are very inefficient and ineffective in what they do. They lack vision, mission, and a concrete plan with which to accomplish these visions and missions. Mexico's poor and frail educational programs continue to fail to help people develop all their human abilities and potentialities. As such, the core of the Mexican problem is the state of individual personality characteristics (Adjibolosoo 1995a).

Because a significant proportion of the Mexican population lacks well-developed HF traits, most of them perceive themselves as big-time losers in life. When one travels around most of Mexico and interviews people, one gets the general feeling that most rural and urban dwellers of Mexico have given up on life. They feel that there is very little they can do to affect their current conditions of life and economic well-being. As such, people have little motivation to see to it that positive changes come into their society. The strong negative attitudes of Mexicans deny people the ability to continue dreaming and looking for real ways to make their dreams come true. Since people's perceptions and views about change in Mexico are very narrow, many do not believe that Mexico could achieve any significant progress in its development program.

To most Mexicans, corruption is an accepted way of life. Those who do not have the necessary tools to make the best out of life usually go out of their way to engage in corrupt behavior to acquire additional financial resources to supplement their work incomes. Those who are in positions of trust continue to extort money from others before serving them. For example, while some people can obtain a driver's license easily, without having to take the necessary driving tests because they paid the required amount of bribe, those who do not have the money to bribe the officials usually have to go through the driving test several times. In many cases, people still fail the driving test, not because they do not know how to drive, but because the official in charge sees such people as a means of making additional bribe income. Their hope is that when such people fail a few more times, they will be more willing to pay the bribe and get a driver's license. This phenomenon is highly pervasive in Mexico as well as other developing countries (see detailed discussions on this issue in Adjibolosoo 1994).

To the corrupt Mexican, it feels good to cheat a system that has continuously cheated him or her for decades. In colonial days, most Mexicans saw the colonizers as looters. They were a bunch of people who usurped Mexican birthrights and denied them the ability to enjoy the riches of their own homeland. Mexicans viewed the Spanish colonizers as people who came in, exploited Mexican resources, and shipped these resources out to Spain. Thus, even many decades after independence, Mexicans still see their own governments as foreign bodies (see the case of Africa in this regard as discussed by Adjibolosoo 1995a).

People know very well that the Mexican system is excessively corrupt. As such, they do not think that this corruption will go away that easily in Mexico. Some Mexicans believe that the best way to effectively deal with corruption in Mexico is to engage oneself in corrupt activities to acquire some financial resources for one's use. There is the belief among many rural and urban Mexican populations that regardless of how hard one tries to alter his or her current state of well-being, one will never achieve any lasting positive results. Some people have come to the understanding and conclusion that if you try hard, you will get nothing, and if you do not try at all, you will lose nothing. Thus, why try at all? This is one of the primary reasons why most Mexicans have very little desire to see to it that things change for the better in their country. People have lost hope in the system. The ongoing lack of trust and loyalty evident in the whole country continues to rob people of the desire to work hard and fight for positive changes.

It is, therefore, understandable why many Mexicans would engage themselves in such activities as illegal drug trading, prostitution, and child labor. The continuing HF decay and underdevelopment in Mexico continuously promote social decay, economic stagnation, and political uncertainties. As these problems continue to escalate, they create additional problems that are usually much more complicated to deal with successfully. The policies being pursued continue to ignore the fact that the primary foundation of these problems are HF decay and underdevelopment in Mexico.

DEALING WITH MEXICO'S PROBLEMS: A SET OF ORTHODOX SOLUTIONS

The Mexican economy has experienced many difficulties for decades. The overall current account deficit is approximately $23 billion (approximately 7% of Mexico's GDP). Recall that between 1972 and 1975, Mexico's GDP grew at an astronomical rate of 16 percent. President Echeverria traveled to Germany, Austria, Italy, and Yugoslavia in February 1974 to forge economic relationships with these nations. He also visited Costa Rica, Ecuador, Peru, Argentina, Brazil, Venezuela, and Jamaica in July 1974. His major objective was to improve both economic and political relations. He was also committed to encouraging these countries to support the proposal for a U.N. Charter of Economic Rights and Duties of states. He was able to secure agreements with Brazil for technological and scientific cooperation. In addition, both countries agreed to improve tourist activities and sea and air transportation systems between them. They also considered the establishment of a joint committee to see to how to improve and strengthen economic ties between the two nations. There were agreements between Mexico, Peru, and Ecuador to pursue technical cooperation in the petroleum sector. Indeed, many other agreements were signed with other Latin American countries involving different areas of technical and economic cooperation.

The government pursued a program of action to reduce inflation. Some of these measures included tightening control on money supply and government expenditure, promoting private investment, and strengthening price and income policies. These programs seemed to have been successful in the first quarter of 1974. Indeed, while Mexico was experiencing a significant expansion in its economic activities, increases in domestic prices were beginning to slow down slightly. But by the middle of 1974, inflation began to escalate once again. At this point in time, the official trade union organization, the *Confederacion de Trabajadores Mexicanos*, requested a 35 percent increase in wages. It was ready to support this request with a strike action if the government did not yield to this demand. The government responded immediately by freezing prices of fifty-three basic consumer items in June 1974. The activities of the federal agricultural marketing agency were expanded to include dealing with speculation and hoarding (*Britannica Book of the Year* 1975, 482). As has always been the case, Mexico's external trade balance continued to weaken. In May 1973, the government promulgated a law to promote Mexican investment over foreign investment. At this point in time, it was made known that Mexico had become self-sufficient in crude oil production. It was believed that the newly discovered oil wells in the states of Tabasco and Chiapas would place Mexico in a viable position to become a net exporter of crude oil.

In 1974, Echeverria's administration was confronted with political problems. Terrorist activities escalated in the country. These activities led to several kidnappings and ongoing demands for excessive ransom fees. Guerrilla activities dotted the surface of the whole country.

To deal with Mexico's ongoing difficulties, Salinas attempted to attract foreign capital into the country. Foreign direct investment was excessively low in the 1980s. In the attempt to attract foreign investment into the country, domestic interest rates were raised excessively high. He pursued free-trade agreements with Canada and the United States. In addition to these programs, massive privatization programs were also pursued. Indeed, there were moves to privatize the Mexican banking system. The government did its best to encourage capital inflow by reducing restrictions on foreign investment.

Levy and Szekely (1983, 3) note that Mexico has experienced significant levels of "poverty, malnutrition, disease, unemployment, underemployment, illiteracy, and inadequate education." These problems have been passed on from one Mexican generation to another—with each generation not being able to deal successfully with these problems. Mexico also experiences severe unequal income distribution. Some are excessively rich, but many are very poor and live in poverty-stricken areas and can hardly ever fend for themselves.

The revolution in the south has been staged by Mexicans who believe that they have been cheated for far too long. This group of Mexicans is fighting for their own independence from the rest of Mexico. They want to be treated like any other Mexicans and be given the chance to make a decent living for themselves. As such, they are fighting for land, freedom, liberty, and human rights. If nothing is done to deal successfully with the economic problems of the south, the revolution will never come to a permanent end.

POLICY RECOMMENDATIONS

Mexico is very rich in natural resources. As such, what Mexico needs today to achieve a sustained human-centered development is not necessarily huge financial resources and ongoing technical assistance from abroad. Mexicans have all the necessary resources and the required human capital they need to develop. What is missing is the requisite HF characteristics (Adjibolosoo 1995a, 1995b). Until Mexican leaders and citizens come to that point where they perceive clearly that they must drop their masks of ignorance, there is very little they can do to achieve sustained human-centered development. Mexicans need to develop their HF characteristics so that they can perceive that the problems they experience today are due to ongoing HF decay and underdevelopment. The people need enlightenment, encouragement, and continuing motivation. Mexicans need to cease blaming their problems on other people, especially the Spanish colonizers. Instead, it is critical to develop aspirations and wake up the Mexican conscience and psyche once again. What is foreign may not always be better than what is domestic. The mere fact that Mexico is so close to the United States and Canada and yet cannot develop is not really a puzzle. This is so because the Mexican HF is not as developed as those of Canada and the United States. When one studies Mexican society in detail, one can see that if Mexico continuously fails to develop the necessary HF characteristics in its citizens it will never accomplish the goals of its development program.

Mexicans have to stop running away from their problems of corruption and pull their heads out of the soils of ignorance and apathy. It is now time to face the challenges of HF decay and set up education and training programs to help them prepare the population for a life of integrity, accountability, responsibility, loyalty, trustworthiness, and so on (Adjibolosoo 1996). The rottenness that currently roosts in the hearts of Mexican leaders and civil servants has to be expunged through well-designed, organized, and carefully implemented educational programs. It is one thing to learn religious dogma and catechism, it is quite another issue to live one's life by the standards prescribed by the learned dogma. Mexico needs a long-term non-military-led social revolution that will focus on continuing HF development. Such a revolution must, of necessity, bring every Mexican to the point where he or she will perceive that individual inputs into the nation's development program count significantly. People need to be trained and educated to perceive that it is people who make development happen (Adjibolosoo 1995a).

Exposed corrupt political leaders, civil servants, and citizens should not only be arrested and put into prison for a few years, but they must also be assisted to comprehend the depth of the damages their corrupt activities have unleashed on Mexican society. A program of personal reformation must be designed and used to develop positive HF traits in these fallen national leaders, civil servants, and citizens. Any successes achieved through the new HF development curriculum will go a long way in preparing every Mexican to participate in the national development program. Mexico needs education for citizenship development and nation building (see details in Chapter 13) that continuously concentrates on HF development. Every Mexican needs to rise up and help rebuild the decaying society and stagnating national economy. If Mexico, however, refuses to focus on HF development programs in the years ahead, its social, economic, political, and educational future will be bleak indeed.

NOTE

1. A Mexican legend has it that when they arrived they beheld a royal eagle that was perching on the stem of a prickly pear with a serpent in his talons and his wings broadly opened to the rising sun. The migrating Mexicans perceived this as a sign for them to discontinue their migratory journey and dwell here, and they did (see details in Prescott 1843, 37–38).

REFERENCES

Adjibolosoo, S. 1993. The Human Factor in Development. *The Scandinavian Journal of Development Alternatives* 12 (4): 139–149.

Adjibolosoo, S. 1994. The Human Factor and the Failure of Development Planning and Economic Policy in Africa. In *Perspectives on Economic Development in Africa*, edited by F. Ezeala-Harrison and S. Adjibolosoo. Westport, Conn.: Praeger.

Adjibolosoo, S. 1995a. *The Human Factor in Developing Africa*. Westport, Conn.: Praeger.

Adjibolosoo, S. 1995b. The Significance of the Human Factor in African Economic

Development. In *The Significance of the Human Factor in African Economic Development*, edited by S. Adjibolosoo. Westport, Conn.: Praeger.

Adjibolosoo, S., ed. 1996. *Human Factor Engineering and the Political Economy of African Development*. Westport, Conn.: Praeger.

Britannica Book of the Year. 1971. Chicago: Encyclopaedia Britannica.

Britannica Book of the Year. 1975. Chicago: Encyclopaedia Britannica.

Callcott, W. H. 1965. *Liberalism in Mexico 1857–1929*. Hamden, Conn.: Archon Books.

Castaneda, J. G. 1995. *Mexican Shock: Its Meaning for the US*. New York: The New Press.

Cline, H. F. 1968. *The United States and Mexico*. New York: Atheneum.

Levy, D., and G. Szekely. 1983. *Mexico: Paradoxes of Stability and Change*. Boulder, Colo.: Westview Press.

Prescott, W. H. 1843. *History of the Conquest of Mexico with a Preliminary View of the Ancient Mexican Civilization and the Life of the Conqueror Hernando Cortes*. New York: Hurst and Company.

Sarmiento, S. 1980. Mexico City: A Troubled Giant. In *Britannica Book of the Year, 1980*. Chicago: Encyclopaedia Britannica.

Thompson, A. T. 1992. Children and Schooling in Guanajuato, Mexico, 1790–1840. *SECOLAS Annals* 22 (March): 36–52.

Vaughan, M. K. 1994. The Educational Project of the Mexican Revolution: The Response of Local Societies (1934–1940). In *Molding Hearts and Minds: Education, Communications, and Social Change in Latin America*, edited by J. A. Britton. Wilmington, Del.: Jaguar Books.

The Human Factor in a Small Developing Country: The Case of Bolivia

Carlos Aguirre B.

Bolivia is one of Latin America's least developed countries. It is a well-pre-served multicultural, multiethnic, and multilingual society. Its population of nearly 7 million is divided into different ethnic groups, each keeping its own cultural identity. Since 1982, when a democratically elected government was installed, the country has enjoyed a stable political climate and there are no indications that this situation will be altered in any way in the near or long term. The present government has launched important reforms to consolidate democracy. The level of commitment to democratic values has risen, changing the image of political instability which has characterized the country through-out its history. This level of commitment was due, in part, to profound struc-tural changes that have been taking place in the near past and is also a sign of the improvement of the human factor, as defined by Adjibolooso (1995).[1]

Accompanying the political situation, Bolivia has also enjoyed economic stability. Since 1985, the macroeconomic indicators have shown improvements. Gross domestic product was approximately U.S.$7 billion in 1995 and has grown at the rate of about 4 percent per year. Per capita income is around U.S.$800, and inflation has been held below 15 percent annually. In the 1990s, private investment grew moderately and public investment fluctuated around U.S.$500 million per annum, of which nearly 50 percent had its origin in Official Development Aid, representing 14 percent of GNP.

Raw materials and intermediate goods constitute 91.6 percent of exports. By 1995, exports had reached U.S.$1 billion. The commercial balance has a deficit of about U.S.$200 million, of which 60 percent are high-technology products. The lack of diversification of exports, in particular manufactured goods, is an indication of the low level of industrialization of the country. The latter, as will be discussed further on, is influenced strongly by the human factor. In spite of improvements in the economy, social indicators continue to show the difficulties affecting a great majority of the Bolivian society. It is felt by some groups that gains in the consolidation of democracy and economic stability may be lost if such conditions are not reversed in the very short term.

The population growth rate is 2.1 percent, 58 percent of the population is urban, the economically active population is 50 percent, women's participation is 38 percent, the fertility rate is 4.6 percent, child mortality stands at 91 per 1,000, the mean population age is twenty-four years, life expectancy is 60.7 years, and the number of doctors per 10,000 inhabitants is 10.1. In view of these statistics, there are at least six immediate challenges that confront Bolivia. These are all related to the human factor:

1. Alleviation of poverty

2. Elimination of the coca–cocaine circuit

3. Reduction of the present overdependence on official development aid

4. Improvement in the production of goods of higher value added and increasing the nation's level of active participation in the world economy

5. Reduction of environmental degradation

6. Expansion and improvement in education

HUMAN FACTOR DEVELOPMENT: PAST AND PRESENT

The causes of the economic and social underdevelopment and today's challenges have a strong human factor dimension. Their origins can be found in the history of the country. Before the establishment of the Spanish colony in the early sixteenth century, several cultures had superseded and coexisted, often clashing violently with each other. Some, like the Inca Empire, constituted vertical political systems where dissension and other means of popular expression were not encouraged. Others, like the Aymara culture, were more decentralized and thus prone to internal developments as seen from the human perspective.

The Spanish colony brought a new culture which intermingled with the existing ones and became the dominant force for nearly three centuries. It represented a vertical political system much like what it had replaced. Independence was obtained in 1825 after a long period of armed struggle, and the new republic, though based on the principles of equality, was a form of continuation of the rule of the more powerful elites.

The human factor dimension was strongly influenced by the culture of each period and had little chance to develop. In fact, with a few notable exceptions brought about by some governments and the Catholic Church to improve educational conditions, there have been no national objectives regarding the existence of human factor development throughout Bolivia's long history of existence as a nation. There are at least four reasons that explain the causes of underdevelopment that are of more recent nature and are, in a way, common to many countries in Latin America (ul Haq 1995):

1. Lack of incentives to invest in the education and health of the people, technological advancement, and the improvement of performance of vocational institutions
2. Uneven distribution of wealth and land
3. Lack of export-oriented vision and its impact on creativity
4. Lack of government leaders who will assume a real supporting role in public and private institutions that are dedicated to the advancement of production, knowledge, and culture

THE BOLIVIAN PERCEPTIONS OF DEVELOPMENT

In order to understand the human factor in Bolivia, it is interesting to mention the present perception that the Bolivian society has about the economy and other key social issues (U.N. Development Program 1996). Nearly 29 percent of the society has a very strong regional identity, which may lead to significant ethnic conflicts in the case of worsening socioeconomic conditions. Seventy-nine percent of people currently believe that the country's economic condition has worsened in the last ten years. Ninety-two percent believe that only the elites are benefiting from the present economic stability. The latter indicates a growing state of social inconformity. Regarding employment, the situation is still bad; 89 percent of the people believe that the situation is either the same or has deteriorated further in the last decade. In their perception, the idea of stability is associated not only with inflation or other macroeconomic variables, but is also measured and evaluated by parameters that relate to economic certainty or uncertainty.

The political class is under heavy criticism. Fifty-three percent of the population believe that politicians should be changed. Seventy-three percent of the Bolivian population know that acts of corruption have increased. As such, they demand justice. Seventy percent of Bolivian society perceive that their opinions are not taken into consideration because of a faulty administrative system. On the other hand, 86 percent of people are confident that a concerted action between government and society can be a real and positive source of economic problems in the country.

From these perceptions, several facts are clear. The first is that there is a tendency to look at everything negatively. Thus, enthusiasm for transformation is limited. Second, people still depend significantly on the state. Third, society recognizes few mechanisms for social integration, especially when dealing with the more vulnerable groups. Fourth, there exists a restricted national cultural logic whose capacity to adapt to modern change is limited. Fifth, there is credibility in state and political institutions. Finally, the number of channels of communication between state and society are insufficient. Unless these problems are dealt with successfully, long-term development will continue to elude Bolivia. To achieve continuing, sustained human-centered development, the importance of the human factor has to be recognized and made an integrating core of Bolivia's development program (see Adjibolosoo 1993, 1994, 1995). Its development can trigger a definite turnaround in the economic and social progress of the country.

THE EDUCATIONAL SYSTEM

Knowledge plays a key role in shaping the human factor. Thus, every society needs to develop and use relevant knowledge systems. A knowledge system is defined as a system which "comprises institutions that control and regulate the flow and use of knowledge in the economy and society, together with the linkages among them and the outside world. The system includes the stocks and flows of knowledge, its sources and uses, and identifies leverage points— those institutions whose creation or strengthening is likely to promote the wider diffusion of knowledge in the population and lower barriers to its assimilation and use" (National Research Council 1996).

Though a thorough assessment of the system in Bolivia needs to be made, it is relevant to point out briefly the situation of at least two of its key elements: education and science and technology. The existing model of education in Bolivia has not been efficient. As such, it is not able to respond to the changes being brought into being by both international transformations and national challenges. The Bolivian education system has produced generations of scholars who pursue extensive theorizing rather than paying specific attention to practical issues relating to people's lives and well-being. Such people are more dreamers than activists, idealists in words and usually weak in action. Such scholars despise manual work, commerce, and industry (Medinacelli 1977). About 33.7 percent of the population of school-going age does not have access to the educational system. Teacher training is inadequate. Technical education schemes have not been created, and significant efforts have been accompanied by low social prestige and high costs.

The Bolivian higher-education system, a key element for shaping the human factor, is in crisis. The university has always given a high priority to the transfer of knowldege and not to its generation and transformation. Massification has been one of the main causes of the declining quality of teaching and research. Lack of financial resources is a heavy limitation. Private universities and organizations have emerged and many of them are offering low-quality training. Thus, they continue to contribute to the creation of more problems.

Postgraduate studies are not well developed and, with exceptions, are only a remedy to inappropiate undergraduate education. It has been considered urgent that universities insert themselves in the process of international transformation and look for concentration and innovation with the rest of the academic, economic, and social agents.

Considering such a critical situation, the government has launched a dramatic effort to reform the educational system. In 1994, a new law relating to the reform of the educational system was enacted. It provides, among other things, for multilingual education, evaluation and accreditation of curricula and schools at all levels, the adoption of differentiated reward scales according to continuous education of teachers, and so on. It is being implemented, but not without opposition from many interest groups. In the recent past, public investment in education has grown from about 4 percent of GNP in 1992 to 6 percent in 1995. Approximately 90 percent is still being used for salaries. Of the total, primary education takes up 41 percent, secondary 9 percent, teacher training and other services 29 percent, and higher education 30 percent.

A detailed overview of the science and technology system shows that it is also weak and not well articulated with other agents of innovation. Very little investment is taking place—0.33 percent of GNP. There is a lack of financial mechanisms for innovation and technological development. Scientific production is about 0.2 percent of regional output, which is only between 4 and 5 percent of the world total. The output resulting from technical development is also negligible. Between 60 and 70 percent of Bolivia's research infrastructure is concentrated in the public universities. There are about 1,000 full-time researchers in all, probably the smallest scientific community in the region. Research services, though slightly improved in the past years, are still weak. Enterprises do not contribute significantly to research funding. In spite of this disturbing reality, there are continuing efforts being made in research and development.

The existing state of science, technology, and innovation in Bolivia reflects the view of enterprises and government that research activities in these fields belong to more advanced countries and, as such, are not relevant. As a consequence, key players in development are marginal to the national decision-making process. Such an attitude of indifference and lack of vision indicate the absolute need for developing the human factor in Bolivia.

This situation is reflected in innovation and production. For example, in agriculture, because of the lack of innovative capacities, productivity is low in most regions of Bolivia. The land reform of 1952 provided a sense of proporty in rural communities. This reform has been an important element in the cohesion and peace experienced throughout the last forty-five years. Such a reform was made possible because the Bolivian leadership perceived that times were changing and that it was necessary to abandon old paradigms. The leader of the reform, the former President, Victor Paz Estenssoro, demonstrated his well-developed human factor characteristics. His three terms of office (1952–1956, 1960–1964, 1985–1989) marked distinct epochs in the country's history. The first era brought about a far-reaching social revolution that led to land reforms, nationalization of mines, universal votes, and much else. While his second mandate focused on the social content, the third epoch concentrated on a radical change toward extensive economic transformation. The emphasis on economic pursuits were achieved at a high social cost.

Another important productive sector which is yet to develop is manufacturing. This sector has been characterized by its small contribution to GNP (i.e., 14%). In addition, the sector is poorly diversified. It concentrates mainly on nondurable imported consumption goods. This concentration is due, in part, to the sector's low dynamism and lack of innovation capacities. One key characteristic of the industrial sector is the weak linkages among its different segments. The main ones do not possess an important multiplier effect. As a result, the country has not been successful in generating sustained industrial growth. The diffusion of technology has been a slow process in the productive sector in general, and policies designed and implemented to improve it are nonexistent in practice. Very little consideration is given to the existence of markets for exports. These were not made an active part of past industrial development strategies. This gap is, however, being modified more rapidly. When analyzing the productive sector, it is important to note that small- and medium-sized (SME) firms constitute the bulk of the productive units (99%). They absorb two-thirds of total employment. About 79.4 percent are family businesses, employing from one to four workers. From the human factor perspective, the understanding of the characteristics of such a large number of very small enterprises is essential, because for these enterprises to contribute to development they should be transformed into more innovative and environmentally aware entities. They also need to develop the human factor. Otherwise, the chances of developing an effectively working economy is severely limited.

It is interesting to note that significant efforts have been made in the past to understand the difficulties confronting SME firms. None of them, however, has looked at the role of the human factor and its significance to the innovation process. Different recommendations attack the obvious financial problems, such as lack of access to credit and the lack of technical information. Yet these recommendations fail to recognize the relevance of the human factor to social, economic, and political development.

Different analyses show that one of the most important technological weaknesses in the industrial sector in general is poor technology management. This problem is a direct result of continuing human factor decay and underdevelopment (Adjibolosoo 1993, 1994, 1995). It has led to inadequate capital resources for innovation, organizational difficulties, scarce contacts with larger industries and R&D organizations, and the absence of financial mechanisms to support precompetitive stages of the innovative process.

Though human factor characteristics usually affect the extent to which the management function can be successfully carried out, there is hardly any extensive analysis on this issue in Bolivia. This oversight has to be corrected. In reality, human factor development must be made one of the key objectives of the Short Term Plan of Action of the National Council for Science and Technology. By so doing, Bolvia will be begin to prepare its labor force for national development in the twenty-first century.

THE PROCESS OF REFORM: LOOKING INTO THE TWENTY-FIRST CENTURY

To overcome many of its problems and face future challenges, Bolivia has adopted, since 1993, an explicit sustainable development policy and strategy within a free-market economy. The policy has four goals. These include the following issues.

Accelerating Economic Growth

To achieve this objective, the focus must be on export-promotion programs, the capitalization of state-owned enterprises, and the establishment of continuing support for SME firms. The capitalization policy is destined to increase the capital of public enterprises by inviting as partners strategic private investors (foreign or national), while at the same time transfering shares to Bolivian nationals, including workers. This policy is being complemented by the privatization of industries which were operated by regional state development organizations. Also complementary to the economic component is the proposal to establish pension funds as a way of revamping the whole social security system. The primary objective of the government must be to look for an economic program capable of utilizing existing natural resources as efficiently as possible. These programs must also be aimed at facilitating the rate of assimilation of new technologies and the most effective use of the existing qualified labor force (Calderon and Laserna 1995).

Achievement of a Better Distribution of Income

For this purpose, the present government established extensive structural reforms. Education and popular participation are of particular importance. The latter is addressed to transfer to local communities investment and decision-making capabilities to provide a base for power decentralization and to strengthen democratic values. To complement this, a new law on decentralization was adopted in mid-1995 and a new law on land reform is currently being discussed.

Protection of the Environment

From the conservation point of view, the government has created an important network of national reserves, contracting international credit to support its development. At the same time, it has created specific financial mechanisms to fund R&D projects. For the latter, it has used debt-for-conservation swaps. At the more general level, it adopted a far-reaching law on the environment in 1993, and has started implementing regulations addressed to productive activities. On December 9, 1995, formal regulations to the law were enacted. Other important laws are related to tropical forests, and Parliament is debating a law on the use of biodiversity. In general, in the past, government has made a very significant effort to bring environmental sustainability into development planning.

Creation of a Better Governance Structure

To achieve this goal, several measures are being put in place to accompany the decentralization and popular participation procesess. Bolivia has taken a leading role in the developing world with its initiatives for creating susbtantive institutional changes to support the sustainable development policy and strategy. The adopted policy faces enormous constraints and limitations which must be overcome in the shortest possible time. Many of these constraints have origins in weak human factor characteristics. It is quite clear that the reforms affect many interests and, as such, there is opposition to it. On the other hand, the opposition stems from the feeling of the great majority of the society that the adjustment policies of the 1980s did not translate into improved standards of living.

Another source of opposition is the lack of credibility of the public sector and its institutional system. Opposition comes from a badly informed and poorly educated group of people. Bolivia's society in general has not yet clearly understood that the ongoing process of globalization is a fact of life and that every society must learn to live with it. Some Bolivians still believe that the world will wait for the country's institutions and enterprises to develop and then Bolivia will be allowed into the world's globalization dynamics. The country is still believed to be an island, and there are political leaders who take advantage of this view and demagogically offer solutions to problems.

THE ROLE OF THE HUMAN FACTOR
IN SUSTAINABLE DEVELOPMENT

Sustainable development is brought about essentially by the capacities that a society can develop to transform, mobilize its potential, and reaffirm its cultural identity. Sustainable development is not an imported "turn-key" item. It requires fundamental changes in thinking, living, producing, consuming, and the forms of human interrelationship. It requires, in sum, the following:

1. A political system that secures an effective citizen participation.
2. An economic system that generates surplus and technical and scientific knowledge.
3. A social system that provides solutions to distortions created by nonconcerted development efforts.

4. A productive system that respects the ecological base.
5. An innovation system that is aimed at continuously looking for new solutions.
6. An international system that provides sustained frameworks of trade and financing.
7. A flexible administrative system that is capable of managing the complexity of social institutions and systems and correcting distortions.

Regardless of how relevant these items may be, many of them are still non-existent in Bolivia's development policies and strategies. It should be noted that when a country is creating local capacities to serve as the base for sustained development, the globalization of markets and financing introduce severe limitations. That is, it minimizes the degree of autonomy of national policies in relation to those of other countries. It is, however, important to know that regardless of the intensity of the globalization process there is still a huge potential for formulating valid strategies for sustained development.

To do so successfully, the human factor must be developed. Successful programs aimed at human factor development will produce more creative individuals and improve labor productivity. Human factor development programs will promote innovation capacities in the productive sectors. They will also contribute to the development of a more dedicated, committed, responsible, and accountable visionary leadership. Indeed, it will be difficult to achieve sustained development through a national leadership that suffers from severe human factor decay and underdevelopment. In considering human factor contributions, it should be recognized that self-confidence in the capacity to choose one's own way and see it through successfully is a precondition for sustained development. This requires profound convictions and enormous commitment on behalf of the whole society. Technical capabilities that have been developed cannot bring about sustained development in the presence of severe human factor decay and underdevelopment. Human factor development must therefore be stressed as Bolivia strives to meet the challenges facing it in relation to the full utilization of the potential of its citizens.

HUMAN FACTOR ENGINEERING: AN AGENDA FOR ACTION

It is quite clear that, in spite of the limitations that still exist, the present social, economic, and political achievements of the decades since democracy took hold in 1982 have been strongly influenced by a small and selected group of individuals with high levels of accountability, responsibility, integrity, and commitment. Such development must now be extended to a much larger portion of the population through a human factor engineering program which will further contribute to the ongoing positive turnaround and continuing growth in the national economy.

An improvement of Bolivia's human factor will require further insights into issues that are not well understood at the moment; for example, the role of innovative enterprises and their evolution, including the design of recommendations for the adoption of support policies and instruments. Universities and institutions of higher education must be involved in the discussions regarding the ways and means of introducing programs to promote innovation and its effective management.

A key element in the characterization and further development of innovative capacities is a process in which all stakeholders take part, discuss and build consensus on needs and priorities, decide on investments, and so on. This serves, in turn, to constitute the ample social base needed to support the system. This is equivalent to generating an environment under which an innovation culture develops as a base for sustainable development.

The experience of such an approach reveals that integrating criteria based on consensus among stakeholders in the development process can help bring equilibrium among sectoral priorities. This will also help to formulate better national policies. In this way, Bolivia will be able to create the environment for more orderly international cooperation. This will be the case because the whole process will promote clear understanding among all people involved in creating the development program and strengthening Bolivia's innovative capabilities. On the other hand, one of the most basic programs to be initiated and implemented to help develop the neccessary human factor for the nation's development program lies within the education sector. Though several important objectives in the process of Bolivian educational reform already exist, there are still three longer-term goals that need to be pursued as national priorities:

1. It is necessary to advance in the creation of an entrepreneurial culture, a culture of innovation. This cannot be done with entrepreneurs alone. Society plays a key role as a whole. It has to create a spirit open to innovation and ready to take risks, and it has to value and reward work and creativity that has the capacity to incorporate new technologies.

2. Labor training must be enhanced to adapt workers, technicians, and managers to the new conditions of the world and local economies. The acquisition of human factor characteristics must be stressed and people assisted to pursue these human qualities.

3. Productive education is absolutely neccessary to expand the economy. The engineering capacities play a key role in a world of technology. Graduate engineering education is going to be the key issue over the next few years and the need to create new degree structures will have to evolve, particularly combining engineering and management. Again, if this program fails to promote human factor development, it will produce scholars who will be well-equipped with knowledge and skills, but will lack the appropriate human factor characteristics (see details in Adjibolosoo 1995, 1996).

Human factor development programs must be operated hand in hand with science and technology programs. Without an appropriate strengthening of these together, science and technology programs alone cannot lead to the achievement of sustained development in Bolivia. It is therefore a must that conditions for human factor development be seen as *sine qua non* to the attainment of long-term national development objectives of ongoing progress in science and technology. Public understanding of science is also a key issue. Society must be able to understand its output. Two of the most serious limitations to science and technology development stem precisely from little political support and the lack of an ample social base which understands the goals and objectives of the development of knowledge.

The latter has a strong human factor component. It is absolutely essential to create an ample social base to support science and technology-driven sustainable development. For this to happen, such a base must be constructed from the economic, social, and cultural characteristics of the country. The execution of policy dialogues is key in this respect. Dialogues can have a direct effect on society. The capacity of a society to participate actively in development debates, the election of technology, or the use of natural resources and many other aspects that are related to participative democracy is based not only on research or legal instruments, but fundamentally in its capacity to act and be active; that is, to understand situations.

CONCLUSION

Few small developing countries have produced sustainable development strategies in which the science and technology components are introduced explicitly and specific actions taken to create a base which will enable the integration of economic, social, and environmental dimensions of sustainable development. This is precisely the purpose of the action plans of the National Council of Science and Technology. From the social dimension, the main long-term purposes of the plans are to use science and technology as instruments of development and to fight against poverty; to articulate its actions with the educational reform and in particular with actions addressed to the transformation of higher education; and to allow science and technology to support the popular participation process and administrative decentralization. One key human factor development program that has to be examined is that related to the need for developing the management components of innovation under a sustainable development concept and defining the role of enterprises. Such an approach is fundamental if policies are to exert significant impact on the country's sustained development with local entrepreneurs as its main actors.

For a country with a limited industrial tradition, objective sustainable development conditions can only be created by strong policy decisions with long-term views. On the other hand, international experience has shown the need for an ample and continuous action of establishing educational and technological mechanisms among entrepreneurial sectors, principally small and medium-size industry. Enterprises must create a more complete overview of those problems of an economic and technological nature that affect their operation and the means they have at their disposal to overcome severe limitations to their growth which are present today. This is an issue strongly based on the human factor.

In conclusion, one cannot do otherwise but emphasize the need to develop the human factor in Bolivia and build the capacity for its management. By so doing, a well-developed human factor will facilitate sustained development. If, however, the Bolivian leadership fails to promote ongoing human factor development, it might cripple future progress (see details in Adjibolosoo 1995).

NOTE

1. Adjibolooso (1995) defined the human factor as "the spectrum of personality characteristics and other dimensions of human performance that enable social, economic and political institutions to function and remain functional, over time. Such dimensions sustain the workings and application of the rule of law, political harmony, a disciplined labor force, just legal systems, respect for human dignity and the sanctity of life, social welfare, and so on. As is often the case, no social, economic or political institution can function effectively without being upheld by a network of committed persons who stand firmly by them. Such persons must strongly believe in and continually affirm the ideals of society." The contents of this chapter are based on this definition of the human factor.

REFERENCES

Adjibolosoo, S. 1993. The Human Factor in Development. *The Scandinavian Journal of Development Alternatives* 12 (4): 139–149.

Adjibolosoo, S. 1994. The Human Factor and the Failure of Economic Development and Policies in Africa. In *Perspectives on Economic Development in Africa*, edited by F. Ezeala-Harrison and S. Adjibolosoo. Westport, Conn.: Praeger.

Adjibolosoo, S. 1995. *The Human Factor in Developing Africa*. Westport, Conn.: Praeger.

Adjibolosoo, S. 1996. *Human Factor Engineering and the Political Economy of African Development*. Westport, Conn.: Praeger.

Calderon, F., and R. Laserna. 1995. *Pautas para el Fortalecimiento del Desarrollo Humano* (Guidelines for the Strengthening of Human Development). Proceedings of a U.N. Development Program seminar for high-ranking officers of the Bolivian government. La Paz: UNDP.

Medinacelli, C. 1977. El fracaso histórico de la enseñanza universitaria (The Historical Failure of University Eduaction). Quoted by Mariano Baptista in *Salvemos a Bolivia de la Escuela* (Let us Save Bolivia from School). 4th ed. La Paz: Los Amigos del Libro.

National Research Council. 1996. *Prospectus for National Knowledge Assessment*. Washington, D.C.: National Academy Press.

ul Haq, M. 1995. *Desarrollo Humano Sostenible* (Human Sustainable Development). Proceedings of a U.N. Development Program seminar for high-ranking officers of the Bolivian government. La Paz: UNDP.

United Nations Development Program. 1996. La Seguridad Humana en Bolivia: Percepciones Políticas, Sociales y Económicas de los Bolivianos de hoy (Human Security in Bolivia: Political, Social and Economic Perceptions of the Bolivians of Today). *Claves* 2 (8): 27–39.

Chapter 12

Zimbabwe's Human Factor Balance Sheet: An Analysis of the Causes of Corruption

Claude G. Mararike

At the center of Zimbabwe's social, economic, and political development is an enigma. The attainment of political independence in 1980 was an important development that many people rightly described as a restoration of the indigenous people's power. But this historic event remains problematic, in that it raised the expectations of a people who were once oppressed and deprived of higher standards of living, but its prospects of fulfilling such expectations remain largely remote. We need to know why this is the case.

It is pertinent to review the events which eventually led to the attainment of political independence to contextualize our presentation on Zimbabwe's human factor balance sheet. Note, in particular, the areas which stand out as problems to the development of the human factor and why the country seems to continue to slide deep into human factor decay and its associated impact on the disintegration of the much needed institutional and organizational framework under which positive development can take place.

THE PRE-INDEPENDENCE PERIOD

Like many other African countries that have experienced colonization, Zimbabwe's present problems are a combination of the colonization process and the newly emerging problems being faced as the new government attempts to formulate development strategies. In Zimbabwe, like in many other countries which were once colonized, colonization was a process of socialization, the main agenda of which was to produce subservient and serviceable "clients" out of the indigenous African population (Adjibolosoo 1995). Colonization was not only a mere attempt by the colonizers to plunder material resources for Europe's industrialization, it was also a process that affected every sphere of the African lifestyle in many ways.

European settlers who came to Zimbabwe in the 1890s had hoped to find large deposits of gold and other minerals as had been found in the Rand area and other parts of South Africa. However, after realizing that mining was not going to be as profitable as in South Africa, the European settlers turned to agriculture. This led to the massive removal of the indigenous African population from the rich fertile land to so-called reserves which had poor quality soils and erratic rainfall patterns. The Land Apportionment Act of 1930 legalized the racial division of the country's land and prohibited members of either racial group from owning land in areas assigned to the other.

The herding of Africans into overcrowded reserves and blatant discriminatory policies and practices against African farmers meant that by the end of the 1930s the agricultural economy of the Shona and the Ndebele peoples, like that of the Kikuyu in Kenya and most South African peoples, had been crippled severely. Since control over land was essential to the European settlers' achieving economic and political domination, this issue became the cornerstone of African grievances against the settlers. Land, we must note, was the only workplace of the African people. Land was their mother, their source of economic, social, and political orientation and inspiration. Bakare (1993, 46) accurately explains the issue and notes that for the Zimbabwean, land represents almost everything in life—be it quantitative or qualitative: "It offers them identity, history, and livelihood, and it is sacred." As such, to deprive a Zimbabwean of land was as good as robbing him or her of human rights. Indeed, to Zimbabweans, there is no life without the right to own and work one's own land.

When the indigenous Zimbabweans were faced with continuing declines in the productivity of their land, most of them had no choice but to seek income from other sources, such as formal employment. In addition, the numerous high taxes imposed on them by the European settlers reinforced the necessity for Africans to provide cheap labor for newly created industries. The system worked so well for the European settlers that in the 1930s the then Southern Rhodesian (now Zimbabwe) businesses were said to be enjoying the cheapest African labor, probably in the whole of the British empire (Phimister 1983; Herbst 1990, 18).

The relations between the black population of Zimbabwe and the white settler minority remained sour and progressively led to the intensification of the liberation struggle which led to Zimbabwe's political independence in April 1980. The new government of Zimbabwe took over political power before the background of racial mistrust and animosity. As it turned out, these problems remained and created significant hindrances to Zimbabwe's national development program long after independence.

RACIAL MISTRUST AND THE QUEST
FOR NATIONAL UNITY

The new government, under the leadership of Robert Mugabe and his Zimbabwe African National Union–Patriotic Front (ZANU–PF), attempted to build a new nation with a viable and workable political economy. A culture of mistrust had developed between the European settlers and the indigenous African population. The majority of the European settlers were viewed by the indigenous African population as robbers, exploiters, and oppressors. It was therefore regarded as proper if the displaced African population, who then worked as employees, stole from their European employers. This belief was based on the philosophy that one could not be viewed as stealing from someone who had stolen from him or her in the first place (Adjibolosoo 1995). Besides, years of physical confrontation between African freedom fighters and the European-controlled army had made the quest for national unity a very difficult task. During the first few years of political independence, the main priority of the new government was to build a united nonracial Zimbabwe. At the same time, the new government had to fulfill the high expectations of the indigenous majority. The government's quest for unity was severely threatened by the eruption of acts of politically motivated banditry in Matabeleland, west of Zimbabwe, in the mid-1980s. The Prime Minister, Robert Mugabe (1984, 10), immediately declared total war against banditry. He noted that "those who hope that the dissidents will succeed in achieving by violence and lawless means the political power they cannot achieve through constitutional means of an election ballot are in for a rude shock."

From 1984 to 1987, when a unity agreement between the ZANU–PF and the Patriotic Front, Zimbabwe African People's Union (PF–ZAPU) was signed, the wave of violence in Matabeleland intensified and resulted in the loss of many lives. Scores of people were tortured and left disabled. Property worth tens of thousands of dollars was burned down. During the same period, employees in the private sector, and to a lesser degree those in the public sector, either went on strike or began to be corrupt and lazy at work. Mugabe (1984, 11), in describing workers' performance in an address to the nation in December 1984, noted that "another evil of a criminal nature is the proneness of some workers in responsible positions to fraud, forgery, theft and corruption. We cannot spare any of you who offend against the people of Zimbabwe in any of these dishonest ways. Gaol is what such offenders deserve!" At stake in both incidents which President Mugabe spoke against were the human factor characteristics. If the human factor refers to a range of personality characteristics and other dimensions of human performance that enable organizations and institutions to function smoothly and remain so over time, what was gradually happening in Zimbabwe during those stressful years was the start of an end to the efficient functioning of the country's organizations and social institutions.[1] A relevant question to address, therefore, is why people in positions of trust would resort to fraud, forgery, theft, and corruption.

HISTORICAL FACTORS:
EDUCATION AND MORALS

It has already been mentioned that the indigenous African population of Zimbabwe saw nothing wrong in stealing from their European employers who denied them the right to their lands. As it turned out, this historical influence was not going to be easily shaken from the memories of most Zimbabweans. To most people, it would take time to accept the fact that there was a new government which represented their aspirations, and the type of education which colonial governments had introduced emphasized individual and personal achievements as opposed to the types of education which the indigenous people emphasized. That is, to the indigenous African peoples one is viewed as being human only when he or she is among other human beings and shares with them in all circumstances. The emphasis here was on human factor characteristics such as integrity, accountability, responsibility, honesty, commitment, and love for other people. Though personal wealth was valued among the Shona people of Zimbabwe prior to colonialism, it was not to overshadow one's commitment and appreciation for the needs of others. To perform acts of violence against fellow human beings was viewed as a sure way of inviting misfortune into one's life.

The content of formal education which was given in Zimbabwean schools during the colonial period and even after independence emphasized the accumulation of "book knowledge" at the expense of moral and spiritual knowledge.[2] This form of education does not necessarily address the human factor aspects of human development. It was therefore not surprising that people who were put in positions of trust soon after independence (and even later) resorted to corrupt behavior. As such, the colonial educational and training machinery had failed to adequately prepare Zimbabweans for the tasks of social, economic, and political development.

THE PROBLEM OF CORRUPTION

It may not be an exaggeration to state that efforts to establish a just and efficient administration in Zimbabwe since the attainment of political independence in 1980 have continually been frustrated by varying magnitudes of corruption. The evil of corruption, as pointed to earlier by President Mugabe, existed and still exists at almost every level of Zimbabwean society (see also Dabengwa 1996). In what follows, I examine two forms of corruption in Zimbabwe, systematic corruption and individual corruption.

Systematic Corruption

Carden and Carden (1977, 306) described systematic corruption as "deviant conduct which is so institutionalized that no individual can be personally faulted organizationally for participating, and dysfunction is actually protected." The main characteristic of systematic corruption is that an organization adopts an external code of ethical behavior which is continually contradicted in the course of its day-to-day activities. Organizational practices support and cover up violations of the external code. Individuals who contravene the code are protected and, if exposed, treated with leniency. On the other hand, those who blow the whistle are criticized for exposing organizational malpractice and are likely to be severely punished. Those persons who wish to reform the system by drawing outside attention to the irregularities are threatened and intimidated into saying nothing. Those whose duty it is to reveal corruption only do so when forced by external pressure. To illustrate this form of corruption, let me refer to the 1988–1989 distribution of motor vehicles scandal which later prompted President Mugabe to appoint a commission of inquiry on January 3, 1989.

From 1980 through the early 1990s, the production of motor vehicles in Zimbabwe was low. It was estimated in 1989 that Zimbabwe needed between 20,000 and 25,000 new motor vehicles per annum. Because of a shortfall that had grown since the late 1970s, the country had a backlog in the supply of new motor vehicles estimated at 100,000, and the demand for new vehicles at that time in Zimbabwe exceeded the supply. As a direct consequence of this supply and demand imbalance, certain undesirable trading practices developed within the motor vehicle distribution network on a wide scale.

One such practice was conditional selling, which allowed car dealers to require customers to trade-in their own cars at an artificially low price in order to buy new motor vehicles from the dealers. Another corrupt trading practice was the selling of new motor vehicles by car dealers through second or third parties at a price far in excess of the controlled price. A third undesirable practice was the abandonment of waiting lists for new motor vehicles. This was done to enable the car dealer to manipulate the selling of new motor vehicles to preferred customers, usually at prices far in excess of the controlled prices.

Indeed, these practices were forms of systematic corruption. According to evidence submitted to the Sandura Commission,[3] a number of Cabinet Ministers, members of Parliament, senior civil servants, and prominent businesspersons were involved in the undesirable motor vehicle trading practices. During the investigations and thereafter, a number of Cabinet Ministers and senior civil servants lost their jobs. One senior Cabinet Minister committed suicide. He had been directly implicated in the illegal procurement of vehicles.

From January to December 1995, 237 cases of corruption were reported in the country. Out of this number, only 107 convictions were made. The figures for the period running from January to June 1996 indicate that there has been a significant increase in the instances of corruption. Out of the 170 cases reported, only 54 convictions were made (Dabengwa 1996). It is usually the case in Zimbabwe, as well as in other countries, that most corrupt activities happen secretly, and a victim of corruption is usually less willing to report to the law enforcers or government officials who engage in such corrupt practices. Presenting a paper at the Second International Conference on the Human Factor and Development, held at the University of Zimbabwe, Harare, Dabengwa, the Minister of Home Affairs in the Zimbabwe government in 1996, maintained that one cannot discuss this subject (i.e., corruption) fully without making reference to corruption in high places (i.e., in government officialdom). If a government official diverts funds meant for the development of the human factor into other activities of lesser importance, or engages in outright embezzlement, the effects will be felt in the long run.

The long-term effect of such official and systematic corruption is that the whole nation is engulfed by it. When everyone begins to do it, the future of Zimbabwe's development program will be in doubt. To avoid this situation, Africans must not sit aloof and watch their own leaders gamble and squander the future of their nations. Indeed, this problem can be successfully dealt with if the leadership is ready to play its role as suggested by the mandate given to it by society through constitutional means. Every case of corruption must be treated appropriately and as a unique case. The police must do everything possible to make sure that people who engage in such practices are punished, including their own leaders and colleagues (see a detailed discussion on this issue in Adjibolosoo [1994a] and Dabengwa [1996, 17–18]).

Individual Corruption

Individual corruption occurs when a small number of organizational members contravene norms of honest administration and public accountability which are observed by the organization as a whole. An individual may tamper with official records and other types of information, for example, by removing or destroying important files to conceal the payment of bribes. These forms of corruption vary from place to place and from situation to situation. Salary computerization fraud, fraudulent use of official stationery, payment for letters of recommendation, and the like are a few examples of individual corruption that occur frequently. All these happen because of the severe human factor decay and underdevelopment being experienced in Zimbabwe today.

LEVELS OF ACCOUNTABILITY: LEADERSHIP AND MORALITY

Normally, accountability refers to a requirement whereby an individual is expected to justify his or her conduct or behavior in relation to other people's behavior or expected societal norms. In this regard, every citizen is expected by society to account for his or her actions in all situations and circumstances. For example, leaders at all levels of society are expected to follow and adhere to the laid-down rules and procedures. They are also expected to uphold certain personal principles which guide their actions (Mararike 1995). In the motor vehicle scandal described earlier, a number of important factors which relate to people's personality characteristics deserve further attention.

People's Anthropic Space

In Shona philosophy, the term *munhu* (a person or human being) has two meanings. One such meaning is that of a body; that is, you who are reading this book or a person walking along the road. Another meaning refers to what the body "contains"; that is, the human factor characteristics. Every person, according to Shona philosophy, occupies a position or some geometric space at every point in time. A leader occupies a position. That position implies that he or she must do a job. But every position is relational. It has meaning only in relation to other positions. A minister's position has meaning to him or her because he or she relates to other people who hold positions. These positions may be comparatively lower than his or hers. This hierarchy, however, does not matter. What is important is that such positions relate to his or her position and therefore give his or her position its meaning.

Geometric space is fixed. One can literally vacate it and allow someone else to occupy it. But all people have anthropic (i.e., human inner) space. This space is supposed to be elastic. It can expand or shrink. It can be good or bad. Anthropic space, according to Shona thinking, explains a person's *unhu* (personality). If one's anthropic space is bad, the Shona people say, "*hapana munhu*." This implies that there is no person. If people behave in the manner as revealed by the motor vehicle scandal, Shona people will maintain that "there are no persons." This idiom graphically summarizes the collapse of people's morality and integrity in society.

The Shona idiom can be used to describe a whole family, a village, or a country (*hapana vanhu*, meaning there are no people). There may be dozens of people in the family or in the village, but when their anthropic space is full of corruption (i.e., the case of the motor vehicle scandal), then *hapana vanhu*. A nation can also drift toward a state of "no people" if levels of accountability drop. Worse still, if leaders are described as *hapana vanhu*, then the logical conclusion is that even those whom they lead cannot be expected to be people who possess the HF.

PEOPLE'S TRADITIONAL REFERENCE POINTS

Property ownership normally goes hand in hand with accountability and responsibility. In connection to the Shona custom that governs property ownership, property or items usually belonged to someone—an individual, a family, a clan, a tribe, a community, ancestral spirits, or the gods. Every item in the home belonged to someone. This someone could either be father or mother or children or others. This sense of property ownership usually helps to enhance personal accountability and responsibility. Collectively owned property or communal property such as land, forests, or all God-given resources were managed by community leaders on behalf of such communities. There were rules and regulations which guided the utilization of such resources. There were also forms of punishment for those who violated rules that helped to control the utilization of natural resources. Such punishments ranged from fines imposed by community leaders to more severe punishments handed down by guardian spirits of the area.

Contrary to this Shona custom, in Zimbabwe, as well as many other African societies, people tend to think that property which belongs to the government is "no one's" property. Indeed, the concept of government in Zimbabwe was first associated with oppression. Colonial governments were oppressive and therefore needed to be punished or fought against. The property which such governments owned was therefore an enemy's property. Anybody who stole or damaged government property was regarded as a hero who was fighting to remove a repressive system of government. He or she could not therefore be referred to as *hapana munhu*. The indigenous African people did not consider it their responsibility to care for government property as much as they would care for their own property in their villages or communally owned resources in their communities.

Indeed, the failure of both the Zimbabwean leadership and the average citizen to successfully deal with the problems of human factor decay and underdevelopment will continue to deny the country both the ability and the opportunity to develop. Zimbabwe is still significantly rich in many natural resources, and the nation also enjoys significant external assistance from governments and nongovernment organizations from all over the world. Unfortunately, however, if Zimbabwe continues to fail to develop the appropriate human factor in its citizens, it will deny itself the opportunity to develop in the twenty-first century. In the final analysis, the corrupt behavior of both leadership and citizens will lead to continuing social, economic, and political problems. It is now time for every Zimbabwean to learn and practice both accountability and responsibility. By so doing, people will learn to discharge their duties with significant honesty and integrity (Adjibolosoo 1995).

CONCLUSION

This chapter helps to place in context the state of leadership accountability and individual commitment to duty, as well as the state of human factor development in Zimbabwe before and after independence. We should note that the development of the human factor in Zimbabwe must be viewed as the primary concern of all institutions of education. When we consider training, we must have in mind the molding of the human being to prepare him or her to conscientiously perform his or her assigned duties and responsibilities in a professional manner. The examples in this chapter suggest that the incidence of corruption within Zimbabwe's public sector is indicative of the ineffectiveness of the training given to students in the country. As such, Zimbabwe is failing to produce the kind of employees (i.e., those who have acquired the appropriate human factor characteristics) required for the attainment of development in Zimbabwe.

NOTES

1. See detailed discussions on this issue in Adjibolosoo (1993, 1994a, 1994b, 1995).

2. On this issue, refer to Adjibolosoo (1996) for an extended discussion regarding the contents and intents of colonial education in African countries.

3. The inquiry was popularly known as the Sandura Commission because its chairman was Justice W. R. Sandura.

REFERENCES

Adjibolosoo, S. 1993. The Human Factor in Development. *The Scandinavian Journal of Development Alternatives* 12 (4): 139–149.

Adjibolosoo, S. 1994a. Corruption and Economic Development in Africa: A Comparative Analysis. In *Perspectives on Economic Development in Africa*, edited by F. Ezeala-Harrison and S. Adjibolosoo. Westport, Conn.: Praeger.

Adjibolosoo, S. 1994b. The Human Factor and the Failure of Economic Development and Policies in Africa. In *Perspectives on Economic Development in Africa*, edited by F. Ezeala-Harrison and S. Adjibolosoo. Westport, Conn.: Praeger.

Adjibolosoo, S. 1995. *The Human Factor in Developing Africa*. Westport, Conn.: Praeger.

Adjibolosoo, S. 1996. *Human Factor Engineering and the Political Economy of African Development*. Westport, Conn.: Praeger.

Bakare, S. 1993. *My Right to Land: In the Bible and in Zimbabwe*. Harare: Zimbabwe Council of Churches.

Carden, G. E., and N. J. Carden. 1977. Administrative Corruption. *Public Administrative Review* 37: 301–309.

Dabengwa, D. 1996. Corruption: Its Impact on the Development of the Human Factor in Africa. Paper presented at the Second International Conference on the Human Factor and Development, 20–22 September, at the University of Zimbabwe, Harare, Zimbabwe.

Herbst, J. 1990. *State Politics in Zimbabwe*. Harare: UZP.

Mararike, C. G. 1995. Indigenous Leadership Styles: Can Grapes be Picked from an Orange Tree? In *The Significance of the Human Factor in African Economic Development*, edited by S. Adjibolosoo. Westport, Conn.: Praeger.

Mugabe, R. G. 1984. Address to the Nation. 31 December, Harare, Zimbabwe.

Phimister, I. R. 1983. Zimbabwe: The Path of Capitalist Development. In *History of Central Africa*, edited by D. Birmingham and P. M. Martin. New York: Longman.

PART III

THE HUMAN FACTOR: ITS SIGNIFICANCE

The Human Factor in Developing Civil Society and Nation Building: Some Suggestions for Practical Applications

Senyo B-S. K. Adjibolosoo

It is true that many individuals, nongovernment organizations (NGOs), and groups have been involved in different activities and programs aimed at making development happen in developing countries. These people and their organizations have been committed to seeing positive change and progress in all nations. It is therefore always important to provide ourselves with ideas that are relevant to the development of nations. Many individuals would agree with me that in many countries people have either been highly schooled or trained or educated in certain academic areas. While in school, most people have come across many ideas, ideologies, principles, and theories. As is always the case, all these ideologies and theories are aimed at providing explanations to the various sources of social, economic, political, and educational (SEPE) problems and difficulties being faced by people all over the world. While some people have gained the most basic school diplomas through various formal education and training programs, others have received either bachelors, masters, or doctorate degrees in selected disciplinary areas. People go to school for many years, hoping that at the date of school completion they will find worthwhile employment opportunities from which they can gain sufficient income to live. While some of us enter into industry, others find employment in areas such as teaching, plumbing, building, agriculture, politics, transportation, retailing and sales, construction, and so on.

The ongoing partnerships that exist between governments of the LDCs and those of the developed countries and a countless number of international development organizations (i.e., NGOs), though aimed at bringing progress to the underdeveloped communities of the world, seem to have failed in accomplishing their intended missions. Few of these alliances seem to have fully comprehended the magnitude of the world's problems of underdevelopment. If the actual sources of these problems are not identified correctly and dealt with successfully, the desire of all nations to develop might not be realized.

In many ways, those who have been deeply involved in the development programs of the LDCs seem to be oblivious about the real sources of these countries' inabilities to develop. The views of scholars regarding both the sources and realities of the problems can be likened to the experience of the blind people who were called in and assigned the task of defining what an elephant was by using the remainder of their senses. When the experiment was completed, the examiners realized that each blind person perfectly described the specific area of the elephant he or she touched, but none of them was successful in providing an accurate description of what an elephant really is. As such, anyone who does not know what an elephant is cannot rely on any single blind person's misleading description of what that person perceives an elephant to be, but if we were to amalgamate the various individual descriptions, we might obtain a better picture of what an elephant is.

Recasting this phenomenon in terms of getting a firm grasp on the problems of underdevelopment in the LDCs, scholars who attempted in the past (and even in the present) to decipher the true dimensions of these problems usually fell into the same tunnel-visioned traps as did the blind people. Each scholar who tries to define and describe the intensity of the problems of the LDCs comes out with his or her own views regarding their plight. Much of this work has come to suggest that the ongoing problems of the LDCs are the result of overpopulation, the practice of inferior cultural practices, harsh climates, low incomes and lack of savings, inadequate capital and the use of inappropriate technology, excessive and systemwide corruption, gross inefficiency, poor infrastructure, and so on.

By accepting the views propounded and debated by scholars from the DCs, the LDCs, as well as advanced country governments and many NGOs, international development agencies, and financial donors, have continued to focus their human energy and financial resources on tackling what they have come to view as the true sources of underdevelopment in the LDCs. The intensity of these efforts and the depth of financial commitments are highly impressive. Their results, however, leave much to be desired. They have hardly ever achieved the lasting and self-reproducing results that are required to improve peoples' livelihood and overall welfare in the LDCs.

Where failure has been experienced on a continuing basis, both plan and policy makers on one hand and program and project designers on the other usually quit getting involved with existing programs or projects in one geographical location and move on to others, rechanneling their resources into these newly selected regions of the world.[1] They continue to blame other LDCs for not being ready for the changes deemed to be necessary for the LDCs' economic emancipation. Those groups whose activities fail to accomplish their missions usually leave in shame, yet with little remorse, not being humble enough to acknowledge their significant contributions to plan, policy, program, and project failure in the LDCs. No sooner do they quit than zealots from other groups come in to replace them and hope that they may make a real difference in the lives of the poor people. A little later, when failure begins to stare them in the face, they too begin to plan for terminating their activities and make final plans for their departure.

The remainder of this chapter presents, defines, and discusses the heart of underdevelopment in the LDCs. Future directions for all countries that desire to develop are pointed out. Policy recommendations regarding the critical changes that need to be made on an ongoing basis to achieve human-centered development are also presented. This chapter not only discusses the misperceptions regarding economic underdevelopment in the LDCs, but also concludes that effective human factor development programs are extremely critical to the building of the necessary foundation for sustained progress everywhere in the world. A few policy recommendations are put forward regarding what has to be done from the HF perspective to place the LDCs en route to lasting progress. Additional suggestions are made regarding the various practical ways whereby the HF can be developed.

DEFINING THE HEART OF
UNDERDEVELOPMENT IN THE LDCs

In real-life situations, problems present themselves in many different forms. Indeed, problems that linger for long periods of time may reveal themselves through many different symptoms. In medicine, for example, doctors who are keen on curing certain ailments need to correctly diagnose the true sources of the diseases they attempt to cure. Unfortunately, however, many sicknesses exhibit symptoms that are similar to others. As such, every doctor's task is much more complicated than most people imagine. This makes it difficult for doctors to deal with certain diseases successfully by observing existing symptoms with high levels of confidence. To overcome this problem, doctors who desire to be successful in their everyday practice need to pursue continuing studies in their areas of specialization (Adjibolosoo 1996). It is through these studies that they learn to differentiate between different diseases and therefore pin down their accompanying symptoms.

Unlike doctors, development theorists and practitioners do not necessarily delve deeper into related issues and events to identify and fully comprehend both the sources and depth of the problems of underdevelopment in the LDCs. The causes of these problems are usually wrongly attributed to those factors listed earlier. Yet in many countries where the population is struggling to achieve development (i.e., Cuba, Mexico, Philippines, Nigeria, Ghana, North Korea, Zaire, Zimbabwe, etc.), inherent problems are deeply rooted in continuing HF decay and underdevelopment.[2] Throughout the centuries, many countries continued to fail to initiate effective programs to develop the necessary personality characteristics that are critical to nation building. As more and more people lose their flair for personal accountability, responsibility, integrity, trustworthiness, and commitment to principles of life and work, few tasks get accomplished. This phenomenon breeds personal mediocrity, which in turn leads to low input productivity, low incomes, and many other problems. Taking a cue from this observation, certain scholars of orthodox development theory have looked at the problems and classified them as constituting permanently inscribed vicious cycle of underdevelopment.

Though the traditional view and concept of a vicious cycle of economic underdevelopment in the LDCs is sensible and intriguing, it focuses on incorrect premises and variables (see Figure 13.1). This view about the vicious cycle postulates that low incomes usually lead to a low savings rate, which in turn produces low investment. Low investment rates also foster continuing lower rates of capital formation and accumulation. Consequently, people's incomes are usually low. This process repeats itself, producing continuing economic underdevelopment. This being viewed as the primary problem of most LDCs, the orthodox solution to the problem is to either disarm or dismantle the forces of an already entrenched vicious cycle. To do so, it is usually suggested that the LDCs receive help from elsewhere so that they can raise incomes, savings, investment, and capital formation. These are expected to provide the foundation for an ongoing human-centered development.

However, by viewing the orthodox concept of the vicious cycle from the HF perspective, one realizes that its foundation principle, premises, and key variables are not actually correct. Indeed, though a vicious cycle may exist, it does not necessarily have its initial beginnings in low incomes, as postulated by traditional development theory. Instead, the primary factors that initiate and sustain it are HF underdevelopment and its ensuing decay. Thus, what the orthodox view of this cycle ignores is the significant role the HF plays in the whole development process. As shown in section 2 of Figure 13.1 and the left-hand side of Figure 13.2, HF underdevelopment gives birth to continuing HF decay (leakages). As the process of HF decay deepens and entrenches itself, it not only releases productivity-diminishing human characteristics (represented by the negative signs in Figure 13.2), but also creates the environment for negative rent-seeking activities. As these activities are left to continue unchecked and then become endemic in society, more and more people get involved. In this way, as the whole society experiences the ongoing systemwide HF decay and underdevelopment, productivity stagnates in the short term and then plummets precipitously in the long term. As this phenomenon becomes more endemic, the chain of reactions resulting from the various hindrances to

Figure 13.1
The Vicious Cycle of Underdevelopment: Two Different Views

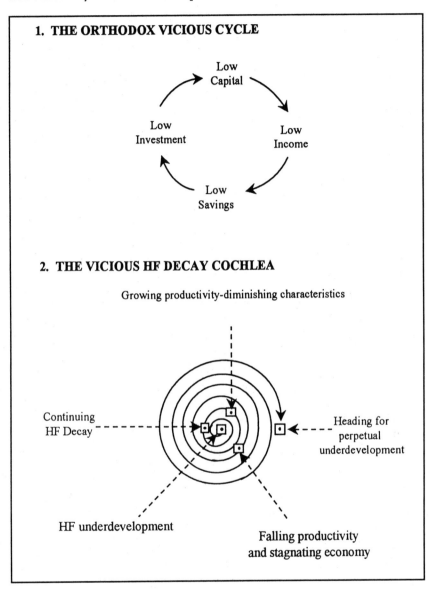

1. THE ORTHODOX VICIOUS CYCLE

Low
Capital

Low
Investment

Low
Income

Low
Savings

2. THE VICIOUS HF DECAY COCHLEA

Growing productivity-diminishing characteristics

Continuing
HF Decay

Heading for
perpetual
underdevelopment

HF underdevelopment

Falling productivity
and stagnating economy

development unleashed on an ailing economy produces and sustains underde-velopment permanently (see Figure 13.2). This in turn brings about severe SEPE problems, which finally lead to crises of immense and unmanageable proportions. Alternatively, HF development (injections) will lead to successful

Figure 13.2
The Intensity of the Impact Sequence of Human Factor Characteristics on Economic Growth and Development

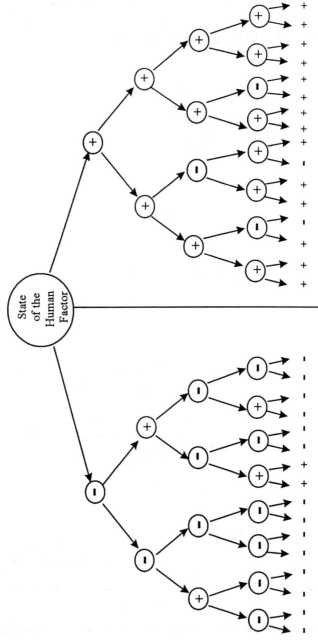

Human factor development (injection) exceeds human factor decay (leakage) and leads to varying levels of economic growth and development.

Human factor decay (leakage) exceeds human factor development (injection) and leads to varying levels of economic stagnation or decline and underdevelopment.

development programs (see details in the right-hand section of Figure 13.2).

Given the HF view of the vicious cycle, LDCs that focus on how to increase national income by putting effective programs in place to raise the low rates of incomes, savings, investment, and capital formation and its accumulation will underdevelop their whole economy and place it in a trap of permanent stagnation and decline. There may be no way out. Indeed, only countries that pay keen attention to programs aimed at HF development will achieve development in the long term. They will be more successful in breaking the vicious cycle of poverty and, if possible, turn it around in their favor.

SOME STUNNING OBSERVATIONS AND REVELATIONS

Upon achieving independence, most LDCs begin to feel and enjoy the winds of hope, personal liberty, and human fulfillment. They have always believed that they could work harder to carve a future of comfort and good living for themselves and future generations. With this in mind, they enter into schooling activities like ants and termites would do with their programs of food collection preparing diligently for the winter and rainy seasons, stockpiling sterile academic knowledge for any present or future eventualities. Yet, as time passes by, seconds changing into minutes and minutes into hours and hours into days and days into weeks and weeks into months and months into years and years into decades and decades into centuries, they lose sight of the original vision with which they began at independence. As the going becomes tough, these countries find themselves in extremely difficult and excruciatingly painful circumstances. As such, they forget about their initial ideals, dreams, and visions. In cases where this has happened, many nations are more than willing to completely abandon the very principles that form the unshakable foundation of the visions and dreams held by previous generations for political independence—freedom in every regard and true justice for all. Thus, from the youngest to the oldest, from females to males, from the most powerful and authoritative to the powerless and voiceless individuals, many people in these countries yield to pressures that not only erode the very principles of life away, but also gnaw at them and mow down their national vision, mission, and plans (see the cases of Nigeria, Mexico, Cuba, etc.). At this point, they begin to engage themselves in different types of behavior that are extremely inimical to community development and nation building.

The continuing betrayal of the personal trust invested in people who are placed in highly honorable positions by the rest of society, sends signals that most people have decided to pursue activities that stand against collective efforts aimed at the attainment of national dreams. They begin to wonder whether they would not be called fools by the rest of society if they did not jump onto the bandwagon and engage themselves in antisocial and negative rent-seeking behavior. Indeed, as it is often said, "Monkey see, monkey do." Those who can no longer hold firmly to universal principles of life and work begin to yield themselves to unspoken pressures that lure them unsuspectingly to do as their crooked leaders and managers do. People no longer believe in the saying, "Do as I say and not as you see me do." Individuals whose lives were once based on higher ideals and principles finally yield to the excessively mean, blind, and ruthless goddess of selfishness. Their overindulgence in personal desires and self-interest lead many to betray the trust society has placed in them in the first place. As they succumb to both internal and external pressures of wrongdoing, the magnitude of their individual HF begins to decline (see Figure 13.2). Productivity-diminishing HF characteristics balloon and thereafter continue to militate against social progress, economic growth, and development and political maturation.

This, in turn, leads to ongoing HF decay and underdevelopment. People who suffer from ongoing HF decay fail to perform effectively in society. They become more interested in embezzling and abusing (i.e., destroying) national wealth than creating it. To these people, it is always better to misappropriate, mismanage, and misapply scarce national resources. They become like excited honey birds who grow bolder and more aggressive as they poke their long and sharp proboscises deeper into flowers, drawing nectar. They scarcely ever care about the flower's welfare. Because these individuals have already lost their shame and cast off their garments of accountability, responsibility, integrity, commitment, and trustworthiness, they go after activities and events that provide them with the opportunity to illegally empty the pot of national financial resources and unload the embezzled funds into their own personal domestic or overseas bank accounts. The more successful they are in these activities, the more underdeveloped their home countries become.[3] This process continues to gather momentum until it becomes systemwide. This terrible vicious cycle of HF decay and underdevelopment not only becomes entrenched, but also facilitates the development of a nationwide culture of silence and destruction. In the event this stage is reached, everything else goes out of order and control. Few people continue to be loyal, trustworthy, or interested in preserving public property and resources. The bewilderment, hopelessness, helplessness, and confusion unleashed on society by the severe slaying of the national HF on the throne of the personal goddess of excessive human selfishness and avarice lead to total social degradation, economic collapse, political imprisonment, and educational and intellectual dishonesty.

Using the culture of silence as its linguist and policy executioner, the goddess of personal greed that reigns supreme in the hearts of men and women in all countries usually advances its clandestine mission of life destruction unhindered. In the final analysis, as most people resign themselves to their fate, the wildest seeds of underdevelopment and human suffering, sown in the soils of their psyche, germinate, blossom, and produce continuing HF decay and underdevelopment (see the left-hand segment of Figure 13.2). The people's laudable ideals of work and happy life are strangled completely and finally executed.

The complete demise of society is finally pronounced. Expectations wilt and wither. Dreams become frostbitten and forever crippled. There is nothing more worth living for. People accept their current plight and are resigned to their fate. There is little desire to pursue a program of action to bring positive change.

By depreciating the HF, people destroy national dreams and hopefulness. This is sad, because people who should know better continue to fail to recognize that their societies make too many mistakes by allowing others who are not qualified to run their lives by telling them what they think has gone wrong. People in the LDCs lose faith in their own schooling programs, training activities, and education systems, and then run after self-proclaimed experts who do not necessarily know much about the people they plan to help. People spend huge sums of money to bring them in, house them in their best hotels, and pay the bills, only to receive misleading advice. The LDCs have most often disregarded the wisdom bequeathed to them by previous generations. They ignore their wise sayings. Indeed, if the LDCs desire to change their plight and turn the existing sordid situation around, they need to recognize that they cannot accomplish any tasks successfully without recognizing that people who possess the HF make things happen. Expert advisors have failed in the past to alert the LDCs that they are experiencing these problems primarily because of the severe HF decay and underdevelopment prevailing in their societies. As such, they have misled and given the LDCs reasons to convince them to focus on dealing with symptoms rather than the actual causes of their individual and collective problems—human factor decay and underdevelopment (see the case studies of Singapore and Japan in Chapters 3 and 4, respectively).

Since HF development takes a considerable length of time to happen, quick-fix solutions do not have the slightest chance of overcoming problems that are rooted in HF decay and underdevelopment. The problem of HF decay and underdevelopment happens very quickly and becomes entrenched over the years. It has its own roots in the personal acquisition of productivity-diminishing personality characteristics. If the LDCs will achieve any lasting successes in their attempts to develop, they must go through the longer but guaranteed HF development route.

FUTURE DIRECTIONS AND CRITICAL CHANGES

People from the LDCs must be prepared to make the necessary sacrifices to attain development. They cannot eat their cakes and still have them. If this attitude continues to exist and becomes entrenched in any country, little development will ensue. All people in their respective countries must be ready and willing to not only engage in, but also support the necessary types of personal and group transformation required for human-centered development to occur. This fact is also illustrated by an Ewe traditional proverb which points out that if one wants to harvest a bunch of palm fruits, one must necessarily cut off the palm branches that hold and shelter the palm fruits first before proceeding any further to cut the stalk of the bunch of palm fruits. Failure to follow this process will lead the harvester into a great disaster. Thus, in any human endeavor, first things must be done first. No nation can achieve economic growth and development without having first created the necessary conditions that favor and promote development. The society that initially focuses on HF development will realize sooner or later that it has built a permanent, solid foundation on which its ongoing development program will thrive (FYI 1996).

Singapore's nation-building program was couched on the principle of citizenship development. The first generation of Singaporean leadership was not only aware of the significance of the HF in nation building, but also believed that, without well-developed citizens who have acquired the necessary HF, no nation can achieve and sustain development (Adjibolosoo 1995e). Hendry, Arthur, and Jones (1995, 10) point out the following:

People are the actors through whom strategy unfolds, as a result of which firms succeed or fail. . . . People act, among other things, as owners, as entrepreneurs, as sources of skill and expertise, as collaborators, as participants in network and learning activities, as agents of their own carriers. . . . People as entrepreneurs are credited with special qualities, such as strengths in judgment (Casson 1982), a "will to conquer" (Schumpeter 1934) or a "need for achievement" (McClelland 1961), through which they succeed in founding new firms. . . . Economic renewal depends then on the rise to leadership of "New Men" [and women]. (Schumpeter 1934)

Aware of this principle, Lee Kwan Yew and his colleagues pursued a program of development that focused on education and training programs aimed at HF development. Singapore could not have been that successful had its first-generation post-independence leaders ignored HF development (see Adjibolosoo [1995b] and Chapter 4 of this book).

In view of what has been accomplished in Singapore (in approximately three decades) through a carefully orchestrated HF development program, it should be clear to every scholar of development theory that the primary starting point of a national development program is HF development. Indeed, countries such as Ghana, Ivory Coast, Kenya, Nigeria, and many others that were further ahead of Singapore in the late 1950s and early 1960s lost their chances for attaining human-centered development because they failed to recognize the significance of the HF (Adjibolosoo 1993, 1995c, 1995e). These countries still have the chance, however, to develop, but as long as they continue to hang on to programs based on structural adjustment without any concern for HF development, they may never achieve any sustained development. Indeed, one of the greatest problems facing the developing economies is the inability of both the leaders and the people to perceive the significance of the HF to the process of development (Adjibolosoo 1994, 1995c, 1995e).

In view of these observations, it can be argued that it is time for every developing country to wake up to the realities of the closing decade of the twentieth century. It is time to perceive that the future success of people from the developing world will be determined by their own abilities and willingness to move away from old unproductive paths and turn to those ideas and programs that will bring fruitfulness to their efforts. It is time to stop being the perpetual guinea pig on which all tests of orthodox development theories are performed. It is time, perhaps, to move away from the height of national ignorance and seek solutions to problems in the right places. It is time for a change in the social, economic, political, cultural, educational, and intellectual life of the people of the developing world.

How should the LDCs go about their activities so they can bring about positive results? Regardless of what answers one provides to this question, until the sources of underdevelopment in the LDCs are identified and dealt with appropriately, the LDCs cannot develop. Indeed, as observed by Hendry, Arthur, and Jones (1995, 2), "Human resources—like other resources—can be harnessed or neglected, built up or run down over time. As an economic resource, people have a unique capability not only to animate other economic factors (Zan and Zambon 1993), but also to develop new capacities through learning and in the way they themselves combine (Penrose 1959). They differ from other resources in the skills, knowledge and learning—at both individual and firm levels of analysis—which they accumulate." It is therefore the case that nations that fail to develop their people will face severe difficulties in relation to organizing and running their systems, institutions, and projects. To avoid this problem, every society needs to pay continuing attention to the human qualities of its people. In this way, it will be guaranteed the necessary caliber of people required for nation building and industrial progress and successful global competitiveness.

When life is at risk, doctors cannot afford to experiment with people's health. In cases where doctors are proven to have been negligent, they are either sued or run the risk of losing their licenses to practice, so doctors do their best to make sure that they do everything possible to isolate, understand, and articulate correctly the underlying causes of the patient's problems. In so doing, good doctors usually do almost everything possible, looking beyond visible and deceptive symptoms by trying to take a critical look at other related problems. Those problems that cannot be easily defined require thorough professional review, study, examination, and analysis. In cases where problem definition focuses on inaccurate data, the solutions arrived at are either wrong or suboptimal (see Render and Stair 1994, 3–8).

Viewing the LDCs' current state of severe underdevelopment from this angle, it can be argued from the HF perspective that their problems have been extremely misdiagnosed. This misdiagnosis is due to the fact that those who tried in the past to define and find solutions to development problems in the LDCs have not only failed to isolate the actual causes of the problems, but also did not know what to do. This failure has caused a great deal of havoc in many LDCs. Proposed solutions have been directed at dealing with symptoms rather than the real root causes of the problems (Adjibolosoo 1995c).

Dreams die when those who dream them refuse to work to see them become realities. Yet, dreams that have no basis will never materialize. In many cases, people wrongly think that by changing the government of the day, culture, institutions, and much else they will effect positive changes in their societies. For example, historical evidence shows that many coups d'etat in countries all over the world were aimed at correcting the mistakes of deposed governments. The military regimes established have hardly ever brought any lasting and positive gains to the people. Some military leaders become hard-hearted, rule their people with blood and iron, and, above all, chastise them with thorny metal whips and the bullet-spewing barrels of guns. They end up destroying the lives of innocent and unsuspecting citizens. In this way, most of the resources poured into the LDCs for many decades did not lead to any significant results.

WHERE DO WE GO FROM HERE?

The world is continuously changing. Nothing seems to be stable anymore. As we journey into the twenty-first century, permanent residents of the developing world need to wake up to these glaring realities and make the best of them. The LDCs that wait for others to come to do it for them will be left behind forever. It is, therefore, time to review and revise old ideas, procedures, techniques, and methodologies and then throw away those that are no longer relevant to the problems of today. Today's problems are much more complicated than those of yesterday. As such, all old procedures may not necessarily be suitable for dealing effectively with the new problems. Instead of adjusting their agenda to fit the national objectives of other nations, the LDCs need to look into areas from which they can discover workable solutions to their everyday social, economic, political, cultural, educational, and intellectual problems.

The current process of social, economic, political, and educational degradation in developing countries must not be viewed as a mishap that will destroy the future of these people. Instead, each LDC should see these phenomena as viable opportunities whereby new gains can be made for prosperity in the twenty-first century (Adjibolosoo 1995c). While others spend their time trying to predict the magnitude of the bleakness of the future of the LDCs, citizens of these nations must begin to work on viable alternatives that will prove wrong the tunnel-visioned theoreticians who cannot see beyond the nose-length predictions of their shallow theorizing and academic modeling. Indeed, contrary to popularly held belief about the imminent doom of the LDCs, there is incredible hope for these countries.

Many years ago, the LDCs were told that they could not develop because they were too poor and therefore could not amass enough savings to create the investment that was required for ongoing capital accumulation, economic growth, and development (see Figure 13.1). Since these diagnoses seemed palatable to previous generations in the LDCs, they accepted the experts and paid them handsome remuneration to suggest solutions to their problems—which they did gladly. They recommended to them to take loans and use the funds to purchase goods produced by the donor nations. The people in most LDCs tried this policy recommendation for many decades. The only thing that exists today to remind the LDCs of this ever happening is the huge international debt obligations they entered into unsuspectingly. In addition, they have tried many recommendations relating to modernization through the creation of "white elephant programs and projects." These programs, however, have only contributed to serious woes by increasing the magnitude of the international debt and bringing these nations into perpetual debt bondage. The LDCs are constantly being told by scholars of orthodox development theory that their problems continue to persist because they are overpopulated or their climate is blamed for the failure, or they are told that their inability to develop is a positive function of how they suppress their women and children and deny them their inalienable human rights—the right to be human. In recent years, issues relating to democratization, environmentalism, energy, education, training, and so on have been highlighted as being the key issues that each LDC must focus on. Indeed, this list is unending.

As we debate the various causal factors, trying to deal with the difficulties and problems they unleash on the LDCs, these countries are forced to abandon newly created plans, policies, programs, and projects in favor of new ones that are based on new theories or ideologies developed by foreign experts outside the borders of each LDC. Thus, from one period to another, most LDCs go through a barrage of expert solutions that not only fail to achieve their intended objectives, but also drag them more and more into excessively severe and complicated problems of social, economic, political, and educational underdevelopment. Regardless of the fact that external help has failed most of the time to lead the LDCs to finding workable and lasting solutions to their crises and associated problems, the LDCs continue to allow themselves to be experimented on. Their own scholars, intellectuals, and leaders seem to be in deep slumber. They do not seem to perceive that they are not only being misled, but also that when the smoke clears they will be worse off than they began. They are now excessively confused, they have lost all hopes, and every good thing seems to be passing them by.

If the LDCs desire to reverse the continuing problems of underdevelopment, they need to recognize that without developing the HF they cannot make it. They need to turn around and replace most foreign experts and suspend any wrong advice they were given in the past. People living in the LDCs must not confuse goodwill with unfathomable intentions. This is important because in certain cases personal willingness to help others can easily cloud the real motives for doing so. The LDCs need to look much more deeply into themselves and ask the more difficult questions regarding why everything they have tried to date failed. When they do this sincerely and successfully, they will recognize that the primary sources of their own problems are HF decay and its continuing underdevelopment. It is time for everyone to think about how his or her country must go about developing the necessary HF traits as a unified society.

Regardless of the extent of the damage done, the good news is that people who have a strong will and community spirit can rise successfully above the odds and rebuild, bringing long-lasting peace to themselves.[4] A dying society can rebound as long as it possesses a few individuals who possess the HF and are willing to lead others to develop the relevant HF characteristics and use them to benefit the whole society. These individuals are usually unaware that the mere overthrow of a government that has been in power for years cannot achieve any significant successes when the people suffer from severe systemwide HF decay (e.g., Cuba, North Korea, the People's Republic of Congo [formerly Zaire], Nigeria, etc.). Unless the issue of HF decay and underdevelopment is addressed appropriately, such societies cannot achieve any positive and lasting results.

Those who continue to argue that what the LDCs need are structural adjustment, institutional development, capacity building, and programs of democratization are oblivious to the LDCs' many problems of underdevelopment. These people also fall into the trap of development illusion regarding what actually makes positive changes happen in societies. It is unfortunate that their intelligence and many academic laurels are often unable to lead them to discover that, in the presence of continuing HF decay, changes effected in inanimate programs cannot bring any desired results.

SPECIFIC COURSES OF ACTION

What must the LDCs do at this point in time to develop? To answer this question, I propose four critical directions to be pursued by every LDC as all humanity moves into the twenty-first century:

1. Each LDC must of necessity create and develop a workable vision, mission, and plan.

2. Every person living in a developing country must be educated and trained to honor time and personal commitment. The programs of education and training must promote the acquisition of personal integrity, responsibility, accountability, and trustworthiness. These same programs must provide every person with the environment within which he or she will believe that the LDC's development game is just about to commence. As such, it is necessary for every person to stretch his or her arms wide and position himself or herself to focus on practical programs that could bring about lasting human-centered development.

3. LDCs must avoid problem accommodation (see Adjibolosoo 1995d, 22–23). This implies that the LDCs need to concern themselves with problem solving rather than looking for quick fixes.

4. LDCs must institute programs to facilitate ongoing HF development. In this case, only people who have acquired the HF must be allowed to run the court systems, the law, financial institutions, prisons, schools, and so on. Hard work is not neces-

sarily the solution. Working smarter through ongoing HF development programs, however, holds much promise. There is no room for any individual or groups of individuals to either dwell on the mistakes of the past or pursue self-pity. Instead, it will be more productive to learn from the past and use the knowledge gained to pursue progress with a high intensity of courage and tenacity. The idea of perfection is great, but it is usually not attainable. As such, the pursuit of ongoing excellence in all spheres of human endeavor is greater, and worth pursuing.

In view of these suggestions, I now present to all national leaders certain recommendations that could serve as viable starting points for their development planning, policy formulation, program development, and project implementation. When these leaders commit themselves and the whole nation to these ideas and do them with integrity in the presence of personal accountability, trustworthiness, responsibility, and commitment, they will indeed see the true light in the long dark tunnel of underdevelopment in which they have wandered for many decades. It is only through their ongoing successes in this regard that they can begin to smile once again because their intended national dreams at independence are becoming rekindled and clearer.

In regard to changing the course of their plight and past history of struggles and suffering, the LDCs need to come together and pursue well-articulated programs of action that have the capability to not only lead them to the next level of positive changes, but also lead to the development of the requisite HF traits. It is critical that both leadership and citizens agree to make existing institutions become more effective and efficient. For example, the LDCs must make conscious efforts to help every student to know his or her rights, privileges, and responsibilities. In lectures, professors need to educate all students in issues relating to personal integrity, trustworthiness, accountability, diligence, responsibility, and commitment. Every student must be taught to be on the lookout for others who may wish to exercise their personal inclination to destroy institutional property, and let such students be brought under tough disciplinary action (neither violating their human rights nor denying them the right to personal freedom). It is also important to teach everyone to perceive and comprehend that institutional property and resources belong to all members of that institution. As such, everyone who benefits from such property must make sure that others do not destroy it. When they do so, they will be in a strong position to maintain existing structures successfully and also prevent them from experiencing dilapidation. Seminars and conferences must be used to train and educate everyone to engage in personally responsible behavior in terms of caring for both institutional and national property and resources.

It is also useful to encourage students to use their various groupings or associations to educate themselves on how to take care of institutional and national property. Student groups can invite well-known and respected individuals who have demonstrated higher levels of personal accountability, responsibility, integrity, and commitment in society to give lectures, seminars, and conferences regarding how everyone must get involved in the nation-building program. School, college, and university authorities must encourage and lead students to perceive and fully comprehend how their positive contributions could lead society to deal with its ongoing problems.[5] By so doing, the repetition of desired behavior will become entrenched in the long term, and students will take the necessary initiatives to make sure that they build a great future for themselves. Similarly, the ideals and principles on which the founding fathers and mothers established each educational institution must be extolled at every institutional gathering where all students must be challenged to uphold and defend them. Inclinations that may lead to the erosion of such foundation pillars must neither be allowed to grow nor blossom.

The leadership at all levels (be it business, association, or government) needs to provide students with adequate resources to hold their own conventions where they can meet other students from all over the country or the continent to dialogue and encourage each other regarding their individual roles as citizens in nation building. These events will not be complete unless students are given the chance to make meaningful and relevant recommendations to both school administrators and national leaders regarding their concerns and what roles they believe they could play in the nation's development program. It is necessary to create forums where students and institutional and national leaders are able to sit down face to face to discuss and resolve difficult issues amicably. The success of this program requires the possession of critical human abilities that are necessary for successful communication, conflict resolution through peaceful means, the ability to respect the rights of others and treat them as coequals, and the willingness to agree to disagree in peace and friendliness until new information becomes available for going back to the table to continue with dialoguing. Where student demonstrations are called for, every student must recall that patriotism and good citizenship require that every one of them respects the laws of the land. Regardless of the worth of the cause being fought for and the relevance of the issues being addressed, nothing is further from the truth than to think that violence is permitted in certain circumstances.

This whole program must become systemwide, in that it should be promoted and carried out in every place of employment, industry, commerce, government, academia, and so on. There must be friendly and continuing interaction among groups. These must present channels that will allow and facilitate programs and activities that will foster transparent and honest dialogues in and among these groups. Again, seminars, conferences, and roundtable discussions must be used to educate people regarding the ideals of nation building and what every person must contribute to the whole process. To promote and foster HF development in these groups, it is necessary to create national awards of honor that can be conferred on individual citizens who acquire and exhibit positive HF characteristics. Such awards must have concrete and special privileges or financial remuneration attached to them. Their existence alone must create significant incentive for every citizen to aspire to win these prestigious laurels.

When all is said and done, everyone needs to recognize that the success or failure of this agenda depends on every citizen. If citizens fail to perceive that every person's contribution to the program is crucial, the development program may fail miserably. Self-respect and regard for all other citizens must be treated with the highest priority and honor. Personal pursuit of integrity, honesty, and trustworthiness is essential and must not be overlooked. Any developing country that is successful in making all these programs work will prepare its citizens for the task of development and nation building. Bethel (1990, 70) could not have been any more accurate when she wrote "Economic problems are human problems, and so human values must be applied to their solutions. These human values and solutions come from you and me." Bethel noted further that "Societies create general rules of conduct to guarantee their own survival. The rules established by our forefathers and still agreed upon by most of us are what protect us from anarchy, leaving us free to advance without having to decide the same issues over and over again. . . . In our Judeo-Christian society we have many truths that have served us well for generations. Even though we may have lost sight of some of them, they are still there, waiting to be rekindled by people like you who want to make a difference" (p. 63).

World leaders need to develop strong personal ethics based on universal principles to guide themselves to serve as examples for others. These must be passed on to the general public in both word and deed. Leaders who are successful at this will become true inspirations for others to emulate. Their experience (i.e., wisdom and judgment), conscience (i.e., moral character), and integrity (i.e., the basis for building effective relationships on trust and loyalty) are critical to leadership success (Bethel 1990, 64). This is, indeed, the best route toward successful national development in the twenty-first century and beyond.

Drawing conclusions from the discussions presented so far, it must be obvious that every economic system generates and perpetuates certain values. It is also the case that economic development and the industrial progress of nations may not happen and remain permanently sustained without having developed the HF (Adjibolosoo 1995e). The relevance of universal principles and human virtues to the development process is obvious (Adjibolosoo 1998). Indeed, it is around these principles and virtues that individual character is formed and molded. Knight (1951, 47) argued, "Economic activity is at the same time a means of want-satisfaction, an agency for want and character formation, a field of creative self-expression, and a competitive sport. While men [and women] are playing the game of business, they also are molding their own and other personalities, and creating a civilization whose worthiness to endure cannot be a matter of indifference."

It is reasonable to suggest that everyone needs to thoroughly reexamine the influences of the economic system on values, belief systems, attitudes, and character formation. In evaluating the economic performance of the various countries studied in this book, it is important that everyone recognize that development cannot happen in the presence of continuing HF decay. The continuing treatment of business and economic activities as if they were ball games without rules is indicative of HF decay and underdevelopment. The severity of this problem encourages people to strive to win no matter what. To die is sometimes viewed as a better alternative to losing. Knight (1951, 67) noted, "In America, where competitive business, and its concomitant, the sporting view of life, have reached their fullest development, there have come to be two sorts of virtue. The greater virtue is to win; and meticulous questions about the methods are not in the best form, provided the methods bring victory. The lesser virtue is to go out and die gracefully after having lost." Every society needs to pay particular attention to principles and put structures in place to help people get to know and respect these principles. They lay the foundation for effective HF development programs in society. Indeed, the significance of the HF in human action should not be ignored. The significance of the prevailing HF characteristics in every society can be demonstrated in the following:

1. Business and economic operations
2. Global business operations and competitiveness
3. Institutional and organizational effectiveness
4. Politics and government operations
5. Ideological effectiveness
6. Identifying and meeting human needs
7. Human action and performance
8. Religious life and clergy performance
9. Building organizations and strategic relationships
10. Leading change and successful revolutions
11. Conflict resolution and cooperation
12. Vision, leadership, and productivity management
13. Decision making and team effectiveness
14. Invention, innovation and technological advancement
15. Minimizing criminal activities

CONCLUSION

As long as positive HF characteristics remain in force like the walls of ancient cities, a society's development program will flourish and achieve its intended goals. However, when the HF decays and releases continuing productivity-diminishing characteristics into the whole society, development plans, policies, programs, and plans stagger and fail. Societies that suffer from HF decay and underdevelopment will be like ancient cities whose walls have been broken down by enemy forces. Such societies will neither prosper nor develop. In view of these observations, it is important to note that, in the presence of pervasive systemwide HF decay, these suggestions will fall on deaf ears. To avoid this, the educational curriculum at all levels of schooling must provide the opportunity and encourage all teachers to help their students to acquire the necessary HF characteristics by exposing them to nationally cherished principles and ideals.

NOTES

1. A case in point is the ongoing marginalization of African countries by moving resources away from them to Eastern Europe. This process began in the early 1990s, when developed countries' governments, NGOs, development-oriented organizations, and many others came to the conclusion that their previous activities and efforts were not leading to any positive results in African countries. While these groups were trying to decide what to do next, socialism began to lose its hold in Eastern Europe. This created perceived new opportunities for these groups to rechannel their development funds and other relevant resources.

2. See details in the case study of Mexico, as discussed in this book.

3. Examples include the Philippines under Marcos, Uganda under Amin, and Zaire under Mobutu.

4. From the HF perspective, the information presented in this chapter is critical to all nations that are keen on achieving economic growth and development—developed and developing countries alike (Adjibolosoo 1993, 1995c, 1995e).

5. In this case, leading by example will accomplish much more than leaders·using continuing speeches of moral suasion and yet engaging themselves in behaviors that are contrary to what they preach. Continued mentoring of young people will prepare them sufficiently for the tasks of development as long as the mentors themselves are committed to a life of accountability, integrity, commitment, and responsibility. National leaders have to walk the talk.

REFERENCES

Adjibolosoo, S. 1993. The Human Factor in Development. *The Scandinavian Journal of Development Alternatives* 12 (4): 139–149.

Adjibolosoo, S. 1994. The Human Factor and the Failure of Development Planning and Economic Policy in Africa. In *Perspectives on Economic Development in Africa*, edited by F. Ezeala-Harrison and S. Adjibolosoo. Westport, Conn.: Praeger.

Adjibolosoo, S. 1995a. Achieving Optimal Quality and Productivity: The Passions. In *Productivity and Quality Management Frontiers*, vol. 5, edited by D. J. Sumanth, J. A. Edosomwan, R. Poupart, and C. G. Thor. Norcross, Ga.: Industrial Engineering Press.

Adjibolosoo, S. 1995b. Book Review. *Review of Human Factor Studies* 2 (1): 141–146.

Adjibolosoo, S. 1995c. *The Human Factor in Developing Africa*. Westport, Conn.: Praeger.

Adjibolosoo, S. 1995d. Rethinking the Sources of Economic Underdevelopment in Ghana. *Review of Human Factor Studies* 1 (2): 1–35.

Adjibolosoo, S. 1995e. The Significance of the Human Factor in African Economic Development. In *The Significance of the Human Factor in African Economic Development*, edited by S. Adjibolosoo. Westport, Conn.: Praeger.

Adjibolosoo, S. 1996. Human Factor Engineering: The Primary Mission of Education and Training. In *Human Factor Engineering and the Political Economy of African Development*, edited by S. Adjibolosoo. Westport, Conn.: Praeger.

Adjibolosoo, S. 1998. *Global Development the Human Factor Way*. Westport, Conn.: Praeger.

Bethel, S. M. 1990. *Making a Difference: Twelve Qualities that Make You a Leader*. New York: Putnam's Sons.

Casson, M. C. 1982. *The Entrepreneur: An Economic Theory*. Oxford: Martin Robertson.

FYI. 1996. *Forbes*, 23 September, 12.

Hendry, C., M. B. Arthur, and A. M. Jones. 1995. *Strategy through People: Adaptation and Learning in the Small–Medium Enterprise*. New York: Routledge.

Knight, H. F. 1951. *The Ethics of Competition and other Essays*. London: George Allen and Unwin.

McClelland, D. C. 1961. *The Achieving Society*. Princeton: Prentice-Hall.

Penrose, E. 1959. *The Theory of the Growth of the Firm*. Oxford: Basil Blackwell.

Render, B., and R. M. Stair, Jr. 1994. *Quantitative Analysis for Management*. Toronto: Allyn and Bacon.

Schumpeter, J. A. 1934. *The Theory of Economic Development*. Cambridge: Harvard University Press.

Zan, L., and S. Zambon. 1993. Strategy, Change, and the Strategic Approach: Making Sense in Process. In *Perspectives on Strategic Change*, edited by L. Zan, S. Zambon, and A. M. Pettigrew. London: Kluwer Academic.

Index

About the Editor and Contributors

SENYO B-S. K. ADJIBOLOSOO is a full professor of business and economics at Trinity Western University. He graduated with a Ph.D. in Economics from Simon Fraser University, Burnaby, British Columbia in 1988. His current interests include the significance of the human factor development, development education, history of economic thought, and international business and trade. He has published several articles on econometrics and economic development and has edited, coedited, and written numerous books on economic development. He is the founder and director of the International Institute for Human Factor Development (IIHFD), an institute solely devoted to researching the HF and its role in economic development.

FRANCIS ADU-FEBIRI is a sociology professor at Camosun College, Victoria, British Columbia. He obtained his Ph.D. from the University of British Columbia. His research interests include sociological perspectives on the human factor and development, the state and racism, ethnoracial minorities and tourism, tourism and development in developing countries, and social inequality in contemporary Africa. Dr. Adu-Febiri is a senior research fellow at the International Institute for Human Factor Development.

CARLOS AGUIRRE B. graduated from Oklahoma State University and pursued postgraduate studies at the Centro Brasileiro de Pesquisas Fisicas in Brazil. He was admitted to the National Academy of Sciences of Bolivia in

1976 and became its president in 1992. He is a professor of Science Policy at the Faculty of Sciences of the Universidad Mayor de San Andres in La Paz and holds executive posts in numerous national and international organizations. Professor Aguirre is actively engaged in international consulting in the areas of science, technology, and innovation policies in developing countries, including Bolivia, Peru, Ecuador, Colombia, Venezuela, Mexico, Indonesia, Namibia, and Tanzania, and has been a visiting researcher in Japan, Argentina, the former Soviet Union, and Germany. He has published over 200 papers, monographs, and books on cosmic-ray physics, science and technology policy and planning, and other related subjects.

JOE AMOAKO-TUFFOUR is an assistant professor of economics at St. Francis Xavier University, Antigonish, Nova Scotia. He received his bachelor and masters degrees from Simon Fraser University and his Ph.D. from the University of Alberta. Dr. Amoako-Tuffour has published works on the demand for public goods and on corruption. Since 1994, he has been a research fellow at the Center for Policy Analysis in Accra, Ghana, working on the government of Ghana's public finances and debt. Dr. Amoako-Tuffour is a senior research fellow at the International Institute for Human Factor Development.

MAHAMUDU BAWUMIA is an assistant professor of economics at Hankamer School of Business, Baylor University in Waco, Texas. Dr. Bawumia obtained his Ph.D. from Simon Fraser University, Burnaby, British Columbia. He has presented a number of papers at scholarly conferences and published a number of papers in well-known journals in his field. He is a senior research fellow at the International Institute for Human Factor Development.

SHEKHAR CHAUDHURI is a professor of strategic and international management in the International Management Group and the chairman of Research and Publications at the Indian Institute of Management, Ahmedabad. Professor Chaudhuri's teaching and research interests are in the areas of strategic management, international management, management of technology, international transfer of technology, and Japanese management. He has been a visiting scholar at the Twente University of Technology, Enschede, Holland, a Fulbright Fellow at the University of California, Berkeley, and a visiting professor of strategic management in the College of Business and Administration at Southern Illinois University, Carbondale. Professor Chaudhuri has published a number of papers in India and abroad, has been a consultant to a number of business organizations and departments of the Government of India, and was the leader of the Indian team in a major international research project sponsored by the World Bank.

SANTO DODARO is an associate professor of economics at St. Francis Xavier University, Antigonish, Nova Scotia and lecturer at the Coady International

Institute of St. Francis Xavier University. Born in Italy, he is a graduate of the University of Toronto. In addition to research on international and regional development, Dr. Dodaro is currently working on a book on the Antigonish Movement and the economics of grassroots development with Dr. Leonard Pluta.

JUSTUS HAUCAP is a research associate at the Center for the Study of the New Institutional Economics at the University of Saarland in Saarbrücken, Germany. He has been a research scholar at the Haas School of Business at the University of California, Berkeley, and holds an economics diploma from the University of Saarland. His research interests include the development and organization of market exchange, signaling, and reputation models, as well as the integration of economics, anthropology, and sociology. His most recent articles deal with reputation and signaling models in international trade.

DAVID E. HOJMAN is senior lecturer in Economics and Latin American Studies at the University of Liverpool. He obtained his Ph.D. in economics from the University of Edinburgh. He has published articles and books on agriculture, mineral exports, the Dutch Disease, open-economy macroeconomics, economic integration, labor markets, education, poverty and inequality, infant mortality, public choice and rent seeking, and the political economy of recent conversions to free-market, open-economy policies. Dr. Hojman is currently doing research on the interpretation of differences in economic performance among emerging-market economies, the determinants of the stock market evolution in these economies, and the reasons behind country differentials in direct foreign investment in the Third World.

SUNIL KUMAR received his engineering degree at the Indian Institute of Technology, New Delhi and his Ph.D. at the Indian Institute of Management, Ahmedabad. He is presently employed as a Senior Personnel Manager in the Indian Railways, and has worked with Bharat Heavy Electricals Limited in project management and done extensive work on strategic human resource management, international human resource management, and project management.

CLAUDE G. MARARIKE is a lecturer at the Department of Sociology, University of Zimbabwe, from which he holds an M. Phil. He is the author of the book *Grassroots Leadership: Understanding the Process of Rural Development in Zimbabwe*, and is currently working in collaboration with the School of Oriental and African Studies, University of London, on a research project entitled, "African Food Systems under Stress." He has worked as a journalist for the ZBC, and been a correspondent for the BBC, Reuters, AFP, and the Daily Times of Nigeria. Mr. Mararike is a senior research associate at the International Institute for Human Factor Development and the Regional Director of the Zimbabwe Chapter of the IIHFD.

LEONARD PLUTA teaches in the Department of Economics, St. Francis Xavier University, Antigonish, Nova Scotia and is a former lecturer at the Coady International Institute of St. Francis Xavier University. Born in Poland, he is a graduate of Queen's University. In addition to research on economic systems and economic thought, Dr. Pluta is currently working on a book on the Antigonish Movement and the economics of grassroots development with Dr. Santo Dodaro.

CHIKWENDU CHRISTIAN UKAEGBU received his bachelors degree at the University of Nigeria, Nsukka, and his Ph.D. at Northwestern University. A senior lecturer at the University of Nigeria, Nsukka, he is currently a visiting scholar at the Department of Sociology, University of Wyoming. He has researched and published on science manpower utilization, entrepreneurship, and the politics of ethnicity. Dr. Ukaegbu is a senior research fellow at the International Institute for Human Factor Development.

ISBN 0-275-95967-8

HARDCOVER BAR CODE